**DID THE MURDER HAVE TWO VICTIMS—
ONE PUT IN A CASKET ... THE OTHER IN JAIL?**

Stunning Laurie "Bambi" Bembenek, ex-cop, feminist, and former Playboy bunny, was sentenced to life imprisonment for the murder of her husband's ex-wife—on what the presiding judge called "the most circumstantial evidence I have ever seen." But after serving eight years, Bambi escaped, fleeing to Canada with the help of her young lover. She made worldwide headlines and captured the hearts of supporters everywhere.

This riveting true story provides a wrenching look at Bambi's fight for freedom. And it tells of the dauntless private investigator who uncovered a trail of altered evidence, hidden testimony, pornography, illicit sex and drugs, and misguided justice. But most important, this chilling tale asks one terrifying question: Could what happened to Bambi, happen to anyone?

RUN, BAMBI, RUN

"Kris Radish has done a credible job of exposing what looks suspiciously like an attempt by the male establishment to get rid of an annoying female."

—*Publishers Weekly*

Run, Bambi, Run

Kris Radish

AN ONYX BOOK

ONYX
Published by the Penguin Group
Penguin Books USA Inc., 375 Hudson Street,
New York, New York 10014, U.S.A.
Penguin Books Ltd, 27 Wrights Lane,
London W8 5TZ, England
Penguin Books Australia Ltd, Ringwood,
Victoria, Australia
Penguin Books Canada Ltd, 10 Alcorn Avenue,
Toronto, Ontario, Canada M4V 3B2
Penguin Books (N.Z.) Ltd, 182–190 Wairau Road,
Auckland 10, New Zealand

Penguin Books Ltd, Registered Offices:
Harmondsworth, Middlesex, England

Published by Onyx, an imprint of New American Library, a division
of Penguin Books USA Inc. This is an authorized reprint of a hard-
cover edition published by Carol Publishing Group.

First Onyx Printing, September, 1992
10 9 8 7 6 5 4 3 2 1

This book is for Laurie,
who trusted me to tell her story

CONTENTS

INTRODUCTION

Injustice anywhere is a threat to justice everywhere.

—Martin Luther King

When Kris asked me during one of many long-distance phone calls to write an introduction to her book, I hesitated only because I felt the timing was bad. Of late, my mood has not been very positive and I didn't want this to be evident, since I am certain my rather pensive state of mind is temporary. Usually I'm okay, and I realize I am extremely fortunate right now to have the best lawyer in the solar system (Frank Marrocco and his team) plus an enormous number of kind, wonderful friends. In the United States I also have Attorney Mary Woeherer and Investigator Ira Robins working tirelessly in my behalf. Attorneys Dave Dubinsky and Ron Lester also helped work miracles for me. Sometimes, however, I get very tired in my ten-year struggle. As usual, the nature of my future is totally uncertain, and even though I take life one day at a time, the big picture is that I don't know if I'll ever be free again, or where I'll be. I should almost be accustomed by now to such uncertainty, because this has been my lot since 1981, when I was arrested for a murder I did not commit. I spent most of my twenties in prison, and I've been in a Canadian jail since my capture last October, after a mere glimpse of freedom.

The worst part about those three months as a fugitive was not being able to have any contact with my family and friends—not knowing if my mom and dad were all right; but the greatest joy was being someone other than Laurie Bembenek. No one had any false, preconceived notions about me when I was Jennifer. I was simply the woman next door, and strangers couldn't accuse me or gossip maliciously or condemn me before meeting me. People judged me by my interaction with others and on my personality, rather than on some totally untrue "killer bunny" media story. In Thunder Bay, people liked me for *me*. I hope Kris's book will allow the reader this perspective as well—to look beyond the headlines and sensationalized exaggerations at the real pain and torment of individuals directly involved. You may even be surprised to discover that the human side to this case will show you that similar injustices could actually happen to anyone. A great number of people suffered needlessly throughout this seemingly endless ordeal, and perhaps this book will help to promote changes within the system that could prevent something like this from ever occurring again.

—Lawrencia Ann Bembenek
June 1991

ACKNOWLEDGMENTS

It's impossible to thank everyone who helps you write a book like this. The friends and relatives who couldn't visit for months on end; the neighbors who called to tell me to shut off the computer because there was a tornado in my backyard; the other folks who left beer on the doorstep when they saw the basement light on all night; the friends who listened to every piece of evidence, every new development in the story over and over again. But some people deserve mention: Ira Robins, for sharing his notes, files, sources, and the fire in his heart; Joseph and Virginia Bembenek, for acknowledging my sincerity and becoming my friends; Peg Kelly, for knowing this book had to be written; Hillel Black, for using his master editor's pen to whip my words into shape; Malcolm McIntyre, for his professional guidance; Mike Witos, for his computer expertise; Meg Glasgwyn, for her talent with words; Greg Gent, for his artistic eye; Ginny Lord and Nancy Kuehl, for their mother's arms, and Bob Jozwiak, for telling me twenty years ago I could do this. Most important, my thanks, apologies, and love to Andrew and Rachel, who gave me up for way too long, and to my husband, Stephen Carpenter, who held the babies, locked me in this office, sacrificed his tennis, and made my greatest dream a reality. This is your book, too.

CHAPTER 1

The Heart of the Night

Christine Jean Schultz ran her fingers through the warm dirt behind her Milwaukee home and imagined what her barren garden would look like at the end of the summer. It was May 27, 1981, just a few minutes past 3 P.M. She closed her eyes and in an instant saw ripe tomatoes, flowers in bloom, and herself sitting on the patio and not worrying about a damn thing.

The idea of not worrying pushed her back into reality and made her smile. Christine, an attractive dark-eyed brunette, had more than her share of concerns. Divorced in November of 1980 from her husband, Elfred O. Schultz, Jr., her life had quickly developed into a complex web of men, women, and children.

Christine, then thirty years old, was never really surprised when friends told her they had seen her husband around town with other women. The marriage had been on the downside for years. Schultz, two years older, was tall and blond and had looked more than handsome when he wore his Milwaukee police officer uniform before he became a detective. Women were always after him, and he loved the attention. When Christine asked him about the other women, he admitted he had been seeing them and said that's just the way it would continue. When Schultz quickly remarried a gorgeous younger woman, twenty-one-year-old Lawrencia Ann Bembenek, Christine was surprised. She was certain her ex-husband wasn't through running around.

Her close friends, many of whom had seen Schultz become violent with Christine, told her she was lucky to be out of that relationship. But the relationship was far from over.

The Schultzes' two sons—Sean, eleven, and Shannon, seven—quickly became a constant source of arguments for the estranged couple. Schultz demanded to know everything about his ex-wife's life. He wanted to be in on every decision she made about the boys. It was important that he maintain some kind of control over the children and their mother. Christine wondered if she would ever really be totally divorced from the man she had once loved and grown to fear.

When Schultz continued to show up at the home he had built for her on the south side of Milwaukee, despite a court order that he stay away, Christine finally had the locks changed. She also informed her divorce attorney, Eugene Kershek, that she was worried that Schultz might try to kill her.

"He told me he wants to blow my fucking head off," Christine had told her attorney just a few weeks earlier. She had also told Kershek that someone had been following her and she didn't know why. She suspected that the internal affairs division of the Milwaukee Police Department had been keeping tabs on her latest boyfriend, who was also a Milwaukee cop. But she wasn't sure, and she was frightened.

On that May 27 she was also worried that

Schultz would find out she had taken the boys up to northern Wisconsin for Memorial Day weekend without telling him. While her visions of an early summer garden quickly faded, Christine Jean Schultz prayed that Elfred O. Schultz, Jr., wouldn't flip out when the boys told him about the trip.

Christine got up from the ground when she heard her youngest son Shannon come home from school. She was a slender woman who still turned more than a few male heads, a woman who vowed daily to try to quit smoking so she could live longer.

"Sean's at baseball practice, Mom," Shannon yelled to her as he raced across the street to play baseball with the neighborhood kids. Christine loved her sons very much and she tried hard not to let her feelings and fears about their father interfere with their own perceptions of him. She had become a good pretender.

By six, when her forty-one-year-old boyfriend, Stewart George Honeck, Jr., showed up to help her rototill the garden, Christine was looking at another major problem. Honeck, twice divorced, had once shared an apartment with her ex-husband and now lived just down the street. Honeck wanted to marry her. Christine had dated other men since her divorce and wasn't sure she was ready for another marriage. A tall, burly man with a low, often gravelly voice, Honeck also had a drinking problem, a fact that her ex-husband reminded her of constantly. The two men had become bitter enemies since Honeck started dating Christine.

About seven-thirty, just after the sun had dipped

out of sight, Christine went inside to cook dinner. She mixed Honeck a vodka gimlet and had one herself. They had another drink and sat down with the boys to eat. It was nearly nine. They talked about the yard work, about how things were going at St. Roman's, where both boys attended school, and they had some wine. The boys skipped their baths and showers that night, said good night to Honeck, and went upstairs to the bedroom they shared.

Their room was directly across the hall from their mother's, and Sean would often lie awake and look across the hall into his mom's room. That night his little brother, who was supposed to sleep in the top bunk, called down, "Big brother, can I sleep with you?"

Sean was used to this routine. Hardly a night passed that Shannon didn't ask to sleep with him. That night Shannon said he saw something in the closet. A light sleeper, Sean was on the outer edge of the bed and he barely moved as his brother cuddled against him and fell asleep. He heard Honeck come back into the house after he'd gone home to check on his dog, Ginger. Christine and Honeck had a few more drinks and then Sean heard his mom ask Honeck to lock the door as he left for home.

As Sean drifted slowly toward sleep, Christine cleaned up the kitchen and washed the dishes. He was used to his mother's routines and he wasn't surprised to hear "M*A*S*H" on television in her room a short time later. His mom came in to check on the boys and sat down on the bed to talk with Sean. He knew she was upset. She had been all day. Sean was sure she had talked to or seen his father sometime that day.

"Mom, can't Shannon and I see Dad more often?" he asked her. Sean knew the question would upset her even more, but he missed seeing his dad. He knew his father was mad, too, that they had all gone up to the cabin without telling him. Sean also asked his mom if she was going to marry Stu Honeck. His mother didn't answer, and soon she got up, kissed her oldest son good night, and walked into her bedroom.

While Hawkeye and Radar were trying to save hearts, souls, and bodies in Korea, Sean finally drifted off to sleep. Christine put on a yellow T-shirt and some white underpants, and, with the television to keep her company, she threw a sheet and light blanket over herself and tried to forget about Elfred Schultz, Stu Honeck, and every other problem that she had.

An hour passed and then another. The house at 1701 West Ramsey Street was quiet. The doors were locked. Everyone was asleep. In the master bedroom only the faint glow from the television set flickered in the dark. In the boys' room a tiny night-light threw a slender rod of light across the room.

Just before 2 A.M., someone—perhaps two "someones"—slipped into the almost dark Schultz home. In the early depths of sleep Sean Schultz heard something. He felt something terrible—a rope, some string, a wire—tighten around his neck and he saw a very large gloved hand move over his face. Then his mouth, eyes, nose were completely covered. Terrified, he began to struggle. He pulled at the thing that was around his neck and screamed. Shannon, awake and frightened too, jumped out of bed and started to kick at the person—a large man who had a reddish ponytail and a green army jacket. The man quickly ran from the room, across the hall, and into their mother's bedroom and—for a moment, just a moment—the boys stood still, silent. Then they heard something terrible. First Shannon heard a woman's voice say, "God, please don't do that." Frightened beyond words, the boys then heard, in almost the same instant, something that sounded like a firecracker.

Shannon raced to the door of his room. His older brother was right behind him. He caught a glimpse of a man standing over his mother's bed. Shannon moved just a few inches into the hall, and at that same moment the man who had been standing over his mother ran by him and headed for the steps. Sean saw the man with the ponytail jumping down the stairs, three and four steps at a time. The man's green army jacket was flapping as he flew to the bottom of the steps. When the man landed at the bottom, Sean saw black shoes on his feet. A deep, heavy growling sound came from the man. Both boys then rushed into their mother's bedroom. What they saw will always remain a terrible memory.

Christine Jean Schultz was lying facedown on her bed. Her left hand had a cord around it. There was some kind of scarf wrapped around her head. She had been shot in the back. The boys moved toward their mother's bed, still frightened, worried that the man in the green coat was still in the house.

Sean immediately saw the hole in his mother's

back. He leaned across her still body and asked her if it would be okay if he ripped open her shirt so he could fix the hole. Christine was gagged, but she nodded, ever so slightly. Sean turned on the lights, tore open his mother's Adidas T-shirt and with a washcloth tried to wipe off the blood on her back. When that didn't work, he wrapped some gauze around his hand and pushed hard, directly above the wound. He wanted the blood to stop coming out. He wanted to help his mother.

Shannon watched silently and wrapped himself up in a blue blanket and stood close to his brother. Shivering in the cold room, the terrified brothers stood guard over their dying mother. They had just witnessed her murder.

CHAPTER 2

A Sigh of Relief

In the early morning hours of May 28, 1981, Stu Honeck was sleeping in his own house, just a few blocks from Christine Schultz, when he heard his phone ring. Honeck shook his head and looked at the alarm clock near his bed. It was almost 2:30 A.M. He wondered who in the hell would be calling him.

The person on the other end of the phone was quiet and frightened. Honeck could barely hear the small voice. It was Sean Schultz.

"Stu, come quick. Someone put a firecracker on Mom's back and it blew up."

Honeck sat up in his bed. He told Sean to put his mother on the phone but Sean said she couldn't talk.

"Let me talk to her."

Sean put the phone close to his mother's face.

"She can't talk, Stu. She's gurgling."

Honeck was out of bed. He told Sean to stay in the house and he would call for help and be right over.

Then he called the emergency number at the police department. He said Christine Schultz was hurt or "shot." He told the police he would meet them at the house. Honeck grabbed his pants and woke up his roommate, Kenneth E. Retkowski, another Milwaukee police officer. Both men got into Honeck's van and drove to Christine's house. It took less than two minutes.

The Milwaukee police were quick to respond when they heard Stu Honeck's rough voice on the emergency phone line yelling for help. Honeck was a cop. This woman who could be hurt or shot was a cop's ex-wife, and the Milwaukee men in blue were always quicker to help one of their own.

The Milwaukee Police Department had lots to worry about in 1981. A series of problems, including lawsuits and allegations of brutality, had tainted their nationwide reputation as one of the finest police departments in the country.

In one well-publicized case several police officers beat up a local businessman who had pulled over to the sidewalk to relieve himself against the curb. When questioned about the incident, the police officer said the man had hurt himself after he fell over one of their motorcycles.

In another case a black rape suspect was killed while in police custody. The real rapist was found just a few blocks from the site of the crime. That same year a retired police officer came forward to say that years before, the police had shot a man, Daniel Bell, in the back, then planted a knife in the dead man's hand. Another retired officer was implicated in the case.

Police Chief Harold Breier wanted the men—and the few women who had made it into the department—to be especially careful that spring. Another problem was brewing. All the women and other minorities who were getting fired were starting to raise questions about how Breier operated the department. Breier hated to be questioned about "his" department, and he would do almost anything to protect the department's reputation. The Milwaukee cops were on edge. No one wanted to lose his job, and many of the officers would risk anything to protect a fellow cop.

When Honeck got to Christine's house, he saw a patrol car coming around the corner. Honeck, Retkowski, and the two patrol officers pounded on the front door. Sean and Shannon finally unlocked it and let Honeck and the other men inside. The boys looked like little puppies. Their eyes were wild and they seemed confused and frightened.

Honeck went upstairs but he didn't stay long. He found Christine Jean Schultz lying on her right side, facing west. Honeck saw a huge bullet hole in her shoulder. He moved toward the bed and rolled Christine over. Her hands were tied in front of her and she had a gag in her mouth. When Honeck saw that Christine was not breathing, he quickly left the room.

By the time Honeck got downstairs, the house that Elfred Otto Schultz, Jr., had built for Christine was like a sea of moving blue uniforms. It looked as if every police officer in Milwaukee was in the house, in the front yard, or driving past. The cops were actually bumping into each other. Everyone wanted to see the murder scene.

Fred Schultz also showed up. He talked with his sons for a few minutes, gave them each a quick hug, and called his brother John to pick them up. He was then asked to help in the investigation. An ambulance was finally called, and by 5 A.M. the body of Christine Schultz was headed for the police morgue.

The noise at the end of Ramsey Street woke up half of the usually quiet neighborhood. There were police sirens and red and white lights flashing on every corner. Neighbors were looking out of windows and standing on doorsteps in their bathrobes. No one could imagine what was going on. This part of town was safe. It was a neighborhood of families and a few older, retired couples. There were red wagons and Hot Wheels on the sidewalks, even in the middle of the night.

By the time *The Milwaukee Journal* hit their doorsteps the following afternoon, Christine Schultz's neighbors knew what had happened in their safe little neighborhood. A woman had been murdered. Right next door. Right down the street. Right around the corner. Everyone was frightened. Nothing like this had ever happened before.

Although murders in Milwaukee were not uncommon, they usually occurred miles away in the inner city, the ghetto. Most people who lived on the south side of Milwaukee had never even been to the inner city. That was a different world. The people who lived away from the inner city sent their kids to parochial schools. Their children played soccer and baseball together. There was always a barbecue grill going on the block. They lived next door to their parents and many still spoke the Polish and German phrases their grandmas and grandpas had taught them when they were little boys and girls.

To these people Milwaukee was a wonderful place to raise a family. Most never even bothered to travel past the state line. There simply wasn't any reason to leave such a wonderful community. Famous for "beer, brats, and bowling," it was also a city that followed traditional values. In Milwaukee kids were taught to respect and honor police officers. In a city where the majority of fathers and mothers worked in factories and breweries, policemen were revered and given special treatment.

That is why the frightened neighbors of Christine Schultz knew the policemen would find out who killed her. They simply trusted the cops. The papers said the assailant was probably a burglar. The police already had a good description of the man because the boys had seen the guy who did it. One of the boys had even been strangled. Police were seeking a white male who was wearing a green Army jacket. They said the man had light-colored hair with a six- to eight-inch ponytail.

While mothers and fathers hurried their babies home from their suburban playgrounds and installed extra deadbolt locks, the police were indeed busy. Police officers neatly dressed in their smart black shoes and crisp-collared shirts fanned throughout Christine Schultz's neighborhood. They were asking questions, making notes, and trying to find the man who murdered Christine Schultz. It was good just to see all the police cars in the area.

Because the Schultz home was next to the freeway, the police speculated that the assailant could have run onto the freeway and gotten away quickly. The very morning of the murder, just hours after it occurred, they had even questioned a man, Daniel Gilbert, who was parked on the overpass directly above the Schultz home. The police detectives also had some very interesting leads.

At least twelve area residents, two of them Milwaukee police officers, had seen a man matching the description of the murderer during the few weeks before May 28. Several people had seen a jogger with reddish-brown hair tied back in a ponytail, wearing a green jogging suit. He didn't live in the area, and he was often seen wearing or carrying a blue bandana, just like the bandana that was used to gag Christine Schultz. One boy, the son of a Milwaukee police officer, said he would be able to identify the man because he had seen him numerous times.

Then two nurses who worked at a nursing home less than one mile from the Schultz residence came forward. The night of the murder, in the early morning hours of May 28, they had seen something very strange. They looked across the street and observed someone lying in the parking lot. After they went inside and called police, they came back outside about 2:50 A.M. and saw a man with reddish-brown hair and a green jogging suit standing in the bushes. He coughed. They glanced around the street, then back to the man. He had disappeared. It was just after three on the morning of May 28. Christine Schultz had been dead for thirty minutes.

The ex-husband of Christine Schultz was quickly ruled out as a suspect. He was a Milwaukee police detective, and he had been on duty the night of the murder. Christine's current boyfriend was also a Milwaukee cop. Another suspect was a neighbor of Christine's. His name was Ray Kujawa. He told the cops that the night of the murder someone broke into his garage and stole a green jogging suit and a .38-caliber revolver. A truck driver, Kujawa claimed to have spent the night at a friend's but something about his story sounded strange.

The police detectives investigated most leads but it was impossible to check everything out. Three weeks following the murder of Christine Schultz, they were onto something anyway. They were checking out Lawrencia Ann Bembenek.

She was Elfred Schultz's new wife and an ex-cop herself. Everyone in the department knew her. She was one of those radical women's libbers. The kind of woman who thought females deserved an equal chance. She was also one of the most beautiful cops the department had ever seen. She was tall, with a great set of legs, sky-blue eyes, long, slender fingers, and a head of thick blond hair. She was gone but not forgotten. She had been booted out of the department because of some minor problem, and Chief Breier smiled when he learned of her connection with the Schultz murder. The police department was no place for women. Let them stay home. These women needed to be taught a lesson.

After the first twenty-four days of June the detectives and police officers working on the Christine Schultz murder case stopped looking for the man with the reddish-brown ponytail and green jogging suit. They were interviewing everyone who knew Lawrencia Bembenek. She was an unlikely suspect, but she was the second wife, and that always created problems. Murders had been committed for much simpler reasons.

When Judy Zess, a former roommate of Bembenek's, told the police her ex-roommate had once talked about having Christine Schultz bumped off, the detectives knew they were onto something. Interestingly enough, Zess had also been a Milwaukee police officer. She knew how everything worked and what to say. Then, as if God had popped right out of the sky to help them, the cops discovered that someone had flushed a reddish-brown wig down the plumbing system in the same apartment complex where Lawrencia Bembenek lived with her new husband, Elfred Schultz.

While several cops scurried around Milwaukee and into Chicago looking for some clothesline that matched the rope that was used to tie up Christine, everyone else tried to connect Lawrencia to the Schultz murder. The wig helped, and so did the stuff Zess told them. Lawrencia had no alibi. She was home sleeping. The police pieced together an interesting story, and in their story Lawrencia Bembenek was a killer.

Lawrencia Bembenek was jealous of Christine Schultz. Even though her new husband Elfred was officially divorced, he still saw his first wife several times a week. Christine had given birth to his sons, and she was the first woman he had loved. How did Lawrencia know for sure that he had stopped loving and sleeping with his first wife?

Lawrencia Bembenek also resented the alimony and child-support payments that her husband was making. They cut into her lifestyle. A former model, Lawrencia was used to expensive clothes and eating out in fancy restaurants. She also hated the fact that Fred shared his affections with his two sons. She wanted him and his money all to herself.

Because Lawrencia Bembenek was a tall woman, she easily fit the description of the killer that police detectives had received from Shannon and Sean Schultz. She was also an avid jogger who kept herself in great shape by working out at a local gym. She was even a weight lifter. If Christine or one of the boys tried to struggle, she would be able to subdue them easily.

Trained as a police officer, Bembenek would also know what to do at the scene of a crime. She would wear gloves so she would leave no fingerprints. She would disguise her appearance so that the boys or Christine would fail to recognize her. She even knew the layout of the house because she had been there several times with Elfred to pick up his sons.

So, on May 27, when she knew her husband would be at work, she planned a murder.

She dressed in a green jogging suit, which she probably discarded after the murder, loaded up his off-duty revolver, donned a blond-reddish-looking wig, and jogged two miles to the Schultz residence. She knew the home was secluded in back. She entered through the rear door, without breaking the lock, and headed to Christine's bedroom. When Christine struggled, Lawrencia Bembenek did what someone trained in police work would do. She pulled the trigger. She murdered Christine Jean Schultz, then tucked the gun inside her pants and quickly jogged back to her Twentieth Street apartment.

When Milwaukee County District Attorney E. Michael McCann heard the police scenario, he thought it was a bit farfetched. No one had actually seen Lawrencia Bembenek even near the scene of the crime. No one had observed her with the gun or the wig or a green jogging suit, which was supposed to be a green Army jacket according to the two boys, the only eyewitnesses. The story was totally circumstantial. McCann didn't like it, but the police officers, led by Deputy District Attorney Robert Donohoo, told the district attorney they knew she had done it. It had to be her.

On June 24, 1981, Lawrencia Ann Bembenek, twenty-one, was arrested for the murder of Christine Schultz. When her picture flashed across the television screen that night on the six o'clock news, three-fourths of Milwaukee couldn't believe it.

Lawrencia Bembenek, once a member of the police department, had been nicknamed Bambi by the officers at the police academy. She had been a police officer. Those who saw her deerlike eyes thought the name was perfect. She had been a model, and the male population was happy to hear she had even worked as a waitress at the Lake Geneva Playboy Club near the Illinois border for a few weeks. Throughout the city and into the suburbs everyone was saying the same thing: "Why would someone like that kill somebody?"

In Christine Schultz's own neighborhood, no one felt relieved. This was a hometown girl. Someone who had grown up just a few miles from the scene of the murder. Someone who had gone to school with their sons and daughters. Someone they could have seen at the local store carrying groceries for her mother or buying a six-pack at the corner bar. How could this be? Could the police have made a mistake?

In the next few days Milwaukee and half of the

country learned everything they thought there was to know about Lawrencia Ann Bembenek. She was an unlikely murder suspect, and her face appeared in newspapers across the nation. It was a great story. A beautiful ex-cop kills cop husband's ex-wife. Everyone wanted to know everything about the Playboy Bunny killer. But there was so much the Milwaukee Police detectives never told. So much Lawrencia Ann Bembenek never got a chance to say.

CHAPTER 3

Growing Up Normal

The arrest of Lawrencia Bembenek on June 24, 1981, was an unpredictable turn in her young life. There had never been a hint of danger or evil in the shining blue eyes of the little girl with the quick smile from the south side of Milwaukee.

She was born on August 15, 1959, to Joseph John and Virginia Carol Bembenek. She was a welcome surprise, an "oops" baby, who came eight years after the birth of an older sister, Colette. Another sister, Melanie, was already entering her teenage years when the last Bembenek baby girl came home from the hospital.

The Bembeneks' baby was baptized at the local Catholic church and given the name Laurie Ann. But the Latin translation of her name, Lawrencia, somehow showed up on her birth certificate. The baby would be Laurie to her family and friends. Later, as she grew up and began her own life, Laurie Bembenek would often use her formal, official name, Lawrencia.

Her neighborhood and her family were ethnic mirrors that reflected the hardworking values of Polish ancestors. The small houses on her street were full of babies, and working fathers, and mothers who stayed home. The white frame Bembenek house on South Taylor Street was always filled with laughter, Barbie dolls, and dozens of patent leather shoes.

The Bembenek sisters grew up surrounded by lots of love and good times and were raised on solid Catholic Christian values. There was never a doubt in Laurie Bembenek's mind that her parents loved her.

Her father, Joseph Bembenek, worked for three years as a City of Milwaukee police officer. Disillusioned by the corrupt practices of his fellow officers, Bembenek quit the police force and began working as a carpenter. Laurie would often accompany him on jobs during the weekends and after school. She loved being with her dad and she especially loved to hear the stories he told about his work as a cop.

Although the Bembeneks raised their daughters with old-fashioned values, they were surprisingly modern when it came to encouraging their children to explore nontraditional roles. Laurie and her sisters were constantly told they could do anything they wanted. Even though the Bembeneks chose the mother-at-home, father-at-work way of life, they made it clear that not everyone had to live that way. It was important for Virginia and Joseph Bembenek to instill self-confidence in their daughters. They knew that if their daughters believed in themselves and in their abilities, they could go anywhere and do anything.

Laurie attended a Catholic grade school close to her Taylor Street home. She went to an all-girls high school, St. Mary's Academy, her freshman year and then transferred to Bay View High School for the remainder of her high school days. Ever so gradually Lawrencia Ann Bembenek lost her overtly tall, gangly look, replaced her glasses with contact lenses, and changed into a beautiful young woman.

At five-foot-ten she towered over most of the high school class. She was an interesting blend of mother and father. Her bright blue eyes, high cheekbones, and blond hair gave her the kind of looks that stopped the men who passed her on the street. It wasn't her looks that really set her apart, though, it was her attitude—her sense of independence and self-assurance—that made her seem different and special.

Laurie dated in high school but not excessively. She was a member of the track team and played the flute in the high school band. The inequality of her high school curriculum choices helped lay the foundation for the feminist beliefs that became a strong part of her personality. After her parents told her she could be whatever she wanted to be, Laurie was shocked by the limits society put on her.

"Mom, the girls all take home economics and the boys take shop," she told her mother with disbelief in her voice. "That isn't how it's supposed to be."

Laurie Bembenek would find out that many things in life aren't what they are supposed to be. She dreamed of becoming a zoologist or veterinarian, but then she discovered her Catholic education left her lacking in some of the necessary skills to pursue those dreams.

"The nuns taught math and science to the boys, and girls were supposed to be good at spelling and English," Laurie said. "We could be cheerleaders and play volleyball, but the rest of the world was for the boys."

Laurie fought those stereotypes. When sports

rules were changed, she ran hurdles on the track team, hung out with the "jocks," and worked hard to overcome the "lonely and cloistered" feelings that had been her gift from the Catholic educators. By her senior year Laurie felt pretty good about herself, but she still wasn't sure where she was headed.

A high school guidance counselor talked her out of graduating early. Instead, she worked part-time at a Milwaukee department store and attended classes the rest of the day. She also had to deal with an ever-growing problem. There was a line of boys at her door who wanted to go out with her. Not interested in a serious relationship, Laurie was selective about whom she spent time with.

Still undecided about a career, Laurie took a test for a scholarship at a local business college and was surprised when she received it. For the next two years she attended school and worked toward a two-year business degree in fashion merchandising. She also served as a waitress and did some clerking.

Laurie did some modeling too. Friends and family members had been telling her for years that her long legs and arms would make her a hot commodity. The girl who had been nicknamed "flatsy" in high school decided to give it a try. She signed on with three Milwaukee talent agencies. The money was good—thirty-five dollars an hour—and Laurie could work her modeling around her class schedules. Modeling wasn't as glamorous as it appeared, though, and lugging around forty-pound garment bags was not her idea of an ideal job.

Laurie's feminist beliefs were still in the formative stages, and she justified her modeling by refusing to pose nude or in underwear. She wasn't that kind of girl. Her most risqué shot was for the Schlitz Brewing Company. She posed as Miss March in their 1978 calendar. In the photo she is lying on a velvet couch and wearing a low-cut dress.

When Laurie started to work as a display artist at Boston Store, a major department store in Milwaukee, she knew almost instantly that she had chosen the wrong career. She was bored, unchallenged, and ready for something different. A second job at a local gym helped convince her she needed a solid career. She did not want to work at two low-paying jobs for the rest of her life. Laurie Bembenek decided she wanted to become a police officer.

Her idealistic motivations carried her through the months of preapplication planning for entrance into the police academy. While her high school friends married, moved away, and slowly drifted apart, Laurie was busy doing push-ups and jogging. Active in various feminist groups throughout the Milwaukee area, Laurie Bembenek thought that working as a Milwaukee police officer would help solve the terrible problems she saw around her every day. She wanted to help prevent sexual assaults. She wanted to comfort the female victims of crime. She wanted to be a role model for other women and girls.

In 1979 Laurie Bembenek was idealistic, twenty years old, and ready to start chasing her dreams. She thought the whole world was waiting for her.

CHAPTER 4

On the Inside

From the very moment Laurie Bembenek entered the world of law enforcement, she was subjected to sexist jokes and comments. It wasn't exactly the kind of career she had planned. Dressed in a nondescript T-shirt and blue jeans, Laurie had an appointment at the downtown Milwaukee police station. She had just celebrated her twentieth birthday. It was August 1979.

"Don't tell me you're waiting for an interview?" the first cop who saw her asked. "You mean a pretty little thing like you wants to be a big, bad policeman?"

"Police officer," Laurie corrected him, unsmiling, her stomach already in knots.

In front of her another cop sneered. "Hey, assign her to my squad," he bellowed. "I'll teach her a few things."

While the male cops laughed, Laurie rose silently and went in for her first interview.

The Milwaukee police chief, Harold Breier, did not hesitate to express his feelings about women and minorities on the police force. He had definite ideas about what women should be doing, and police work did not appear on the list. Stories about harassment were pervasive throughout the city. Female cops, black cops, Hispanic cops, all but white male cops were always in for a hard time.

Back in 1979 federal investigators were secretly and eagerly building a case against the City of Milwaukee for discrimination and misuse of federal funds.

Laurie tried to ignore her first encounter with the Milwaukee cops and felt elated when she was notified that she could take the written test that could qualify her to enter the police academy. She passed a physical agility test, and several months later was granted an oral examination before the Milwaukee Fire and Police Commission. She scored very high on all her exams and received an appointment date of March 10, 1980, for the Milwaukee Police Academy.

While Laurie was thrilled with her appointment, her current boyfriend was not. Her desire to pursue a law-enforcement career signaled the end of their four-year relationship, and, weeks before her appointment was to begin, Laurie had to choose between him and her new career. Her boyfriend quickly canceled a trip they had planned to Florida, and Laurie decided to go by herself. She knew it would be a year or more before she could get away. Boyfriend or no boyfriend, she had to get on with her life.

Several days later she bumped into Judy Zess, a fellow police recruit, and Zess eagerly volunteered to join her on vacation. Zess was young and, like Laurie, seemed excited about the prospect of being a cop. The two women had met during the physical agility tests weeks before. The Florida trip proved uneventful except for one strange event.

A man that Zess had hung around with at the hotel swimming pool approached Laurie a day or so before the end of her vacation. A New Yorker, his accent hung in the air for what seemed to be seconds after he spoke to Laurie. "There's something funny with her," the man said, referring to Zess. "It's like she's obsessed with you."

Shocked, Laurie responded by laughing. Judy Zess never approached her physically during that trip, and Laurie never said anything to her about it. But the man's comments were so odd Laurie never forgot them.

The following twenty-one weeks were a far cry from the fun and sun of Florida. Laurie cut her hair so it wouldn't cover her ears. She wore no makeup or fingernail polish, and she found out what it was like to go through the rigors of basic training. She was physically and mentally sore every night. One of the officers who had a hard time pronouncing her name immediately decided Bambi was a better name for her. She didn't think the name was half bad considering she felt like a fawn running through the middle of a snarling bear's den.

Instructors were particularly hard on the female recruits. Laurie cringed every time a street lesson was being taught because she knew that one of the female recruits would most likely end up learning the lesson first. The instructors were constantly testing the recruits. Laurie knew she would have to remain quick-witted if she were going to survive—and survive she did.

During one session a detective instructor stopped in front of a female recruit and started yelling. "Well, what do we have here? A pussy cop." The woman shrank down into her seat and was visibly shaken, but the detective continued. "Hey, why are you carrying around that nightstick? Can't you find a man?"

Officer Bembenek joined in the laughter until the detective walked up to her. "Bembenek!" he yelled right in her face. "Is your mother still hooking?"

"Just on weekends, sir," Laurie responded, smiling.

The detective was impressed. Laurie made it to class the next day, but the other woman dropped out and was never seen again.

Four weeks into the training Laurie received good marks on her first evaluation. The sergeants and instructors were particularly impressed with her physical performance on the track and in the gym. Her jogging, weight-lifting, and workouts had paid off. She was holding her own despite the leers and jeers of the male recruits and some of the instructors.

Laurie's feminist beliefs couldn't be left in the backseat of her car when she walked into training each morning. Her thoughts about women and what they could and couldn't do were too important to her. She had decided years ago that she never wanted to have children and that if she did marry she would never change her name. She was always concerned about women and their rights. As she sat through insulting lectures about rape and how to handle the victims, she couldn't forget what she believed and what motivated her.

She felt good remembering the time she had attended a rally protesting Chief Breier's archaic stand against forming a sexual assault unit. Instead of following national trends and local demands, he continued to assign rape cases to his insensitive, male-dominated vice squad.

Everyone in her recruit class knew that Bambi had strong feelings about women's issues. She spoke out in class when the instructors were talking about sexual assault cases, and almost everyone took particular delight in letting Laurie know each time a state had refused to ratify the Equal Rights Amendment.

Undaunted, Laurie Bembenek never considered dropping out of her police recruit class. She plugged away, determined to finish the course and work as a police officer. She was flabbergasted a few weeks into training when Sgt. Orval Zellmer summoned her to his office. She was quickly told she was soon to become part of a confidential internal investigation. It was a set of words she would quickly become accustomed to.

Zellmer and another sergeant named Figer spent the better part of an hour grilling her about a party she had been to the previous week. Laurie was shocked when they told her they had received an anonymous complaint saying that she had been at a police party, with her badge pinned to her shirt, smoking marijuana. Laurie had been at the party, but the allegations were so ridiculous she had to stifle a laugh during her visit with the two men. The laugh didn't last long, however.

Laurie Bembenek had seen the inner workings of the Milwaukee Police Department. Their treatment of women and knee-jerk reactions appalled her. She was beginning to understand why her father had switched careers. She also began to think that the Milwaukee Police Department already had drawn a black line through her name.

Her thoughts were prophetic. Two weeks later, when Laurie accompanied Judy Zess and three friends to a Milwaukee concert, her controversial police career was pushed to the edge. While Laurie used the bathroom, two plainclothes police officers arrested Zess and one of her friends for possession of marijuana. The next day Laurie was back in the same interrogation room with Zellmer and his partner. This time the questioning went on for hours. The men wanted to know every detail of her life. Where she went. What she did. With whom she spent time. Laurie thought the questioning was pretty severe considering her crime was using the john. When they finally let her leave the room, she was exhausted.

By the following Monday the questioning started all over again. This time she was threatened with losing her job. When Laurie approached the Milwaukee Police Association with her problem, they told her there was a rumor she had been running around some party with her badge pinned to her underwear. Then Judy Zess was fired from the department because a tiny marijuana cigarette was found in a Styrofoam cup under her chair.

Lawrencia Bembenek's superiors at the academy continued to badger her to sign a confession and then resign. They tried to get her to say she had smoked marijuana at the concert and at the party. Laurie refused to be intimidated. She would not confess to something that she had not done. Lawrencia Ann Bembenek had her own honor code and she would not go against it.

The way she was being treated, Laurie figured her real crime had something to do with the fact that she had been born female. There were no women working in police administration. There were no female sergeants or detectives, and the way it was going there wouldn't be many female patrol officers either.

When Laurie refused to buckle under the demands of her superiors, things seemed to settle down. For a while she actually started thinking she might even graduate from the academy. In July she received her field-training assignment. She was assigned to District Number Five, which included an all-black neighborhood and some of Milwaukee's fashionable East Side. Her field-training officer was a fat Italian cop, Rosario Collura. His squad partner was Michael Jourdan. Laurie Bembenek was about to be baptized by fire.

From the moment Officer Bembenek presented herself for duty, she became a third-class citizen. Her first night on the job she worked several shootings and armed robberies. If anything went wrong, it was her fault. She did all the paperwork. She became Collura's slave.

On her third night of duty, when she was standing roll call, the sergeant ordered the officers to draw their guns and unload for inspection. Officer Bembenek took a second longer than the veteran officers. Her gun was the last to click as she snapped the cylinder back into place.

"Was that you, Jourdan?" the sergeant asked.

"Nope, it was the dumb cunt," Collura said, laughing out loud.

Officer Bembenek refused to flinch. She didn't flinch the rest of the week either when Collura continued his sexist verbal attacks on her. He constantly joked about women's rights and ordered Laurie to do all the physical jobs they encountered.

"Hey, if she wants a man's job, let her do a man's job," he said when he ordered her to change a flat tire.

When Laurie talked with other classmates who were going through training, she wasn't surprised to find out that they were being treated much differently. Collura was being excessively hard on her, and when her three weeks were up, she finally found out why.

"Bembenek, I'm putting my ass on the line for telling you this, but you've been a good shit, so I figure I owe ya," Collura told her.

"What?" Laurie asked, astounded by this first shred of kind behavior.

"Well, okay, don't let this get around, but I was ordered to give you a hard time, which I did," Collura said. "The stripes were hoping that you would just give up and resign."

Laurie couldn't think of anything else to say. Clearly the department was out to get her.

"Hey, all I have to say is, you took an awful lot these past few weeks. Good luck, kid."

That was the last time Laurie would ever see Collura. Five years later he would be shot and killed while on duty. She would remember him with mixed emotions, the same way she would remember most of the police officers she worked and trained with. Lawrencia Bembenek had discovered that the great police heroes of Milwaukee were not what they appeared to be.

CHAPTER 5

The Beginning of the End

On July 25, 1980, Laurie walked through the doors of the Milwaukee Police Department Police Academy for the last time. She had seen the inner workings of one of the largest police departments in the United States. About 1,800 trained police officers protected 850,000 City of Milwaukee residents. She had seen the other side of the shiny badges. Cops who drank on duty and intimidated suspects. Women treated like animals and constantly degraded. Police officers merely putting in their time so they could pick up a paycheck. It wasn't what she expected, but she was suddenly a part of the great police machine.

Lawrencia Ann Bembenek was now Officer Bembenek. She had made the cut. She was a Milwaukee cop. She attended the graduation ceremonies in August and was assigned to the south side of Milwaukee, District Two. Excited about making it through one of the worst experiences of her life, Laurie was eager to "start over" and prove she was one of the good cops.

What she saw and experienced in the Second District repelled her. When she talked about the cops she worked with, she could only describe the majority of them as brutal, lazy, apathetic, and corrupt. Her new district was a slow crime district, and that meant the officers had plenty of time to kill. They found unique ways to do it.

Bembenek, the rookie cop, witnessed hundreds of rule violations. She saw squads park in the cemetery at night after the bars closed. The officers would sleep away three or four hours on late shift, or drink together in squad parties. Cops who walked the beat were getting free drinks at bars. She saw some selling pornographic films from the trunks of their cars. Others met girlfriends while their wives waited at home. Some used what Laurie considered to be brutal, unnecessary force on suspects already in handcuffs—in the booking rooms away from the public eye.

Milwaukee's finest were using and selling drugs while on duty. They engaged in oral sex with prostitutes. They paid informants with drugs, and Officer Bembenek saw dozens of drunk drivers released from accident scenes to avoid all the extra time it took to process, test, and book them.

Her fellow officers talked constantly about their involvement with these activities. It was an accepted part of their life, and Laurie had no idea what she could do about it.

There was no one to tell. No one to go to. The unwritten police code of silence—of protecting your fellow officer no matter what—hung over everyone like a cloud. The guys Laurie had trained with in the Fifth District may have been assholes, but at least they worked hard.

There were a few moments when Laurie actually liked her work as a cop. Those were the nights when she walked her beat alone. When she didn't have to watch another cop break a rule and tell her to keep quiet. Those were the nights when

Laurie Bembenek knew she was doing what she was supposed to do.

Laurie turned twenty-one that August and started looking for a place of her own. She had decided to buy a condominium, although her social life had all but disappeared because of her second- and third-shift work. A new place to live might help Laurie meet new people. She had no idea when she picked up the phone on August 25 to check on her work schedule that her whole life was about to change.

The captain on the other end nonchalantly told her that Chief Breier had sent out an order for her dismissal from the police force. Laurie wasn't prepared for the news. She thought everything was fine. She had played by all the rules. She had been fair and honest, and she had kept her mouth shut.

Two sergeants came by to pick up her badge, gun, and uniforms. Laurie stood by the door in a state of shock. She couldn't believe what was happening. She didn't understand. That night when her dad came home from work Laurie told him the news and then cried in his arms.

Four day later a small article tucked away in a corner of *The Milwaukee Journal* helped her figure out what was going on.

BRIER FIRES 3 WOMEN IN ONE WEEK

In the last week, Milwaukee Police Chief Harold A. Breier has fired three women police officers.

Bonnie Avant, Patricia Lipsey, and Lawrencia

Bembenek were all still in their probationary periods. The only reason given on the official police orders for Avant and Lipsey was "for the good of the service." Bembenek's order said she was charged with untruthfulness and making a false official report, but no details were given.

Avant and Lipsey are black.

Lipsey was fired Aug. 21, Bembenek Aug. 25 and Avant Aug. 26.

All three apparently plan to appeal their dismissals.

Another officer, Kathleen M. Rodriguez, was suspended this week for three days for neglect of duty. She has not indicated plans to appeal the discipline.

One of the women who was fired said she had been given no reason for her dismissal and she believed it was a case of discrimination against women. One woman said she was merely given a written notice stating she had been fired.

"They just read it off at roll call [the firings] so that everyone can hear," said another of the women. "It's like daily news. They are really railroading the women in that department. Women and blacks are the only ones they pick on," she said.

Tom Barth, president of the Milwaukee Police Association, said the union would investigate the cases if the women file grievances and ask for reinstatement.

CHAPTER 6

Last Chances

Years later Laurie Bembenek would remember the next months and meetings as a constant blur. She would compare herself to a machine. Running on automatic pilot. Doing all the necessary things. Surviving but never really living.

Laurie's dismissal from the police department devastated her. She had no idea what would happen next. But whatever happened, Lawrencia Bembenek couldn't stop it.

Laurie immediately contacted the police union so she could start a grievance for reinstatement. She was eager to read her personnel files and find out the exact reasons for her dismissal. She guessed, but her guess was just a little off.

When the seventy-year-old Breier finally agreed to release her file, Laurie read that Judy Zess had signed a statement accusing her of smoking marijuana at the concert they had both attended. Laurie couldn't believe the report and left quickly to confront Judy.

Judy admitted signing the statement but convinced Laurie that she had done it under duress after hours of interrogation by police officials.

"Laurie, you don't understand. I was drunk," Judy said. "They told me that if I didn't write all those things down, and sign it, then they were going to wake up the chief and take me to see him."

As she continued to explain why she signed the statement, she grew more and more adamant. "You've got to believe me," Zess screamed. "Why do you think I appealed the damn thing? They had me under the hot lights practically. I didn't know what I was doing. They dragged me in there. I fell down and ran my nylons. Then they stood over my shoulder and told me what to write. My rights were violated. I told them that I wanted an attorney but they said no. This is an internal matter. You've got to believe me."

Judy promised she would sign an affidavit for Laurie saying that she had lied. Before Laurie knew what was happening she had forgiven Judy and was listening as Zess proposed that the women move in together. Laurie knew she had to be crazy even to consider Judy's proposal, but she still valued the relationship. It was September 1980.

Moments later, Judy suggested that both women should drive down to the Lake Geneva Playboy Club to apply for jobs. Laurie was baby-sitting for another police officer, Margie Lipschultz. She was barely scraping by. She had also discovered that the unemployment office was appealing her compensation eligibility. If she lost that appeal, she would have to come up with a hunk of money very fast to pay back the unemployment money she had been receiving. She would use the Playboy Club if all else failed.

For the next few weeks Laurie's life was a waiting game. It was good practice for the years that followed. While she waited, she occasionally dated a man from Chicago, someone Margie knew, and she tried unsuccessfully to figure out what had happened and what was happening to her life. She thought her simple dream of working as a police officer was beginning to destroy her image of herself, her relationships, and, sometimes, she thought, her mind.

In mid-October Laurie's downward spiral continued. First there was a letter from the police union saying that her case was to be dropped. Within a week she also had to appear at her unemployment hearing. During that hearing Laurie thought she was losing her mind. She had never heard so many lies in her life. One officer actually testified that Laurie had been arrested the night she attended the concert with Judy.

"How can they get up there and lie?" Laurie whispered to her attorney. "There isn't an arrest record because I was never arrested."

That attorney, Kenneth Murray, would set the standard for other attorneys who would soon follow him. "Don't worry, Lawrencia," he said. "I'll take care of this."

Murray didn't take care of it. Laurie lost her case and had to pay back almost $2,500 in unemployment benefits. Desperate, she made a move that would haunt her for the next fifteen years. Laurie applied for a job as a waitress at the Playboy Club. She had waitressing experience, Lake Geneva wasn't far from her southside home, and the tips were great. She could make $50 for bringing some bozo a cup of coffee. Laurie figured if Gloria Steinem could work at a Playboy Club, she would be able to handle it for six weeks.

Meanwhile, Judy Zess had come up with a more novel idea for making money. Since her suspension she had worked as a waitress and then at a local waterbed store. When the bills started piling up, she developed a quick way to get some money.

"I called all the guys I've been sleeping with," Judy told Laurie, breathless with the excitement of her clever plan, "and told them I was pregnant and needed an abortion. At two hundred bucks apiece, I raked in about eight hundred dollars."

Laurie shouldn't have been surprised, but she was. Then Judy told Laurie something that shocked her even more. All the drug possession charges against her had been dropped. Judy explained that could pave the way for Laurie to get back on the police force. If Judy Zess was innocent, that meant Lawrencia Bembenek was innocent, too.

At that point Laurie couldn't even consider returning to the police force. Her problems with the department had ruined her self-esteem. She was working part-time at a local gym, and she was seriously thinking about joining the Air Force. Laurie Bembenek didn't really know where she belonged or what she wanted to do. She was twenty-one years old, and to her it seemed that she had made every wrong turn, every wrong decision, that a person could make. She needed something or someone to help her put her life back together.

The third week of November, just before Thanksgiving, Lawrencia Ann Bembenek met just such a person. That's when Elfred O. Schultz, Jr., a Milwaukee police detective, entered her life.

CHAPTER 7

The Dance of Love

Elfred Schultz, or Fred as everyone called him, was having an affair with Laurie's friend Margie Lipschultz when Laurie first met him. It was against the Milwaukee Police Department regulations for two police officers like Margie and Fred to sleep together, but everyone else seemed to be doing it. As long as no one turned you in, everything would be okay. So Margie and Fred sneaked around together even though they were both sleeping with other people.

At first, Laurie couldn't imagine how anyone in her right mind could fall for a guy who seemed to like himself more than anyone else. The first night Laurie met Fred at Margie's she thought he was self-centered and boisterous.

During that first meeting in November of 1980 Schultz immediately started putting the moves on Lawrencia Bembenek. When Margie would leave the room, he would come over and sit by her. Later, Fred told Laurie he was instantly attracted to her and felt an immediate bond. He told Laurie he thought she was one of the most beautiful women he had ever seen, and he was captivated by her quick wit and great sense of humor.

That November evening, while the two women and Schultz talked over gin and tonics, Laurie learned all she thought she needed to know about

Schultz. He was divorced and had two sons. He had had a vasectomy. He was sleeping with so many female Milwaukee cops, he mixed up their names in casual conversation. He readily admitted that the only reason he had married his former wife, Christine, in the first place was that she had been pregnant.

Before Laurie left her friend's home, Schultz had already asked her for a date. Laurie couldn't believe he had the guts to do it in front of Margie.

"Save your breath, Schultz," Laurie told him. "You'll need it to blow up your inflatable date tonight."

Laurie left Schultz standing in the doorway and hoped she would never see him again. Schultz was hoping for something else as he watched Lawrencia Ann Bembenek move across the yard and into her flame-orange Camaro. He knew they would meet again. The sooner the better.

The following week Laurie made good on her promise to enlist in the United States Air Force. She was tired of her seemingly aimless life and she wanted to get as far away from her police department memories as possible. She was signed into a delayed-entry program that would eventually train her to become an airport fire fighter.

Just after Thanksgiving Laurie ran into a man she had trained with at the police academy. Over a drink the man told her that a police aide was the blond woman who had been smoking marijuana and running around half naked at the party Laurie had attended earlier in the year. The man admitted that the other police trainees at the party had been afraid to come forward with the truth.

Disgusted, Laurie slammed her drink down on the table and left the bar. She wondered how she could have been so näive about upholding the law, protecting the public, and doing what is right.

She walked into an East Side club and saw Margie and two men sitting at the bar. They were looking at a stack of photographs. They were photos of naked men and women dancing on picnic tables in a park.

"Where are these from and who are these people?" Laurie asked the two men.

"Don't tell me you never heard of the Tracks picnic," one of the guys said. "They have this picnic every year and it's pretty damn wild."

"Obviously," Laurie said as she shuffled through the photos. "How come no one arrests these people? I can't believe this all happened at a public park. Look at all the people standing around."

"Because half these people are cops," the other man said. "Look, you know Fritz, don't you?"

Fritz was Fred Schultz. The men he worked with in the police department had nicknamed him Fritz because he was German and talked about it often. In the photo Laurie saw of Fred he was posing with his arms flexed in front of a large crowd of people. He was naked.

Laurie learned that the Tracks, a popular Milwaukee tavern, had been having their annual picnic for years. Because the bar was a popular hangout for Milwaukee cops, the picnic was always well attended and well protected by Milwaukee police officers. The parties always started out with free beer and quickly degenerated into wet T-shirt contests and naked debauchery.

Totally disgusted, Laurie was happy she didn't

have to tell anyone she was a Milwaukee police officer. If this was their idea of an outdoor sporting event, then she was sure it was better not to be a Milwaukee cop.

During the first week of December, Laurie decided to talk to a representative of the Equal Employment Opportunity Commission. Laurie was convinced that her treatment by the MPD was a blatant example of sex discrimination. After talking with the commission representative, she felt sure she could prove that female and male officers were treated much differently. She could even get the photos from the Tracks picnics to prove her point. Laurie had been fired for mere rumors, and regular male officers were dancing naked in public. The representative felt she could have grounds for a good case against Milwaukee, and he sent her to see James Morrison, an assistant United States Attorney for the Eastern District of Wisconsin.

Her meeting with Morrison, a tall, quiet black man, was the first positive thing that had happened to Laurie in months. He told Laurie that he had been documenting the way that minority and female police officers were handled by the MPD. He said an obvious pattern was developing and Laurie's story fit the pattern. Morrison told Laurie that in order to get federal money the MPD had to meet guidelines for hiring minorities. He said the city was quick to turn in those figures but that large numbers of women and minorities who were quickly fired were never reported.

Morrison would never forget his meeting with Laurie Bembenek. After years as an assistant district attorney in Milwaukee, where he had heard every conceivable excuse for crime, he had a good sense of who was honest. Laurie Bembenek seemed to be telling the truth. He had heard enough to know that her treatment by the MPD was standard. He thought Laurie Bembenek would have been a great cop, too. She was determined and had a sense of justice. After the way she had been treated, he thought it took courage for her to even pursue a grievance against the MPD. Maybe they could help each other.

Bolstered by that meeting, Laurie borrowed the photos of the Tracks picnic and went to see her old buddy, Sgt. Orval Zellmer. Zellmer almost fainted when he saw the photographs.

"I was dismissed for little more than a rumor," she told Zellmer, "when there are cops out there getting away with things ten times worse than what I was accused of."

Zellmer was silent. He was thumbing through the photos as fast as possible.

"It's not fair," Laurie told him. "How could this picnic and all the other picnics have gotten so out of hand, right out in the open in a public park. Where were all the squads?"

At that moment Zellmer didn't seem to care about what was fair and what wasn't. He wanted to get Bembenek out of his office as fast as possible and take the photographs upstairs. Zellmer recognized several policemen in the photos, but he was certain Bembenek didn't know that. He kept the photos and told Laurie he would check everything out.

* * *

While Laurie had resurrected her battle against the MPD, her friend Margie Lipschultz continued her battle with Fred Schultz, who at the same time was sleeping with several other women. Margie even offered Laurie a litany of names.

Laurie knew that her pal was also sleeping with other men, and she reminded herself of that fact. Margie complained that it was other things, too. Schultz's roommate, Stu Honeck, another Milwaukee cop, told Margie that Schultz was the greatest bullshitter alive.

"Come on, you can't believe that," Laurie said, surprised that she was even bothering to defend Schultz. "You know what department gossip is like."

Laurie wondered why she was defending Fred Schultz. Maybe I'm more attracted to him than I want to admit, she told herself.

When she unexpectedly met Schultz in a Milwaukee restaurant the following week and agreed to go jogging with him, she felt that there must be something there. Fred was an older man and that appealed to her. Even though she hated to say it, Laurie also admitted that Fred was very attractive. He was tall, blond, muscular, and he had beautiful blue eyes. She also liked the idea that he was a police officer. Laurie missed the department. There was still a part of her that wanted to get back into law enforcement. A part of her wanted to prove that a woman could make it as a cop, no matter how tough it got.

On their first date they jogged along the frozen shores of Lake Michigan near downtown Milwaukee. Fred was a perfect gentleman. He talked about his feelings and said he was tired of dating Margie because she drank too much and seemed emotionally unstable. Laurie liked being with him. After they finished running, they hopped into his van.

"Where to?" he asked.

"I'd really like to shower. We can go to my parents' house and have some coffee. You can wait while I change into some jeans."

"Okay," Fred said. "If you'd like to, maybe we can go to a tavern. I know one that has some fantastic imported beer. Do you like beer?"

"Do I? It's my only weakness."

"Is that your only weakness? What about men?"

"Oh, they're nice as pets." Laurie laughed.

Fred pretended to give her a dirty look and they both laughed.

By the end of the night Laurie found that she was falling in love. She tried to fight the feelings she had for Fred Schultz, but they were very real to her. He immediately asked her to go out with him the following night. She agreed and they attended a lavish party sponsored by the municipal court. Everyone who was anyone was there, and that suddenly included Lawrencia Bembenek. Fred had shown up at her door with a dozen red roses. Laurie couldn't believe this was the same man Margie had been complaining about just a few weeks ago. He was absolutely wonderful.

After the party, Fred took her dancing at a downtown Milwaukee club, and he talked about everything. Fred made Laurie feel that they were alike, compatible, and by the end of the evening she felt as if she had known him all her life. A man had never made her feel like that before. He never disagreed with her once the entire evening.

That night Fred could have asked her for anything and she would have given it to him. He was incredibly handsome in his dark suit, and her heart was beating so fast she felt weak. Out on the dance floor, when the music slowed down, Laurie couldn't even see anyone else. Fred kissed her, and she felt like she was falling through the middle of the earth. When she looked up, there was Fred Schultz, his blue eyes sparkling, his blond hair combed just the right way, his arms strong and gentle.

CHAPTER 8

Sacraments and Sins

Fred Schultz became an important part of Laurie's Christmas plans in 1980. Following the municipal court party, Laurie just declined when anyone else asked her out. All she could think about was Fred.

Just before Christmas Fred called her and said he needed to talk to her as soon as possible. Laurie agreed to meet him near the lakefront in the same place where they had their first date. As Laurie sat in her car, waiting for Fred, she wondered what was so urgent. Maybe he wants to stop seeing me, Laurie told herself. I suppose that would be good. It would make my leaving for the Air Force much easier.

Fred finally showed up and ran from his van around the side of Laurie's car. He opened up the door and jumped into the passenger seat. He wasn't smiling. Laurie had never seen him so serious. Usually he was loud and always joking about something.

"What's up? You had something important to tell me?" Laurie asked him.

"You're ... different," Fred said, talking slowly and deliberately. "I want it all with you. I want a long-lasting relationship."

"Look, Fred ... you and Margie ..."

"I don't care about her," Fred said, cutting her

off. "And neither should you. You should hear how she talks about you."

"You're not telling me anything new. I know she's not a true friend. She gets drunk and says nasty things. That's why I don't see her much anymore. But she still calls me."

Laurie and Fred got out of the car and started walking next to the huge ice floes along the lake. The sky was a deep, dark blue. The snow on the lake was totally white.

"Would you like to hear what she told me about you? She said that you used to beat your kids with a hammer."

"What? That's bullshit," Fred shouted. "Who told her something as outrageous as that?"

"Do you have a roommate named Stu?"

"That bastard. He's always trying to ruin any decent relationship I've ever had with anyone. He's seeing my ex-wife, for chrissakes."

Fred said he was trying to find a new place to live but could not come up with the money. He said he was doing some work for Honeck instead of paying rent. He said there was another divorced cop living with them, too.

"What about us?" Laurie asked him. "I'm scheduled to go into the Air Force in February. We'd have two months together, that's all. What about Margie?"

"She told me it's over. Can't you see what she's been doing? She's been bad-rapping us both so we wouldn't be interested in one another."

Everything Fred said made sense to Laurie. She wrote Margie a short note and said it would be a good idea if they didn't see each other anymore. She started spending every evening with Fred

Schultz. Laurie found him endlessly interesting, humorous, and pleasantly assertive. He was always at her elbow and always interested in whatever she was doing. It seemed as if they wanted the same things out of life and were headed in the same direction. Fred said he didn't want any more children and that he wanted an independent partner, a career woman. To top it all off, Elfred Schultz was a cop. Laurie was beginning to feel as if she had found her perfect match and the ten-year age difference didn't matter at all.

Laurie started brooding over her decision to enter the Air Force. She was trying hard to ignore her feelings and emotions. I must close my heart like a tight fist, while I still can, she said to herself over and over. Then something happened that made her realize it was impossible for her not to love Fred.

Just days before Christmas, Fred took Laurie on a drive to Pewaukee, a small town on a large lake about twenty-five miles west of Milwaukee, to see his parents. They weren't home but Fred had a key. They went in, and he made a fire in the fireplace and poured two glasses of wine.

"Did your dad build this house?" Laurie asked him.

"No, he bought it. They have a smaller house that they rent out in West Allis. My parents used to live there."

Suddenly the conversation shifted. Fred sat down right next to Laurie, so close she could feel his breath against her face.

"I think you love me as much as I love you."

It was the first time Fred Schultz had mentioned

the word *love*. Laurie thought she was in love with him, too.

"Yes. I do. It's just too bad that I made those plans to join the service before I met you."

"You're not going anywhere."

"I'm afraid I am."

"But you can't. We get along so well, we like all the same things, we feel the same way about everything. This past month has been so wonderful. Laurie, I feel like . . ."

"We'd better go."

They closed up the house and walked back outside to Fred's van. After Laurie got in, Fred walked up to her closed window and put his hand up against it. Laurie put her hand up on the other side and lined her hand up with his. When she looked across the tops of their fingers, she saw tears in Fred's eyes. Laurie wanted to cry, too. She thought it was ironic that just when she met a man who was everything she ever wanted, she might not see him again.

Laurie did see Fred again, though. She couldn't stay away from him. They went everywhere together, and Laurie couldn't remember a better Christmas.

Her favorite present that year was a tiny red-and-white wooden rocking horse, a special gift from her mother to make up for the rocking horse she was supposed to have received seventeen years earlier.

The glow of Christmas faded fast just after the holidays. Laurie received a phone call from a police friend warning her to be careful. The discrimination charges she had filed against the MPD were making lots of cops mad. Her friend said police officers were verbally threatening her.

"It's the guys. Boy, are they pissed," her friend said. "We were standing roll call last night and Sergeant Zellich told us that all because of you, we have to make our marks now."

Beat cops and squads are required at the Milwaukee Police Department to make their "mark" every hour while on duty. That means using the police call box to contact the station. The marks help keep track of the officers. If an officer fails to make a "mark," that could be a sign that he or she is injured or in trouble. At Second District, the late-shift workers were not required to make their marks. They could do whatever they wanted all night long. Until Lawrencia Bembenek told on them.

Within moments Laurie's phone rang again.

"Bembenek, your mother's dead," a man's voice growled.

Then she discovered that someone had tucked a dead rat under her windshield wiper. There were more threatening calls, and a few days later someone let the air out of her tires. When Laurie called internal affairs at the MPD, they said, "There just isn't anything we can do."

By the end of January Laurie was seeing Fred Schultz constantly. He called her several times a day and sent her cards and flowers. She met his sons, Shannon and Sean, and the four of them would often spend time together. Laurie never talked to Christine when she went with Fred to pick up his sons, but the women always waved to each other. Laurie thought she must be a good mother because the boys were always well behaved.

During the last week of January Laurie started to make plans for basic training camp. She wondered over and over if she had made the right decision. If I leave, will I ever find anyone like Fred Schultz? Laurie asked herself. The last time I gave up a man for a career it got me absolutely nowhere. I don't want to make the same mistake again.

When her Air Force recruiter called to tell her that she couldn't go to training camp with her suit pending against the City of Milwaukee's police department, Laurie couldn't believe it. "The Air Force can't accept anyone with any litigation pending. Nothing. Not a criminal litigation, not a civil action, a divorce proceeding, a custody petition. Nothing. Not even a complaint or claim with a government agency that involves a hearing," the recruiter told her.

"So what are you telling me? I can't leave for basic training next month?"

"Not unless your complaint is dismissed or decided by then." Laurie hung up the phone and immediately called Fred. He met her for lunch and she told him the news.

"That's great," he said, grinning. "I'm sorry if you are disappointed, but this means that you are not leaving. That's all that matters to me."

"The only thing I can do is drop the claim," Laurie told him, "and I can't do that. Not after all this time. Maybe I should. I don't know."

Laurie was torn by her feelings for Fred and desire to do what was right and the need to get on with her life and continue with her Air Force plans. She knew her women friends in the various women's organizations that she belonged to—the National Organization of Women, Women Against Rape, and the Women's Political Caucus in Milwaukee—were all supporting her. She did not want to let them down.

As their lunch hour stretched into two and then three hours, Laurie could feel the wine affecting her. She loved talking with Fred. When she was with him, nothing else seemed to matter.

"Does it bother you that I'm divorced?" Fred asked her.

"No. Your past is your past. As far as I'm concerned, you're a single guy."

"What about the Air Force now?"

"Everyone I know thinks I was nuts to enlist in the first place. I don't know. The commitment is scary, four years, you know. Even my dad doesn't want me to go. He said if it's anything like the Army, I won't like it."

Laurie told Fred she really didn't want to drop the suit against the MPD because of all the time and energy she had invested in it. She said the department was getting away with things it shouldn't.

"So?"

"So, I guess I won't be leaving next month. I just have to get my career back on the ground. I have to have a direction. I have to work."

Fred poured her some more wine and leaned across the table.

"You know, Laurie, we are so much alike. When are you going to ask me to marry you?"

"Ha," Laurie said, laughing hard. "When hell freezes over."

"Then I'll ask you. Do you want to get married?"

Laurie was caught off guard. A marriage proposal was the last thing she expected that day. Her mind started to race. For years she had been saying she wouldn't marry until she was at least thirty years old, but she felt a strange sense of urgency. She hated the thought of losing Fred Schultz.

"Of course," she finally said. "I'd love to get married."

Once the decision was made, the plans followed even faster. They both agreed they wanted a private, quiet ceremony. They also agreed not to tell anyone and met the following morning—their wedding day, January 30, 1981—to drive to Waukegan, Illinois. It was Fred's idea to cross the state line for the ceremony. He said he knew a judge who would marry them.

Laurie and Fred exchanged simple gold wedding bands. He promised her he would buy a diamond as soon as he saved up the money. They kissed, and the judge congratulated them. When Laurie signed her marriage license, she wrote Lawrencia Ann Bembenek. She had already told Fred she would be keeping her own name. He said he didn't care, just as long as they were married.

On the way back to Wisconsin, Laurie and Fred stopped at a small park to take some photos. Laurie could hardly believe she was married. This was supposed to be the most exciting day of her life but something was missing. She wasn't sure what it was. As they drove north, she kept staring at her wedding ring. I'm married, she said over and over to herself, testing out the words before she would have to start saying them out loud. Laurie kept turning to look at Fred. She wanted to be sure she wasn't dreaming. She couldn't believe she was actually married to this handsome cop.

CHAPTER 9

Building the Web

Lawrencia Ann Bembenek and Elfred Schultz spent their first day as man and wife moving in with Judy Zess. Judy lived in a high-rise condominium close to the shores of Lake Michigan just a few minutes from downtown Milwaukee. The Bay View Terrace Condos on South Shore were nice, but it wasn't exactly a honeymoon arrangement.

Fred had planned on moving in with Judy before he proposed to Laurie. He wanted to get away from Honeck. One night, just before his second marriage, Fred and Honeck got into a fistfight and Honeck ordered Fred out of the house. Judy told Laurie that she was looking for a roommate to share expenses, so Laurie suggested the arrangement to Fred.

Fred said they should go on a honeymoon, and he made arrangements for them to fly to the West Indies for a week, but first they had to tell their parents about the wedding. They decided to do it at a local restaurant.

When Laurie told her mom about the wedding, she initially thought her daughter was joking. Marriage had always been the last thing on Laurie's list. In fact, Laurie told her more than once she would be surprised if she ever got married. There were too many other things to do. Her mother was also hurt that Laurie hadn't invited anyone to the ceremony and disappointed that the wedding hadn't taken place in church. Fred's parents seemed pleased when they heard the news.

"We're legally married and everything," Laurie said. "We just didn't have a reception, so we might have a little thing in the spring."

"You're having a little thing in the spring?" Laurie's mother asked. "Is that why you eloped?"

"Impossible. I married Fred for his vasectomy."

"I suppose you kept your name," her mom added. "You've been pontificating about that for years."

"You know better than to argue with me about that. Yes. I kept my name for feminist reasons."

"I hope you know, Fred, you got yourself an independent little cuss here."

Fred said he knew what he was getting into and couldn't wait.

Just before Laurie and Fred left for their honeymoon, Fred called his ex-wife Christine to tell her he had gotten married. Laurie was standing right next to Fred and he suddenly handed her the phone. Laurie didn't know what to say and she felt awkward.

"I heard you collect butterflies," she told Christine.

"I put them on velvet and make wall hangings."

"Maybe I can buy some tropical butterflies and bring them back for you."

"That would be nice. Could I talk to Fred again?"

Laurie told Fred she didn't appreciate being put on the spot like that. Fred said she would get used to it because she had no choice. He said Laurie would be seeing Christine a lot because of the children.

"I just don't have any experience with this kind of situation," Laurie said. "Just give me a little time."

"You know what?" Fred asked. "I only wish that I could have met you ten years ago."

"But, Fred, I was only twelve ten years ago."

The incident with Christine was quickly forgotten. The entire honeymoon week in Jamaica was like one page after another from a travel brochure. Laurie and Fred stayed at a hotel right on the beach. They spent afternoons sailing around coral coves and past swaying palm trees. They drank wine and walked up and down the white sand beach. They held hands constantly and talked for hours about all the wonderful years they had to look forward to. They were together every minute, and Laurie was certain she had made the right decision when she ran off to marry Fred. There was only one unhappy event all week.

Fred accidentally left his expensive Nikon camera in the dining area of the hotel and when he went back to get it, the camera and all of their film were gone. Fred had left the camera in the restaurant and he was blaming everyone but himself for the mistake. He began yelling and screaming. Laurie had never seen him act that way, and she couldn't believe what her own eyes told her.

Once Fred calmed down, things got back to normal. They spent their evenings dancing and it seemed as if the Caribbean were made for new lovers. Everyone, including Laurie and Fred, was always kissing and hugging. For the first time in months Laurie was happy. She was very much in love.

Back in Wisconsin the honeymoon glow faded the minute their plane landed. Judy Zess and a friend she called "Gene, Gene, the Dancing Machine" picked them up at the airport. After they all said hello, Judy told them they had to look for a new place to live. Judy said she had had a party while they were gone, and the landlords, who lived directly below them, said they were being evicted because of loud music.

"Oh, Zess, we just moved in. Do you mean to say that we're going to have to move all over again!"

"At least everything of yours is still in boxes," Judy said.

Fred said legally they had to be served with an eviction notice. He added that would take a few weeks and give them time to find a new place to live.

While Fred worked the third shift, from midnight to 9 A.M., as a detective, Laurie and Judy spent most of their evenings together. They drank wine, did the laundry, talked. Zess commented often that Fred was a little possessive of his new wife. He called her several times a night and he wanted to know where Laurie went, whom she went with, and what she did when the two of them were not together, which occurred rarely.

Their high-rise apartment was in a nice neighborhood that had a great park and lots of jogging paths. Fred's sons would often come over to spend time with their father and with Laurie. She was slowly getting used to the kids and she had had a few conversations with their mother.

One Friday night, over a bottle of tequila, Fred talked about his first wife. Schultz had expressed bitter feelings about his ex-wife before but never like this. He confessed to Laurie that he had been forced into marrying her when she claimed he had gotten her pregnant.

Laurie listened quietly as her husband talked about Christine. He blamed the failure of the marriage on her. He thought his wife was lazy, a bad mother, a terrible housekeeper. Laurie listened. She was certain there had to be another side to the story. Schultz was also angry that his ex-wife was dating his old roommate, Stu Honeck.

"I can't stand the thought of them sleeping in the house that I am paying for," Schultz said. "It makes me very angry."

Schultz had more than one run-in with Honeck, but the two avoided each other as much as possible.

A few weeks later when Fred received word of his property settlement, he came home from work sobbing. He had been ordered to continue making house payments of $383 a month, and he had to pay child support of $363. He was bitter and angry. "I built that house with my own hands and now she gets everything," he said. "It's not fair. It's just not fair."

While Fred and Laurie adjusted to married life, Judy Zess started dating someone new, Thomas Gaertner, a bodybuilder who lived above them in the condominium complex. Judy did not offer much information about Gaertner. Laurie wanted to know what he did for a living. He was living on a large inheritance. Judy wouldn't say much more than that.

When Judy finally received an eviction notice, they had already found a new apartment at 4612 South Twentieth Street number 5, in Milwaukee. The apartment was just under two miles from the home Fred Schultz had built on West Ramsey Street for Christine and the boys.

While everyone settled in, work continued on Laurie's complaint against the city. For once, Judy Zess actually agreed to help her. Judy wrote and signed a statement that Laurie turned in to the Equal Employment Opportunity Commission. In her short affidavit Judy said that she had been coerced into making a false statement on May 2, 1980, when she said Lawrencia Bembenek had smoked marijuana. She also said that Laurie didn't know anything about a marijuana cigarette butt under Judy Zess's seat. Zess said that the report filed by Lawrencia concerning what actually happened the night of the concert was factual and correct. Judy said the possession charges that had been filed against her had been dropped following a jury trial. Judy went on to say that she and Lawrencia had been discriminated against and that white male police officers are afforded preferential treatment.

Laurie had other statements that the commission was eager to see. One year following her appointment to the police academy, five black males, four white females, three black females, and one overweight white male had already been forced off the police force.

While the status of her complaint seemed positive, her relationship with her new husband had troubling moments. Laurie noticed that Fred talked excessively about his first wife. Then Laurie discovered his old wedding ring in a pair of his pants she was about to wash. When she showed him the ring, a swell of anger hit her. She was tired of his constantly talking about his Christine. She hoped she didn't have to spend the rest of her life listening while Fred complained about a set of circumstances that were probably his own doing. She felt as if he had never really left his first wife.

"All I understand is that she must have something on you and it must be something good, because when she puts her pretty little foot down, Fred jumps," Laurie said.

"What do you want me to do?" Fred argued. "I've done all I can do, and that's just the way the divorce laws are set up in this state."

Laurie knew differently. She knew Fred could have gotten more than a dresser and his clothes out of his marriage.

"What has that woman got on you?" Laurie demanded.

"You just don't know, Laurie. She has me by the balls. She could have had my job."

Fred never explained what he meant by those remarks, and his ex-wife Christine Schultz would never get a chance to tell her side of the story.

CHAPTER 10

Madness Descends

Fred Schultz solved his problems that April with his new wife by escaping to Florida for a week. Just after Fred and Laurie returned to Wisconsin, she received notice that the Equal Employment Opportunity Commission was ready to hold a fact-finding conference.

City Attorney Scott Ritter attended the meeting as well as a lieutenant and the commanding officer of the Second District station. Laurie's complaint and the separate charges were presented orally, step by step. The attorney was given a chance for rebuttal.

Laurie maintained that she was dismissed for reasons of sex discrimination. She said the report she filed about the concert she had attended with Judy was truthful. She gave them Judy's signed statement. She also told them she had never been arrested that night.

Ritter claimed to have numerous witnesses who had seen her being arrested. However the district attorney had not issued charges against Laurie, and there was no record of an arrest. When Ritter finally checked his files, he admitted that Laurie was right about the arrest but wrong about the sex discrimination charges.

"Cunt refers only to a woman, doesn't it?" Lau-

rie asked them. "That was uncalled for and was done to me deliberately."

"You can't prove intent," Ritter said.

"I know it was deliberate because my field training officer later informed me that he was told to give me a hard time per his superiors."

After she divulged their names, Ritter said that field training is a vigorous period of training that occurs before a recruit is allowed to graduate. He said giving a recruit a hard time is part of the training. He said street slang and name-calling are part of a police officer's jargon.

The hearing continued for several more hours, and Laurie realized she was getting absolutely nowhere. The city wanted her to find a man who had the same problems she had encountered. If she could prove the man had not been disciplined, her case would have some merit.

Laurie knew that would be impossible because she didn't have access to personnel files. She also knew it was unlikely that a similar case against a male officer existed.

"This is impossible," Laurie said. "They judge whether a report is false or not, even when it's the truth, as plain as the nose on your face. It's so unfair. That female Puerto Rican from Second District took a rap for falling asleep on duty. They all fall asleep. So I would not only have to prove that a male officer filed a false official report, but that the commanders knew it was false and didn't discipline him. That's impossible."

Laurie was told that the Equal Employment Opportunity Commission would determine soon if she had cause for her claim. If the commission found cause, they would pursue the matter through the Department of Justice. If no case was found, Laurie had the right to sue at her own expense. Determined to do whatever she could to see that her claim was handled properly, Laurie decided she would file a lawsuit if that's what it took for women to be treated as equals in the Milwaukee Police Department.

Back home, Judy confided that her relationship with the bodybuilder upstairs had turned serious. Judy still wouldn't say much about Gaertner, but it looked as if she was slowly moving out.

Tom Gaertner, a one-time Mr. Wisconsin, never worked, and Laurie found it hard to believe that the guy was surviving on an inheritance and good looks. One afternoon when Laurie and Judy went to Gaertner's apartment to pick up some clothes, Laurie discovered the secret of his unclaimed success. His refrigerator was loaded with huge bags of marijuana.

Holy shit, Laurie said to herself as she quietly closed the door. What the hell has Judy gotten herself into this time?

Laurie Bembenek and Judy Zess were headed down parallel and identical paths of destruction, with one major difference. Judy was doing it knowingly, and Laurie didn't have a clue. Laurie's path, already tangled and troubled, would quickly become littered with another incredible discovery. When Laurie discovered the drugs in Tom's refrigerator, she thought she understood why he constantly verbalized his hatred of cops. But a frantic phone call from Zess explained the real reason. "Why didn't you tell me Fred killed Tom's friend," Judy yelled into the phone.

"What are you talking about?"

"Several years ago Fred killed an off-duty cop, and the guy he killed was Tom's best friend, and he is really pissed," Judy said. His death had left Gaertner with a deep hatred of cops. According to Gaertner, Fred had killed the man for no apparent reason.

Fred's version of the story was much different from the one Judy offered. While they stood in their kitchen, he told Laurie how he killed the cop. He said he drove to Glendale, a small suburb adjacent to Milwaukee, when he received a call while on duty.

"I shot and killed a Glendale cop in 1975 named G. Robert Sasson," Schultz began. "It turned out that he was a bad cop who was dealing drugs anyway. See, I was in a squad on that side of Milwaukee when a call came over the radio. Officer Needs Assistance, 10-17. The location was vague. They said somewhere on Silver Spring Road. We kept listening. The dispatcher came back and confirmed the location to be a tavern called The Northway Tap. So anyway, we arrived and a woman in the parking lot waves to us. She tells us to go in through the back door because the front is locked. It was Sasson's wife, Camille."

Schultz said he was followed into the back of the bar by the rookie cop who worked with him.

He continued: "There was a frosted-glass partition right by the door. Rounding the partition all I could see is a guy in a yellow baseball uniform, kneeling over a black dude on the floor. As soon as we approached him, he stood and put his semiautomatic to the rookie's chest."

Schultz told his wife that the next few seconds

were a quick blur of action. He pulled out his gun and fired four slugs into the man wearing the baseball uniform. Then Camille Sasson started screaming. "That's my husband. He's a cop."

Another one of Fred Schultz's secrets was making itself known. Laurie had no idea her husband had ever killed a man. Schultz told his wife he had been cleared of any wrongdoing, even though he was in a city outside his jurisdiction.

"The guy who called the cops called the Milwaukee cops by mistake," Schultz explained. "Everything worked out okay because we found out later that the guy was trigger-happy. That wasn't the first time an incident of that nature involved him. He drank too much and usually got into trouble with his gun."

Everything may have worked out for Schultz, but Tom Gaertner never forgot about Sasson. He hated Elfred Schultz. He would never forgive the man who had killed his friend and gotten away with it.

Two weeks later, when Judy found out that Laurie had told Judy's mother Judy was moving in with Gaertner, there was a big scene at their apartment. Laurie left her friend a note.

2nd week of May

Judy,

First of all I don't know how you can pull something like this. To come home from Florida and find half of your stuff moved out—and then we don't hear from you for another two weeks, not knowing whether or not you're going to pay the next half of rent. When we got this place we were also considering you because you didn't have anywhere to go. Fred wanted to get a small 1 bedroom. BUT NO. I said let's help Judy out. Just like we're coming home from our honeymoon and you tell us we get evicted. Are you going to run from one landlord to another from now on? We signed a year's lease here—you signed it too and then conveniently stayed out in Delafield while Fred and I moved everything in here.

The only reason I talked to your mom was because I was concerned about you because I know how you impulsively rush into things without thinking. I didn't bad-rap Tom. I just think I'd be afraid of someone that big. Besides anyone who hates cops that much obviously isn't advocating decency and good moral law and order. I'm not referring to drugs. I don't care about victimless crimes but I do care if my friend could be a victim. Laugh if you want but I'm just telling you. Cheap tactics? The only reason I didn't want to move in with you before is because I was afraid of something like this and Jan Bauman [a mutual friend] warned me about living with you so she proved me wrong. Thanks for the foil and the sugar. Here's money for your suntan oil Freddy forgot to leave for you before.

Laurie

p.s. What happened with Tom's best friend, (strange—I thought he hated cops) and Freddy shouldn't have anything to do with you and me.

If Tom convinced you otherwise don't be so impressionable.

p.p.s. Cheap tactics is using all my dishes for your dinner making a huge mess and then leaving it all as if to say—"Fuck you."

Oh, better change your court hearing to another judge other than Siefert.

When Gaertner read the note, he became angry and confronted Laurie.

"Listen," he yelled. "We don't give a good goddamn about your finances, and I don't give a shit about the mess Judy left in the kitchen or the little talk you had with her mother. All I know is that your husband is nothing more than a scared, motherfucking punk that killed my best friend. The trigger-happy pig!"

Finally, Laurie had had enough of Judy Zess. She told her to take her things out of the apartment. She didn't care about the lease as long as Judy Zess and her problems were gone. But Judy would not be gone for long. One short week later, Gaertner was arrested by federal agents and charges with possession, and with the intent to deliver cocaine.

Judy came back to the apartment in tears to get the rest of her belongings. She was moving back to the same condominium complex she had lived in with Laurie and Schultz near Lake Michigan. While Gaertner sorted out his legal problems, she would stay in his apartment.

While Laurie helped Judy pack up the rest of her belongings, Fred was busy fighting on the phone with Christine. He found out that she had taken the boys up to northern Wisconsin to see her family over Memorial Day weekend. Fred demanded to know every time the boys left town. Laurie could hear him yelling through the door.

"Ten miserable years and I'm paying through my teeth," he said. "Don't give me that crap, Chris. I know how much you make. I intend to expose your income to a judge just as soon as I can! I'll see you in court."

When Fred finished, he came outside and he was laughing. He told Laurie that someone had turned Honeck in to the department for sleeping with Chris. An antiquated policy didn't allow Milwaukee police officers to cohabit or have sex with anyone but the spouse. Fred also told Laurie that Honeck and Christine thought Laurie was the one who had turned them in.

"Me?" Laurie said, stunned by the idea.

"Isn't that hilarious?" he said. "I'm sure it wasn't you, because it was me."

The next day there was Honeck's gravelly voice on their phone-answering machine. "Fuck you, motherfucker," he had said.

Laurie wasn't as shocked by the phone call as she was by the idea that Fred had given their new unlisted phone number to Christine without asking her first. It was becoming more and more obvious to her that although Fred Schultz claimed to be divorced, he had never really moved out of his last home. Laurie didn't understand why he couldn't let go of Christine.

As Fred slammed the door and left for work, Laurie wondered if there would ever be an end to all the madness, all the despair. It was May 26, 1981. Laurie could only hope that things would somehow get better.

CHAPTER 11

The Nightmare Explodes

On May 27, 1981, the morning air throughout Milwaukee was quiet and warm. It was almost summer. When Laurie left her Twentieth Street apartment late in the morning, neighbors were busy dragging out flowerpots and hosing down sidewalks. The air smelled like freshly cut grass. It was warm enough to wear shorts and T-shirts. Driving to job interviews at two different security firms, Laurie watched the city of Milwaukee wake up from the long winter, and she thought the world looked carefree and vulnerable.

Laurie wasn't sure what Fred would be doing during the day. She had no idea how he managed with so little sleep. When she returned home about five from her interviews, he complained that he had tossed and turned all afternoon and was still exhausted. They ate a quick meal together, and then Laurie's parents showed up with some boxes so Laurie could pack what was left of the apartment for the latest move. Fred had rented a tiny efficiency apartment not far from the Bembeneks' home in South Milwaukee. They thought their involvement with Judy Zess was finally over.

Fred decided to go back to bed. Laurie's dad left, and her mom stayed to help her pack. Laurie enjoyed the time she spent with her mom. They were more like friends than mother and daughter. She knew that no matter what happened, her mother would always be there to help out.

It was after 11 P.M. when Joe Bembenek came back to get his wife. By then everything in the house, except for a few items of clothing, was ready for the move to Fred and Laurie's new apartment. The Bembeneks left and Fred got out of bed. Fred immediately wanted to know if Laurie was still going to go to a local bar, the Tropicana, with a friend of hers, Marylisa.

"No, I think she forgot about it. I tried her apartment earlier, but her roommate told me she went straight to her boyfriend's after work, and I don't have his number," Laurie told him.

She told Fred she was glad she wasn't going out because she was exhausted from the job interviews and from packing all night.

When Fred left for work about 11:15 P.M., he said he might stop by for coffee sometime during the night. If it was a slow night, Fred and his partner would often drive by the apartment and then come in if the light was on. Laurie knew he could show up at any time during his shift. She often kept a pot of warm coffee on the stove just in case he stopped in to see her.

Fred called her three times during the next ninety minutes. Although Fred phoned her frequently when he was at work, Laurie thought that night he was trying to set a record. He said he was worried that Zess and Gaertner might try to get into the apartment when he was gone and do something to her. Laurie thought he was using that as an excuse to check up on her. She thought he was just jealous.

Just a week before she had stopped with Judy Zess to buy Fred a diamond ring with the money she had gotten back from the Internal Revenue Service after she filed her income tax return. When she arrived home, he started to yell at her because she was late. When she disgustedly threw the ring at him, all he could do was stand there with his mouth hanging open.

Just after midnight, following Fred's third call, Laurie drifted off to sleep while she was reading a book.

Two miles away Christine Schultz was also asleep. The small television set that she left on threw eerie shadows on her bedroom walls. Across the hall, her sons—Fred Schultz's sons— cuddled together in the bottom bunk.

While his wives slept, Elfred Schultz, the Milwaukee detective, was having several drinks at a downtown Milwaukee bar, Georgie's Pub and Grub, with his partner Michael Durfee, and the bar's owner, George Marks. Both Schultz and Durfee were on duty. But they drank anyway. Lots of cops drank on duty. The officers and George Marks left George's and went to another bar about two miles away, Tompter's Inn. They used the unmarked detective car.

At 2 A.M. the silence of the night exploded in Christine Schultz's home. There was a gunshot. Footsteps, pounding, pounding, pounding. Two tiny voices crying for help. Sirens. Lights. The madness and mayhem of tragedy. Christine Jean Schultz was dead.

* * *

At 2:42 A.M. on May 28, 1981, Laurie Bembenek automatically reached for a phone she heard ringing. Half asleep, she heard her husband's voice. She thought she was still dreaming. "Laurie, are you awake?" Schultz yelled. "Are you awake? Wake up!"

"What's wrong?" Laurie asked, still on the edge of sleep.

"Laurie. Chris has been shot. She's dead. I'm going over to the house right now to see if the boys are okay. Are you all right?"

"Of course," Laurie said. She thought the entire conversation was a dream. She was asleep again before she hung up the phone.

Fred called back about an hour later. This time Laurie realized that she wasn't dreaming. Christine Schultz was dead. She threw on a robe and went downstairs to wait for Fred and make some coffee, but the coffeepot was packed. Laurie sat on a box and waited.

She called her mom. She called Judy Zess. She called her friend Joanne. She worried. "My God," she said. "What am I going to do with two kids?" She reached over and took a swig out of a bottle of whiskey that was sticking out of a cardboard box.

At 4 A.M. two Milwaukee detectives showed up at her apartment. They wanted to ask her some questions about Honeck and about Fred Schultz. They asked Laurie if she owned a gun. How about a green jogging suit? Laurie answered all their questions. She said she would do anything to help. There weren't many questions, though. The investigation into Fred Schultz's role in his ex-wife's murder had just begun and ended.

* * *

It was another hour before Fred got home. Michael Durfee, Fred's partner, was with him. Laurie let them into the apartment, and they raced for the bedroom. Laurie followed them. Durfee had Fred's off-duty revolver, a .38 caliber, in his hand and was checking the rounds and dumping them into his hand. He smelled the barrel.

"Nope," he said. "This gun hasn't been fired. Fred, why don't you clean this thing once in a while?"

"Yeah," Fred said. "I just wanted to check out this gun right away and make our report on it. That way there'll be no questions asked."

"Besides," Durfee said, "we think the guy used a forty-five tonight."

Laurie gathered up her clothes and walked into the bathroom to change. She was taken aback by Fred's composure. Her mind was flooded with questions. Why was he so eager to have his gun checked? Why was he so emotionless?

Fred then told Laurie he wanted her to go downtown with him. He said he had to identify Christine's body. Laurie thought that was a strange request because Stu Honeck had already seen her. Fred told her that Stu had been at the scene of the murder. But she didn't say anything. She got into the squad car with Fred and Durfee and they sped downtown.

Laurie and Fred entered the morgue alone. Laurie stood back until Fred motioned for her to come closer. She had never been this close to a dead body before. The whole thing seemed unreal to her. Christine was dressed in a pair of panties and a T-shirt that had an Adidas logo on the front. Long strands of rope hung loosely at her wrists.

A blue scarf was around her neck. Fred told her that it had been used as a gag. Then he rolled over his ex-wife's body so he could look at the bullet wound in her back.

Laurie stepped back for a moment. The wound was very large. She wondered if Christine had been sexually assaulted, but she didn't say a word. She just stood there wondering why Fred had insisted she come with him. Then he motioned for her to come closer.

"Look at this," he said, pointing to the area around the gunshot wound. "This is called radial expansion. See how the muzzle of the gun left its imprint on the skin? The gun was right up to her skin."

They finally left the morgue. Laurie didn't know what to say. What she had just seen was tragic and sickening.

Fred talked with the coroner while Laurie waited in a small office with Durfee. She could hear Fred answering questions about Christine.

"How would you describe her physically?"

"Very athletic," Fred said quickly. "Oh, yes, very athletic. She was on the swim team at college."

Laurie couldn't believe what she was hearing. She thought, Very athletic? You once told me that you couldn't even get Chris to go jogging with you. He had told Laurie numerous times that his first wife was lazy, fat, and unmotivated. Now he was telling the coroner something different. Then she heard him say, "It was common for her to run around the house in nothing but a T-shirt and panties."

Next, Fred told Laurie to wait for him in the

cafeteria of the Police Administration Building. He said an inspector upstairs wanted to talk with him. When Fred popped open his briefcase to toss in his memo book, Laurie noticed that he had his off-duty gun inside. It was the same gun Durfee had just checked.

While Laurie waited, she wondered who wanted to meet with Fred. And she wondered who had killed Christine Schultz and why? What would happen to the boys? Where would they all live? What was happening to her?

CHAPTER 12

To Tell the Truth

The day following the murder of Christine Schultz, Laurie and Fred put their energy into taking care of Shannon and Sean. The boys didn't really understand what had happened. They knew their mother had been murdered, and they knew they had seen the man who had killed her. The reality of the murder would hit them later, but on May 28, 1981, they were handling themselves better than expected.

That afternoon Fred and Laurie took them to their apartment. There were boxes everywhere and the boys turned on the television while Laurie and Fred made beds for them. They watched the evening news. A newscaster said police were looking for a tall man with a long ponytail who was wearing a green jogging suit. The man who had murdered their mother.

"But it wasn't a green jogging suit," Sean said. "It was a green Army jacket, without camouflage."

"Sometimes the news gets things wrong," Fred explained.

Other news agencies also started asking anyone who had seen someone in a green jogging suit in the vicinity of the murder to call police. No one could explain how a green Army jacket had turned into a green jogging suit. The police department had a hard time keeping up with the dozens of calls about the murder. Someone said a substitute mailman matched the description.

Just after the news, Sean turned to his father and said he wanted to ask a question.

"What is it?"

"We were all standing there, after it happened, the policemen, Stu, and well ... Stu ... Stu said, 'I bet Freddy did this!' But I know you didn't do it, Daddy," Sean said, bursting into tears.

While the boys continued to watch television, Laurie heard Fred swearing in one of the other bedrooms and throwing boxes around.

"What are you doing?" she asked him.

"Trying to find my leather jewelry box. Where is it?"

"I have no idea. My mother packed this room, so she packed all of your things. Why? You're making a mess."

"It's got to be here."

"Why do you need your jewelry box?"

"Because! I have a ring of keys in there, one of which is the key to the house on Ramsey. I wasn't supposed to have a key to the house at all, Christine didn't want me to have one. So, one day when I picked up the boys, I made copies of Sean's house key. I hid one in my jewelry box."

"One?"

"I had one on my key chain with my keys, but I had to give it to the police, so they could get back into the house to dust for prints."

Fred finally found the key. Laurie stood in the room after he walked by her and wondered how she could live with someone and not know something so important about him. Fred was sneaky.

She had no idea there was a key in the apartment that belonged to Christine Schultz.

Fred then said they needed to visit Christine's house and get some things for the boys. They dropped the youngsters at Laurie's parents. At Christine's home, Laurie packed some of the boys' clothes into a paper bag while Fred paced up and down and apologized for the condition of the house. It smelled like dog urine and the children's room was a mess. There were toys everywhere. Clothes were thrown on the floor and one of the bunk beds had a urine-stained Mickey Mouse sheet on it.

"Don't let this scare you," Fred said. "The boys were never allowed to live like this when I was living here. You have to discipline kids."

When they walked into the den, Fred pointed out a strongbox in the middle of the room. He said it wasn't usually kept there. He also showed her how the stereo had been moved. Fred said it looked as if someone was looking for something. But what?

Laurie wasn't sure it was a good idea to be prowling through the scene of a murder, but Fred was a police officer. She followed him from room to room and listened as he belittled Christine's ability to take care of the home he had spent so many months building.

Fred was certain that Honeck had something to do with the murder. When they went into the bathroom, he looked into the shower and saw that it was stacked with dirty clothes. Laurie noticed a wad of gauze that had fallen out of the medicine cabinet and unraveled across the floor. It was the gauze Sean had used to try to save his mother's life. As they walked out of the bathroom, Fred said he was sure Honeck had lied about what time he had left Christine's house.

"You were with me at the morgue. Chris was perfectly clean," he said. "Her hair was freshly shampooed. It shone under the lights. She didn't look like someone who had been working in the garden all afternoon. When I saw Stu, he was cleaned up, too. They both showered somewhere and it wasn't here. If Chris had showered here, these clothes in the tub would be on the floor. She wouldn't put them back in a wet tub. I bet she spent some time at Honeck's house for a shower and a roll in the hay, and he's not saying."

"What if they don't find traces of semen at the autopsy?" Laurie said. "I don't think you should jump to conclusions. There might be a few holes in Honeck's story, but it doesn't spell murder. Besides, Orval Zellmer lives right across the street from Honeck. He's the king of internal affairs. You know he's the Milwaukee cop who's in charge of internal investigations. If Honeck was under suspicion for sleeping with Chris, I doubt if she'd frequent his house."

Fred continued his search. He found a well-stocked liquor cabinet and cursed Christine for asking him for extra money because she didn't have enough for food. He also went through Christine's purse that was lying on the counter. He pulled out a pack of birth control pills and started waving them around.

"Look at this!"

"Stop snooping," Laurie said. "Let's just go. You are getting yourself all worked up over nothing.

If I didn't know any better, I would say you are acting jealous. My God, Fred, she's dead."

Christine Schultz was buried in Appleton, Wisconsin, and Fred and Laurie drove to the city with Sean and Shannon, rented a hotel room, and attended the services. Fred didn't cry during the two days they were in Appleton and neither did the boys.

When Laurie walked up to Christine's coffin with Fred, they both noticed she had on a diamond ring. Neither of them had ever seen it before. Christine didn't have it on the night they saw her body at the morgue. Later, Honeck was introduced as Christine's fiancé and Fred wondered if Christine and Honeck had argued the night of the murder because she refused to marry him. He said he would mention the possibility to the police when they returned to Milwaukee.

Driving back to Milwaukee, Fred said that he was going to ask Eugene Kershek to handle Christine's estate paperwork. Laurie thought that was strange because he had been Christine's divorce attorney and Fred had ended up paying more money than he thought he should. Then Fred said Kershek was "cool." Laurie didn't understand his reasoning.

Back in Milwaukee Fred was transferred to day-shift hours. Laurie said they should find a place to live immediately because they had to get out of the Twentieth Street apartment and because they needed extra room for the boys. Fred suggested they move into Christine's house on Ramsey Street.

Laurie said absolutely not. She told Fred the house was Christine's home. It was full of her memories, the kids' baby pictures, memories of her life with Fred. Laurie said she could never live there. Fred insisted but Laurie said they could stay a few weeks where they were and then move into her parents' home while they were on the West Coast. Fred said she should take some time to think about Ramsey Street.

Laurie continued to apply for security jobs while working part-time at the gym. One afternoon, just days following the murder, two Milwaukee detectives approached her at work and asked if she would be willing to take a polygraph test. Laurie had just taken a polygraph test as part of a job application and wasn't excited about the idea. She knew the polygraph exams were lengthy and sometimes inconclusive. The detectives said they were asking Honeck, Judy Zess, Laurie, and Fred Schultz to take the tests. Laurie almost said yes when the detectives stood smiling at her, but she thought they might use the polygraph against her because of the discrimination complaint.

She called Fred's attorney, Richard Reilly, and he told her it wouldn't be a good idea to take the polygraph.

"Absolutely not," he said. "I wouldn't advise it. They can misconstrue the results. Don't trust them. They can't force you to submit to a polygraph, either."

Fred told Laurie he was going to take the test, even though Reilly advised him not to.

"This is very foolish," Laurie replied.

"I've got to do it," Fred said. "For the children. The department promised that anyone who agrees to poly will be cleared if they pass. They won't bother me anymore."

"Judy's not taking one, either," Laurie told him. "Who knows what they ask you once you get strapped in the chair. You could get fired."

Fred Schultz took the polygraph. He came back late in the evening, and he looked terrible. He told Laurie they had asked him "everything" and gone back to the time he was six years old. He admitted that he had smoked pot in college and that he had lied once about a traffic ticket. He told the men giving the exam that once he had punched Christine Schultz.

Laurie struggled in her new role as instant mother. She confided in her own mother that it was difficult to have to deal with two young boys. "I never even wanted to have children, and look, suddenly here they are," Laurie said. "I don't know how in the world I am ever going to do this."

The boys clung to Laurie and constantly told her how much they loved her. A child psychologist, Ken Ploch, said the boys' recurring nightmares would eventually go away. Every morning, when Laurie woke up, the boys would be sleeping beside her in bed. The psychologist also said it would really be a good idea for the boys to move back into their own home on Ramsey Street.

Laurie's mom continued to help her with Christine's children when Laurie looked for work. She applied for a job as a public safety officer at Marquette University in Milwaukee and crossed her fingers that she would get it. It would be pretty much the same type of work she had done as a police officer.

When their lease on the apartment ran out at the end of June, Laurie and Fred moved all their boxes and the boys into her parents' house. They continued their argument about moving into the Ramsey Street house. Fred told Laurie that Christine's mother had asked him to make an offer to purchase the estate's half of the house.

"In other words, they expect me to buy half of my own house from my children," he said.

Fred also told her that when he had taken apart the bed in Christine's bedroom, a penis-shaped vibrator fell out.

"I can't believe the police didn't discover it," he said. "But it's no wonder, the crime scene that night was a regular circus, with almost every squad on the south side climbing over one another.

Fred called two detectives when he found the vibrator, but they didn't seem interested enough to confiscate it.

"They could have taken it to the crime lab and tested it for traces of pubic hair or semen," Fred said. "But they acted like, 'Who cares?' "

Fred also said the police were really checking out a man they considered a suspect in Christine's murder. He lived across the street from the house on Ramsey.

"He's been described as a sort of a nut. A strange guy, living alone, and he has a history of emotional problems."

Fred said the man, Ray Kujawa, reported a .38-caliber revolver had been stolen from his garage.

"But the gun used on Chris was a forty-five, wasn't it?" Laurie asked.

"No, ballistics determined it was a thirty-eight."

"Then why was the bullet hole so large?"

"They said the wound was that large because of the close proximity from which it was fired. Right up to the skin."

"So this guy reported a gun of the same caliber stolen, even before the police knew it was a thirty-eight?"

"Yeah, he also made a statement to a neighbor that he's missing his green jogging suit."

"He must be crazy."

"He works second shift at a factory, has long brown hair. He paints cars as a hobby, so he'd have a painter's mask."

"The murderer was wearing a mask?"

"Well, according to Shannon he was. But you know that kid. I really doubt his credibility. He also says he saw a silver six-shooter with a pearl handle."

News of the Christine Schultz murder faded from the front pages of the local newspapers, even though the police hadn't arrested a suspect. Life on the south side of Milwaukee was returning to normal. The people of Milwaukee were confident that the police would find the man who killed Christine.

Laurie got the job at Marquette working as a campus security officer, and she loved it. She actually started to think that maybe everything was going to work out. The director of the department, Carol Kurdzeil, was a wonderful boss and

Laurie liked her instantly. It was a far cry from her work as a Milwaukee police officer.

Then Fred came home from work and told her they were questioning him about the murder. He said they asked him if he had a key to the Ramsey Street house. Fred told them he had a key with him and one was back at the apartment the night of the murder. Some police officers already knew that because Fred had turned over one key the night of the murder.

"They must know Honeck had a key too," Laurie said.

"I don't know. It was like they were trying to establish whether or not you or I had access to the house, because there was no sign of forced entry."

"You or me!" Laurie said, almost shouting. "Why? I didn't even have any knowledge of a key. The first I heard of a key was the time you started opening all those boxes, looking for it."

"I know. I kept it a secret because I wasn't supposed to have a key to that house."

"Did you explain that to them?"

"No. That would make me look bad."

"You! Jesus Christ, what about me? You make it sound like I had a key to that place. Why did you even tell them you had the extra key?"

"I couldn't lie. If the police saw us in the house later on, I would have had to explain how we got back in anyway."

Laurie desperately wanted to believe Fred. He was her husband. But it seemed as if he was shifting the blame away from himself and toward her. She became angry. "No wonder they were hassling me to take a polygraph," she yelled at him.

"You were just too chicken to take the blame yourself!"

"Bullshit," Fred yelled back.

"Bullshit, nothing. It's been nothing but trouble ever since we got married. My mother told me that divorced men were nothing but trouble. I should've listened to her. I thought you were so different."

"So what are you telling me?"

"I'm telling you that I'm tired of being your fall guy and I want out of this whole, nasty situation. I am not moving into the house on Ramsey. I am not playing Susie Homemaker to two kids that aren't mine. I'm tired of being treated like dirt by your family and I'm tired of this whole thing."

"Either you come to live with me on Ramsey in my house, or I'm leaving you."

"Fine. I'll live right here with my parents, and go to my job every day and not worry about washing boys' underwear with shit in it. Go to your damned house."

Fred took the boys and left for baseball practice. Laurie wanted to get in her car and drive away as fast as she could. She felt trapped. When Fred returned with the boys, Laurie finally agreed to move to Ramsey Street until the house could be sold. She felt as if she had no choice. She didn't want to lose Fred at this point in her life. She felt as if he was all she had left.

The following day when she received a call from Fred's lawyer at work, Laurie didn't know what to think. Reilly told her that the crime lab had found blood on Fred's service revolver.

Fred claimed to have only two guns. His off-duty

gun, the weapon Fred and Durfee checked the night of the murder, was a small Smith & Wesson .38 caliber with wood grips and a two-inch barrel. His service revolver, also a .38, had a four-inch barrel and a big black rubber grip. He always used the larger gun when he worked.

That night Fred told her the blood on the gun was type A, his blood type as well as Christine's. Laurie had no way of knowing for sure if his blood was really type A.

"Fred, this has to be a frame," Laurie told him.

"Maybe it's my blood on that gun from a fight I got into at work. We got dispatched to a disturbance at Monreal's . . ."

"You didn't tell me you were hurt at work."

"I wasn't hurt that bad. But I picked a scab on my arm. That must be it. They've been crawling all over me since we were at the lab. They might as well be accusing me, but I was on duty that night. Then they were ridiculous enough to suggest that you might have been able to switch guns that night. Isn't that stupid!"

"Me?" Laurie said. "What are you talking about, Fred?"

"You didn't have an alibi that night."

"Are you crazy? This is a homicide! An alibi?"

"I know, but they were questioning me."

"It's your gun! They found blood on the gun you were wearing that night. Why would they be asking questions about me?"

"I passed the polygraph and you refused to take one."

Laurie shook her head just to make sure she was really awake. What was Fred trying to tell her?

What was he trying to do to her? She quickly decided that the blood on the gun had to be Fred's. It couldn't be Christine's. The detectives were only asking routine questions. Fred couldn't possibly think she had murdered his ex-wife. Could he?

Laurie also remembered how upset Fred had been the morning following the murder when he talked about the meeting he had with police officials just after they had viewed Christine's body. He came into her parents' kitchen and told her and her mom and dad that he had been questioned over and over about Christine's murder and his actions the night of the murder. Fred was almost shaking when he told them about the meeting.

"I told them to charge me or I'm walking out of this meeting," Fred told Laurie and her parents.

Laurie began wondering what had actually taken place at that meeting.

That weekend friends and relatives helped Fred and Laurie clean out the Ramsey Street house. They would move their boxes and pieces of furniture into the house the following week, get everything set up, and then start living there.

Laurie sat on a box in the middle of Christine Schultz's living room and looked out of the window. She told herself that she had to believe that everything would be okay. They would move into the house, fix it up, sell it, and get a home of their own. Somehow she would manage to do what she had to do.

Laurie picked up the box and walked outside. It was hot and the flowers Christine had planted the month before were just beginning to bloom. Laurie stopped to look at them and felt a rush of sadness and sorrow for a woman she had barely known.

"What a waste ... what a waste," she said as she turned her back to the house and walked down the hot asphalt driveway.

CHAPTER 13

Drowning Again

June 24, 1981, was a humid Wednesday. By noon a huge crowd of city dwellers lined the shores of Lake Michigan. Christine Schultz had been dead less than a month. The police still had not arrested anyone.

Laurie left for work remembering the tiny hamster Shannon and Sean had given Fred for his birthday. Laurie helped them put the hamster in a small box, and they all laughed when he opened the top and the hamster jumped out. For those few moments everything seemed normal. So far her work at the university had been routine. As a security officer she patrolled the campus on foot and in a car. That afternoon Laurie was patrolling in a squad car when she realized she had forgotten to take her radio with her. She drove back to the university police headquarters on campus to pick it up.

It was unusual for her sergeant's door to be closed, and she had to knock to enter and get her radio. When the sergeant opened the door, he looked shocked to see Laurie. Seated in his office were two Milwaukee cops, Lt. Carl Ruscitti and Detective Frank Cole. They flashed their badges at Laurie, and Cole said, "You are under arrest for first-degree murder."

Laurie was stunned. Before she could say anything the men took her badge, cap, and university key ring. Then they handcuffed her. It was just like the night when Fred called to tell her Christine had been murdered. "This is a dream," she said. "This isn't happening."

Cole was a big man, over six-foot-five tall and close to three hundred pounds. Laurie was frightened. Driving over to the police administration building, the cops kept saying things like "You sure don't seem surprised" and "You knew this had to happen."

Instead of taking Laurie to the booking room the men ushered her into the deputy inspector's office and removed her handcuffs.

"We really hate to do this, but it's our job," Cole said. "You're such a beautiful young lady. We are going to have the department photographer come up here in a minute to take your mug shots. That way we'll have proof that we didn't beat you up or anything. Is that okay with you?"

Laurie nodded. She had never been this frightened. She knew how the cops worked. How they could twist facts and change documents.

The men offered her a cigarette. Laurie told them she didn't smoke, and then they launched into their investigation.

"All right. Now then, Lawrencia, we think your husband set you up for this. You know he did it. We can make it easier for you. We know you both were in on it."

"I don't understand," Laurie said, and thought to herself, Fred? He wouldn't. He didn't. They're crazy.

The police officers never did tell Laurie what evidence had led to her arrest. She would find that out later. She assumed that the police were using Fred's off-duty weapon as the excuse to arrest her. She had been in the apartment with the weapon on the night of the murder. Years later Laurie would look back and wish she had listened. Wish she had compiled a list of everything that had really happened during the months she met, dated, and married Elfred Schultz. But on June 24, 1981, those thoughts were foreign to her. She couldn't believe that her husband would know anything, do anything, to hurt Christine Schultz.

Cole proceeded to tell Laurie they had enough evidence to lock her up for the rest of her life. He talked about the alimony payments Fred was making to Christine, and then they mentioned that she had threatened Christine. Cole knew that Judy Zess had said terrible things about her friend Lawrencia Bembenek and had implicated her in Christine's murder. She had even told police that Laurie owned a green jogging suit. He also knew that a reddish-brown wig had been pulled from the drain that connected Laurie's apartment to the apartment next door. That evidence was all circumstantial, but at least they had a murder suspect.

Laurie remained silent. These two men had to be making this up.

"Our theory is you two cooked up a plan to scare Chris, but you fucked up and killed her instead."

"That's ridiculous," Laurie finally said.

"You wanted to scare Chris out of that house so that you and Elfred could live there."

Staring at the men in disbelief, Laurie couldn't imagine how a grown woman could be "scared" out of her own house.

Ruscitti and Cole continued. They said if she would cooperate with them they would recommend that the charges be reduced to manslaughter. Laurie told them it was her right to remain silent until she had an attorney.

That angered the two men, and Cole slammed his pen down on the table. They had expected that she would confess and make their jobs a little bit easier.

Cole told Laurie they were also going to charge her with attempted murder for trying to strangle Sean the night of the murder. Cole stood, towering over Laurie.

Before he left the room, Cole took out a ruler and measured the back of Laurie's hair. The suspect in the murder had a six-inch ponytail and Laurie had a ponytail that was barely two inches long.

They must be desperate for a suspect, she thought to herself.

On the way to being fingerprinted, Laurie ran into Richard Reilly in the hall. He was Fred's divorce attorney and Fred called him and told him to rush to the police building. Fred's friends at the department had called him and told him Laurie was being arrested for the murder.

"This is all a mistake, isn't it?" she said, grasping Reilly by the arm. "They're going to let me go home, aren't they?"

"They didn't have a warrant for your arrest," Reilly told her. "It certainly appears to be a mistake, but they mean business. Just hang in there right now, and don't say anything to them. Do you understand? Not anything. I'll get back as soon as possible."

* * *

Laurie was shoved into a dirty holding cell. It was small and dimly lit. There was one metal cot and a metal door with a tiny slit. When Laurie pressed her face against the door, all she could see was the wall on the other side. There were four cement walls, a steel toilet, and a tiny ceiling light bulb enclosed in a wire cage. Her world had suddenly become very small.

She stayed in that cell for three days and three nights. She still had on her Marquette University uniform. The annual city Summerfest festival was going on, and the only thing Laurie heard during those days and nights was the sound of drunks coming and going. Once a day, at 5:45 A.M., she received coffee and a baloney sandwich from a nameless matron. Her shirt became soaked with perspiration. She tried exercising to pass the time. There was nothing to read. No visitors. Laurie would find out later that she was kept in that cell for three days while Cole typed up the criminal complaint against her.

She would also find out that local newspapers and radio and television stations were already sensationalizing her arrest. She was being called a beautiful ex-Playboy bunny. Reporters were scouring the city trying to find anything they could about her. Lawrencia Bembenek, the nice girl from the South Side, was front-page news.

On the third day Reilly finally showed up. Laurie was allowed to leave the cell and walk into the visiting room. The matron had taken away her glasses and she could barely see where she was going.

"You've been charged with first-degree murder. Our next step is to go before a judge, who will set your bail at ten thousand dollars. That amount is a gift. Bail for most murder cases is set around one hundred thousand."

Laurie thought Reilly looked like Orville Redenbacher, the popcorn king. He had a tiny voice that sounded like a humming bee. She hoped he knew what he was doing. Considering that Fred believed he had screwed up his divorce, she wasn't sure he was the attorney she should be talking with. Reilly told her that the case against her was very circumstantial and that's why the bail was so low. He said the conditions of the bail would stipulate that she live at home with Elfred or her parents and that the boys, Shannon and Sean, live out of town with their grandparents. Laurie never thought to ask why Fred was suddenly not considered as an accomplice when just three days ago the cops said he was the guy who had masterminded the whole murder to get out of his huge alimony payments.

Reilly also told her that she should waive her right to a preliminary hearing, a suggestion that would have made most other attorneys cringe. Reilly said that skipping the preliminary would give him more time to prepare for the trial. But, another attorney would have pushed at the preliminary to have the charges dropped. He also said that her boss at Marquette, Carol Kurdzeil, had suspended her with pay.

Laurie sat on the other side of a glassed-in partition and kept nodding. It was as if she were just floating above everything and watching it happen.

"This must be what it feels like to be dead, to

be caught in some kind of terrible, terrible whirlwind," she said as Reilly droned on and on and
on.

"Are you all right?" he finally asked. "Because
I've got a few questions to ask you."

He wanted to know if Laurie had ever owned a
wig. She told him she owned two short blond wigs
that she wore when she worked at the Second District station. Almost all the female officers wore
short wigs, Laurie told him, because they were
constantly getting written up if their hair was below their ears. She remembered selling one of the
wigs to Margie Lipschultz, and she told Reilly the
other one was packed somewhere in a box.

"Did you make the statement 'I hate those fucking kids' in regards to Fred's children?"

"Of course not."

"How did you feel about Sean and Shannon?"

"At first I wasn't thrilled about the whole idea.
But it was working out. I like them. Why are you
asking me these things?"

Reilly seemed rushed. He wouldn't answer any
of her questions, and he kept telling her he would
explain it all later.

"Did you ever tell anyone you'd like to hire
someone to kill Christine?"

"No!"

"Okay. That's it for now. I'll be back to accompany you to the hearing. Just sit back and watch
TV and try not to think too much. I'll see you
later."

Laurie thought she had just talked to a used car
salesman.

Sit and watch TV! What TV? Try not to think?
Am I going crazy? she asked herself.

* * *

Before her appearance in front of the judge, Laurie was placed in a bullpen outside the courtroom. Without knowing it, she had become the biggest freak show in town. Every few seconds someone would run up to the bullpen's window to look in. When she was brought into the courtroom, there were photographers and reporters everywhere. Without her glasses, Laurie still couldn't see, and she didn't have a comb and had not showered or changed clothes in three days.

The guard marched Laurie past all the reporters and photographers. She tried to see if Elfred Schultz was there, but she couldn't find him. Bewildered and confused, she stood in front of the judge with her arms hanging down, one hand resting across the top of the other. Her small gold wedding band glistened every time someone snapped a photo.

Reilly stood next to her and held a pen in his hands. The judge charged her with first-degree murder for killing Christine Jean Schultz on May 28, 1981. As Reilly had said, bail was set at $10,000.

Laurie was immediately transported to the Milwaukee County Jail. She had heard stories about what a terrible place it was, and the stories were not exaggerated. She was ordered to take off her uniform and to change into a lightweight cotton dress. The cellblock was filthy, with a mixture of old food, vomit, and cigarette butts covering the floor. A woman with vacant eyes sat in the corner singing. Laurie sat on the edge of a chair and glanced at the television set. She saw herself walking into court. She felt as if she were drowning.

Years before, when she was just a small girl, she was on vacation with her parents in Canada swimming in the hotel pool. She accidentally went too deep, and because she couldn't swim, she started to go under the water. She went under several times and popped up, gasping for breath. When she was about to go down one more time, her mother pulled her out. Sitting in the Milwaukee County Jail, Laurie felt the same way she did in that hotel pool. Only this time there was no one to save her.

Laurie was finally allowed to make one phone call, and she called Fred. The minute she heard his voice she started to cry. Fred told her none of the banks he contacted would give him bail money, and he didn't have the cash or assets to go to a bail bondsman. Laurie slumped back into the chair and wondered how long she would have to stay in jail. Moments later, a deputy sheriff asked her if she wanted her aunt to post bail for her. She did. Allowed to change into her Marquette uniform, she left the building by the back door.

Back at her parents' house she fell into Fred's arms, and they stood together, both crying. For those few moments Lawrencia Bembenek forgot about everything terrible that had just happened to her and everything terrible that could happen. With Fred's arms wrapped around her, Laurie thought that maybe, just maybe, this terrible predicament would go away.

CHAPTER 14

Searching for Help

Laurie spent her first night out of jail reading newspaper accounts of her arrest and watching what the local television broadcasters had to say about the case. Lawrencia Bembenek's name and photo were splashed across every front page.

"My God!" Laurie said when she read the articles. "They are giving me a press trial. How can they do this to me?"

Fred handed Laurie a drink and said the reporting was sensational and slanted. He said most of it wasn't even true.

"They say that police recovered a red wig from the plumbing of our three-bedroom apartment. That's not true. It came from the apartment across the hall. They said we moved into my house on Ramsey Street and we haven't moved in there yet and they also say you were charged with attempted murder and you weren't."

"They keep quoting a source," Laurie said, scanning the papers, "but they don't say who that source is. A source says she owned a green jogging suit. A source says this. A source says that. Who is this source?"

Laurie was desperate to tell her side of the story, but Fred told her Reilly advised him not to talk to members of the press. Laurie kept reading. She found out all kinds of things she had never known before. The stories she read indicated that the police were basing their whole case on the ballistics report that said the murder weapon was Fred's off-duty revolver.

That's impossible, she said to herself. Fred and Durfee checked that gun that same night! What about the blood on the service revolver? Did they mix up the guns?

Then she read that a wig hair had been found on Christine Schultz's body. Fred quickly said that there had been at least two women at the scene of the murder and they were both probably wearing wigs.

One thing Fred failed to mention was the fact that he told the police on June 2 that Laurie had been playing with the bullets in his off-duty holster just a few days before the murder. Laurie would find out about that soon enough, but it wouldn't be because Fred Schultz told her.

Then Laurie discovered that the police had searched her locker at Marquette University and confiscated her purse without a search warrant. It was becoming obvious that the cops had carte blanche to do whatever they wanted, even if it was against the law and violated her personal rights.

Laurie continued to feel that she would wake up from a terrible dream any minute. Fred and Reilly kept telling her everything was going to be just fine, and she had no choice but to believe them. Reilly had only contacted Laurie once since she had been released from jail, and he was still insisting that she waive her right to a preliminary hearing.

When Laurie's parents returned from a trip to Oregon, they couldn't believe Reilly didn't want a preliminary hearing. They discovered that one of his partners in his law firm was a member of the Police and Fire Commission. After talking with another attorney, the Bembeneks were told that it was a conflict of interest for Reilly to represent Laurie because he was also Fred's divorce attorney. Someone suggested she get in touch with Donald S. Eisenberg in Madison.

Without telling Fred, Laurie drove to Madison with her mother to see Eisenberg. She was immediately impressed by his outgoing personality and somewhat flamboyant style. She was told that his retainer fee would be $25,000. Laurie and Fred didn't have any money and her parents were now living on her father's meager retirement income, but her mother said they would do whatever it took. They hired Eisenberg and Laurie literally put her life in his hands. It was a dangerous move, but no one would realize that until it was too late.

Eisenberg was a handsome man who loved to wear flashy gold jewelry and drive big cars. He had a broad smile, his dark curly hair was graying at the temples, and he always knew what to say and just the right way to say it. Although he had established a winning record as a criminal defense attorney, Eisenberg's tactics were often questioned by his colleagues. He often said publicly that he didn't care if his clients were innocent or guilty. It was his job to get them off. The publicity surrounding many of his cases had elevated his professional, financial, and social status. Donald Eisenberg liked the attention, and he loved having the hottest, most beautiful client in Wisconsin.

Desperate to trust someone, Laurie decided that

Eisenberg would be her salvation. From the moment she met him he seemed very optimistic about her chances for acquittal, and Laurie believed every word he said. "We are going to get this case dismissed at the prelim," he told her. "You won't even be bound over."

While Eisenberg started to work on her case, Laurie took a leave of absence from her Marquette job, and Fred, who was told by his superiors that he was emotionally unfit to return to work, was ordered to take a desk job. He refused. He was going to try to get his detective job back.

To help pass the time Laurie and Fred decided to go camping with some friends. They thought it would be good to get away from phones and reporters. Just before they left, Fred picked up the newspaper and there was Judy Zess's picture on the front page. The night before—July 2, 1981— Judy had been beaten and robbed at gunpoint. Judy claimed to have been accosted by two men as she got out of her car at the Bay View Terrace Apartments, where she lived with Gaertner and where she had once lived with Laurie and Schultz.

Judy said one of the men wore a reddish-brown wig. He pulled out a .38-caliber revolver and demanded the key to her apartment. The other man took the key and entered her apartment. Judy ran when the man wearing the wig tried to handcuff her hands behind her back. The man tackled her and then struck her. Judy said that when she managed to get back into her apartment, it had been totally ransacked and money and stereo equipment were missing.

Laurie immediately noticed the reference to the reddish-brown wig and the .38-caliber. The killer of Christine Schultz had worn a reddish-brown wig and used a .38-caliber revolver. Laurie's spirits brightened a little as she headed out on the camping trip. Certainly the cops would look into the similarities of these two cases. But she was wrong.

The camping trip proved a disaster. It was hot, there was an epidemic of mosquitoes, and Fred's real personality was starting to show. When Laurie accidentally spilled taco sauce in Fred's van, he flew into a rage and ended up hitting Laurie's friend Donna Janke. Fred Schultz had a violent, explosive temper, and Laurie was terrified. Fred apologized, but things could never be the same again.

When they returned to her parents' home, Fred told Laurie something else that made her shudder. "I never loved Chris," he said.

"How can you live with someone for ten years, raise children, build a house, and end up saying you never loved her?" Laurie asked.

"You are wrong. I never loved her."

Laurie told Fred she found it hard to believe he had had sex for ten years without feeling something.

She was still wrong, Fred maintained. He had never loved his first wife, Christine Jean Schultz.

Laurie had seen him break into tears and then stop as quick. She remembered how cold and unfeeling he was the night they went to identify Christine's body at the police morgue. Maybe Fred Schultz was right. Maybe he never loved Christine and maybe he never loved Laurie. Maybe it was just one lie after another.

Laurie wasn't the only person who had begun to

have doubts about Fred Schultz. Christine's relatives had decided that Fred Schultz was an unfit father and they petitioned the court to obtain custody of Sean and Shannon. Without his knowledge several of Fred's family members had been working with the Pennings, Christine's parents, to get the children. Despite frantic phone calls and verbal and physical threats from Fred, he was not given custody. Circuit Court Judge Robert M. Curley ordered the boys to stay with their aunt Barbara Crist, Christine's sister, who now lived in Gresham, Wisconsin. Fred said he would fight to get the boys back.

Laurie's twenty-third birthday was not a grand day of celebration. During the last year her life had totally changed. Instead of working as a police officer, her dream job, Laurie was helping Fred do carpentry work. Because she had worked side by side with her father, Laurie knew all the basics. She could nail up boards, handle drywall, and do rough carpentry work.

Every night, tired and dirty, Laurie would look at herself in the mirror and laugh. "I really look like a sexy Playboy bunny. Where are the reporters who want the real story?"

Wisconsin journalists and writers from around the world would focus on Lawrencia Bembenek's looks and on what she wore. That made better headlines than the facts.

The last two weeks of August went by quickly. Laurie's preliminary hearing was scheduled for September 1. A judge would hear evidence against her and decide whether it was sufficient to charge her with the crime. Eisenberg kept telling her it would be the last time she would have to go to court. Robert E. Kramer, assistant district attorney, had been assigned to the case, and Eisenberg was more than confident that he could stand up to him.

Laurie thought she would be ready for the hearing, too. She knew about the wig and about the crime reports involving Fred's off-duty gun. She couldn't and wouldn't believe that the police department could actually manufacture evidence against her. But there was much that Lawrencia Ann Bembenek did not know.

CHAPTER 15

Preliminary Lies

Laurie quickly found out that the world was not eager to associate with a woman who had been accused of murder. News of her arrest, and the fact that she had been charged with murder, made her a common curiosity. People recognized her everywhere. They pointed at her in the grocery store, and no matter where she went she knew people were talking about what she supposedly had done.

Many of her close friends had also been contacted by the police. Detectives asked if Laurie and Fred had openly talked about murdering Christine. Laurie didn't understand why the cops were still investigating Fred if she was the one who had been charged with murder. Did they know something about Fred Schultz that she didn't know?

Then Laurie received notice from Marquette University that she wouldn't be able to get her old job back. Fred's superiors at the police department told him he was too emotional to work under stress and carry a gun. In the end he took a clerical job in the detective division, a position normally reserved for disabled officers.

Fred was moved to the day shift and he spent hours running off listings of driver's license numbers. It was a far cry from the glamorous job of detective. The days when he could eat free meals at restaurants throughout the city and sign off for free drinks were over. Now he had twenty minutes to eat a sack lunch at his desk. Fred wasn't happy with the new arrangements.

He also spent the weekends with his sons in supervised visits at his family's home in Pewaukee. Laurie had been ordered by the court not to see the boys. After Fred left for work in the morning, she spent the rest of the day alone. She felt aimless and lonely as she wrote and worked on her drawings. Laurie was afraid to call her friends. She did not want to talk about the case. They had already been through enough because of her problems.

During her long days alone Laurie had plenty of time to think. She was becoming more and more depressed, and she felt helpless. She had serious regrets about her marriage. She kept saying over and over again that life had been simple before she met and wed Elfred O. Schultz, Jr.

First I decide on a police career over a man, she thought. Then I decide on a man over an Air Force career, and certainly this isn't right, either. Brilliant decisions, Laurie. How did I ever get mixed up in this?

Laurie had been married less than five months when Fred's ex-wife was murdered. When they married, they barely knew each other. During the first months of a normal marriage, a couple spends lots of time together. But Fred and Laurie were living with Judy and in three months they had had to move twice. When Laurie thought about it, her relationship with Fred had been doomed from the start.

She also was trying to find a job and she had a

discrimination suit pending against the Milwaukee Police Department.

I thought marrying Fred would be the best thing I could do to straighten out my life and it turned out to be the worst thing I could have done, Laurie finally admitted to herself. I was too young and too trusting and too stupid to marry someone that I barely knew.

If Laurie was mentally dysfunctional before the preliminary hearing, she would be totally incapacitated by the end of it. Eisenberg had convinced her that Circuit Court Judge Ralph Adam Fine would never allow her case to go to trial. He told her that the state had to prove there was probable cause for an arrest and he didn't think they could. Fred was there, too, saying constantly that everything would be over soon. But events did not go exactly the way everyone said they would.

September 1 was a warm, early fall day. Laurie dressed in a conservative gray gabardine suit. She felt as if her stomach were in her throat as she drove to the Milwaukee courthouse with Fred. They were both quiet.

Eisenberg met them at the courthouse, bursting with confidence. "Everything will be just fine," he told Laurie for the hundredth time.

There is a pervasive smell in Milwaukee's halls of justice that seems to be a mixture of stale cigarette smoke, old wax, wood, and cold, salty sweat. Laurie would spend the rest of her life trying to get that smell out of her skin. Out of her hair. Out of her mind. But there would always be a lingering scent. A smell she would associate with feelings of evil, betrayal, and hate. At ten o'clock on that muggy September morning, the betrayal was about to begin.

Reporters and photographers were gathered in rows when Judge Fine stepped into the courtroom. Ceiling fans circled overhead and when Laurie closed her eyes, she smiled, thinking they were actually buzzards. The gavel rapped and the preliminary hearing began.

Assistant District Attorney Robert E. Kramer started to speak but was quickly stopped by Eisenberg. Laurie's defense lawyer wanted to know why the state hadn't released exculpatory evidence that could help her. The judge said it was the responsibility of the district attorney's office to make sure all evidence and reports were turned over to Eisenberg. That had not been done. Kramer said he would turn over everything, but there would be no way to make certain he kept his word.

"I will certainly give Mr. Eisenberg all the material required under law, and probably even more, any time that is convenient for us," Kramer said.

Laurie sat next to Eisenberg at a long wooden table. She looked at the stacks of files and yellow legal pads. The words STATE OF WISCONSIN—PLAINTIFF VS. LAWRENCIA BEMBENEK—DEFENDANT, NO. K-0775 were written on everything. Seeing all the legal documents only made things seem less real to her. There was still a part of her that didn't believe she had been arrested and charged with committing a murder.

Kramer led off by reading a list of the witnesses he was going to use that day. There were several police officers, the medical examiner, Judy Zess,

Frances Zess, and five or six other names that weren't familiar to Laurie. Eisenberg said Shannon and Sean Schultz, Virginia Bembenek, Fred Schultz, Lawrencia Bembenek, and Ray Kujawa would be called as his witnesses.

None of Fred's relatives attended the hearing. Laurie's mother and father and her sister Colette and her boyfriend sat as close to Laurie as possible and Laurie turned occasionally to look at them.

At first none of the testimony seemed earthshaking. The state called a witness who had pulled a brown wig out of the toilet in the apartment next door to Laurie, Fred, and Judy Zess. The manager of Laurie's apartment complex also talked about the wig, and Detective James Gauger from the Milwaukee Police Department took the stand. He said on June 18, just three weeks following the murder, he was assigned to go through Christine Schultz's home with Elfred Schultz and look for evidence. Gauger said that while the two men were at the Ramsey Street residence, Schultz discovered a green metal ammunition box that had 200-grain bullets inside. The bullet that killed Christine Schultz was a 200-grain bullet.

When he cross-examined Gauger, Eisenberg was relentless. He got Gauger to admit there was no way to know for certain that the 200-grain bullets were in the ammo box the night of the murder. Gauger also admitted that although Fred Schultz's duty revolver—a .38-caliber Smith & Wesson with a four-inch barrel—had traces of blood on the barrel, no one had bothered to check to see if there was blood on the holster of his service revolver. Eisenberg was doing well, but the prosecution was

just getting warmed up. Their next witness was
Frances Zess, Judy's mother. Laurie was surprised that Mrs. Zess had been called as a witness.
She was even more surprised when she heard
what she had to say.

The questions centered around a dinner party
Mrs. Zess had had at her Delafield, Wisconsin,
home in early February to celebrate the marriage
of Fred and Laurie. Laurie remembered the party,
but the rest of Mrs. Zess's story was not so familiar.

Mrs. Zess said they drank mixed drinks before
dinner and then consumed three bottles of wine
while they ate.

> Mrs. Zess: We were discussing the high cost of
> living and expenses and Laurie said that
> she could relate to the high cost of living
> because a large portion of Fred's payment
> went to his ex-wife, Christine.
> Kramer: And when you say Laurie, do you mean
> the defendant?
> Mrs. Zess: Yes.
> Kramer: Fred, you mean Fred Schultz?
> Mrs. Zess: Yes.
> Kramer: And did the defendant say anything in
> regard to Mrs. Christine Schultz after the
> discussion about the money that Fred had
> to pay her?
> Mrs. Zess: Yes, she said that it would pay to
> have her blown away.

Laurie couldn't believe what she was hearing.
Later in the hearing when Judy Zess was called to
testify, Laurie could only sit staring in disbelief.

Zess agreed with her own mother and said, yes, Laurie had indeed talked about having Christine Schultz "blown away." When Eisenberg was finally able to cross-examine, her story suddenly changed.

Eisenberg: And you were at this party laughing and having a good time?

Zess: Yes.

Eisenberg: And what exactly did Laurie allegedly say?

Zess: We were talking about the high cost of living and she said that it would pay to have Chris blown away.

Eisenberg: How did you respond?

Zess: I don't remember.

Eisenberg: Did you call the police? Did you laugh it off?

Zess: I . . . we . . . the conversation was dropped.

Eisenberg: Did you think she was joking?

Zess: No.

Eisenberg: Would it refresh your memory to read a report that you gave last June, where you told the police then that you thought it was just in jest, and you thought Laurie was joking?

Zess: Yes.

Eisenberg: You thought Laurie was joking?

Zess: Yes.

Eisenberg: But, for the purposes of this hearing, you decided to say that you thought Laurie was not joking?

Judy Zess went on to say that she had seen a green jogging suit in the apartment she shared with Laurie and Fred. Judy said that she had never

actually seen anyone wear it but she knew it was
there. Laurie wanted to ask Judy what she was
talking about. Laurie didn't own a green jogging
suit. She didn't own anything that was green. The
only thing she could think of that was green was
one pair of Fred's baseball pants, and they were
locked in a storage shed to which only Judy Zess
had a key.

Judy said that Laurie also asked Judy's boyfriend, Thomas Gaertner, forty-one, if he knew
anyone who could have Christine Schultz "rubbed
out." Judy failed to tell the court that Gaertner
had become her husband and that he was await-
ing sentencing on federal drug charges. Gaertner
had also been sentenced to three years in prison
in 1975 for unlawful possession of firearms and
for possession of ten pounds of marijuana. In 1977
he was sentenced to eleven and a half years in
prison for smuggling marijuana and evading income taxes.

Eisenberg tried to question Judy's credibility by
mentioning that her relationship with Laurie became strained when Gaertner found out that
Schultz had shot and murdered his best friend in
1975.

Zess also testified that the plastic-coated
clothesline found around Christine's hands was
similar to a clothesline that she had seen in the
apartment. She said Laurie used a clothesline
when she went on her honeymoon with Fred.

Eisenberg was even more stunned by the testimony of Judy Zess than Laurie. Once, Eisenberg
lost control of himself and shouted, "We have a
fabricator on the witness stand."

When Judy finished, she walked past Laurie and Eisenberg without making eye contact.

"What in the hell happened with Zess?" Eisenberg asked Laurie as he leaned over to whisper in her ear.

"I can't understand it for the life of me," Laurie replied. "We had our differences in the past—like I told you about, but it wasn't enough to warrant these lies. How could she do this to me?"

The testimony of Judy Zess proved damaging enough. Then Elfred Schultz took the stand.

> Elfred: Your honor, I have had a conference with my attorney regarding this case and he advises me that I fall under the guidelines of the Fifth Amendment and I will exercise that right at this time.

Apparently no one in the courtroom knew that Fred had planned on taking the Fifth Amendment. He had never mentioned it to his wife or to the attorney defending her. Eisenberg hinted that he had objections about Fred using the Fifth because he was certain the police department did not have the right person who killed Christine Schultz. Despite those feelings he declined to argue when Kramer asked him if he objected to Fred pleading the Fifth.

Kramer did not think the questions he was going to ask Fred would incriminate him, but he told the court that he could understand Detective Schultz's belief that some of his answers could incriminate him. Judge Fine said that before he could allow Fred to take the Fifth he had to know if there was sufficient reason for doing so. It seemed unusual, especially in a murder case like this, to grant immunity to the husband of the suspect.

Eisenberg suggested that Fred's attorney, Joe Balistrieri, be called before they continued. Fine agreed and told Fred Schultz not to talk with anyone or leave the courthouse until his attorney arrived.

Laurie had no idea what was going on. She knew the police had asked her about Fred's involvement in the murder. She also knew he had blood on his duty revolver and that he had access to Christine's house the night of the murder. She knew, too, that Fred had told the Milwaukee detectives things about her that were not true.

Eisenberg told her that if Fred was granted immunity, he could not be prosecuted for the murder of Christine Schultz. Laurie's mind raced. She could not accept the idea that Fred Schultz, her husband of just a few months, could have killed his ex-wife. She told Eisenberg that he was the attorney. He should make the decision.

When Fred was brought back into court the following day he said his attorney had again advised him to plead the Fifth and not answer any questions. Fred was willing to testify if he knew that whatever he said could not be used against him. Without that guarantee, or immunity, his only alternative would be to plead the Fifth.

Judge Fine: All right. The court has previously, in the absence of any request or argument from the attorneys, made the finding that Officer Schultz's invocation of his Fifth Amendment right against self-incrimination is appropriate and authorized by law.

Kramer: Judge, the State at this time would move the court, pursuant to 972.08(1) of the Wisconsin statutes, to grant Mr. Schultz immunity from any of his testimony.

Judge Fine: Mr. Eisenberg, does the defense have any comment?

Eisenberg: No comment, your honor.

Judge Fine then read from part of the Wisconsin state statutes to help explain why Elfred Schultz could not be prosecuted for what he was about to say. Fine said that whenever a person refused to testify because the information he had might incriminate himself, he could be ordered to testify anyway and yet be protected from any penalty. But, the judge made it clear, Fred Schultz had to tell the truth. No one is protected from perjury, he added. The judge then told Schultz he had been granted immunity but that he had to answer whatever questions were asked of him.

Fred Schultz settled back into the wooden chair on the witness stand. He looked comfortable and relieved. They could ask him whatever they wanted. There was no way he could ever be held responsible for the death of Christine Jean Schultz.

Everyone in the courtroom was looking at him, wondering what he was going to say. Did he know anything about the death of his first wife? Did he know if his new wife was a murderer? Fred Schultz had the answers to lots of questions, and it was time to find out what those answers were.

CHAPTER 16

Drama and Death

At first Fred Schultz's testimony on September 2 was not dramatic or revealing. He talked about his years as a police officer and answered various questions about when he married Christine, when they were divorced, and he described his relationship with her. He said that when he moved out of the house on Ramsey Street, he had five guns that he took with him.

He explained how Laurie and her mother spent the evening of May 27, 1981, packing because Laurie's plans to go out with a friend had fallen through. He said he phoned Laurie several times that night and that she was there each time he called. Then he gave a detailed ballistics report about the off-duty gun that allegedly had been used to kill Christine.

His memory of the night of May 27 wasn't much different than what everyone had heard before. He recalled receiving a phone call at the station telling him that Christine had been shot and killed. He said his detective partner Durfee was ordered to drive the car over to Ramsey Street because he was too upset.

When Fred started to talk about how he arrived at the scene of the crime, he suddenly began to cry. He cried so hard, he couldn't continue to talk. The court went into recess, and Laurie and Eisenberg, who were stunned by his sudden show of emotion, were momentarily unable to move.

"He found it impossible to talk about her death?" Laurie hissed through her teeth. "Yet to me all he does is criticize Christine horribly even now. I don't get it."

Laurie thought Fred was putting on an act. The night of the murder she had not seen Fred cry or show surprise that his ex-wife had been killed. She couldn't forget his cold, calculating movements when he identified Christine's body in the police morgue.

Eisenberg had fire in his eyes.

"Goddamn it! If I knew Fred was going to do that, I wouldn't have called him."

Laurie left the courtroom and wandered into the bathroom. She was hurt and confused by Fred's testimony. He had just told a courtroom filled with people that he still loved Christine, and that was completely opposite from what he had said to her in private.

She stood in front of the sink, splashed cold water on her face, and closed her eyes. She could not look in the mirror. Her heart was pounding and all she could see was Fred's face.

Why, Fred, why? she asked herself. What did all those months of vicious criticism and expressions of hatred of Chris mean? Were you trying to fool me or yourself?

When Laurie turned around, her mother was standing beside her.

"What in the hell was that all about?" she asked Laurie. "What's wrong with Fred? Does he still love her? It sure looked that way to me and to everyone in the courtroom."

Shaken, Laurie realized everything her mother had said about Fred Schultz was true. "Please," Laurie stammered, unable to look into her mother's eyes. "Just leave me alone for a few minutes."

As the sound of Virginia Bembenek's retreating high heels echoed in the narrow bathroom, Laurie turned back to the sink and back to her few moments of self-indulgence.

My God, what have I gotten myself into? she asked herself as she walked back into the courtroom.

When testimony resumed, Stu Honeck took the stand. He was chewing a big wad of gum and although he claimed to have been engaged to Christine, he showed no emotion when he was questioned.

He said he had spent most of the evening of May 27 with Christine Schultz. Although the Schultz boys said Honeck walked home that night, Honeck claims that Christine drove him home. The boys told the police they would have heard the car start because it was very loud and parked right in the driveway.

He said that after Christine dropped him at his house, he cleaned up and then called her about 10:50 P.M. He said they talked until 11:20 P.M. Honeck added he fell asleep about midnight, woke up about thirty minutes later, when one of his roommates stumbled in, and then was awakened again about two-twenty by a phone call from Sean Schultz.

Honeck said Sean wanted him to come to the house right away because "someone had thrown a firecracker at his mommy's back and she was bleeding." Honeck said he asked to talk to Christine but Sean said she couldn't talk because she was gurgling.

According to Honeck, he instructed Sean to hang up the phone and wait in the house. Honeck called the Milwaukee Police Department. He told them to dispatch a squad and ambulance to 1701 West Ramsey because someone had been injured severely or shot.

Honeck then called Sean and told him to let the police in when they arrived. Sean said to please hurry because he thought someone was still in the house and he was frightened.

When Honeck got to Christine's house, he said a squad car had just arrived and the ambulance was coming down the road. His roommate was with him and they walked toward the front door with the uniformed policemen who had arrived at the scene.

He said Shannon and Sean opened the door and he immediately went to Christine's bedroom. He said Christine was lying on her right side, facing west. Honeck could see a bullet hole in her shoulder.

When cross-examined by Eisenberg, Honeck admitted that he had a key to Christine's house. Eisenberg wanted to talk about Honeck's chronic drinking problems. He also wanted the judge to know that Honeck drank that evening. Honeck admitted that he had a vodka gimlet the evening of the murder but he said he couldn't remember if he had had wine, too.

According to Honeck, he never saw a weapon or ammunition in the house and he didn't recall seeing a green ammunition box either. He said that the night of the murder he did not argue with

Christine and when he talked with her late that night it was a pleasant conversation.

But Honeck did say that Christine told him several times that Laurie Bembenek didn't like her and once made her stand out in the hall when she came to pick up her children.

All the eyes in the courtroom suddenly shifted from Honeck to Laurie. Laurie kept her eyes on Honeck. She remembered when Christine had come to pick up the boys, but her version of the incident was much different.

Christine came into the apartment and Laurie asked her to look around. Christine felt uncomfortable and said she would rather wait by the door. She handed Laurie a broken blender and said she thought they might be able to use it if they got it fixed.

While the two women stood there, Fred was in the bathroom and stayed there for fifteen minutes. Laurie finally yelled to him to come out.

Laurie remembered the incident as being somewhat difficult. She remembered thanking Christine for the blender and thinking how nice it was for her to bring it over. It was the first time she had really spent more than just a few seconds talking to Fred's ex-wife and she liked her. Christine Schultz was much different from Fred's description of her.

As Laurie sat in the hot courtroom, she felt the walls close in. It seemed as if everyone had come together and decided to make things up so that it would look like she had killed Christine Schultz. She had never heard so many lies. Laurie wanted to get in the car and drive as fast and as far away as possible. When the court finally recessed for the day, Lawrencia Bembenek wondered how she would ever make it through another day of court testimony.

The next day, September 2, Laurie's neighbors in the apartment complex testified that they had not seen or heard a car leaving during the early morning hours of May 28. Carl Templin, a detective who had interviewed Laurie the morning of the murder, said that he had not bothered to check to see whether Laurie Bembenek's Camaro was hot from being used. He said he didn't find a green jogging suit either and that he did not check to see if there were any firearms in her apartment.

Virginia Bembenek was next. She said the night of the murder she was the one who packed Fred's leather jewelry box. She said Laurie was not in the room when she packed the box and there would be no way for her to know where it was. She also said that she would not lie to protect her daughter.

Mrs. Bembenek recalled that on April 14 she and her husband had dinner at Laurie and Fred's apartment to celebrate their anniversary. She said that there was a problem with the plumbing in Judy Zess's bathroom and they had to walk through the apartment and use the other bathroom. The toilet was overflowing and there had been problems with the plumbing for weeks.

Laurie hated seeing her mother on the witness stand. She felt terrible about putting her parents through the trial and the anxiety surrounding it. Eisenberg was rough on Laurie's mother, too.

He didn't want anyone to think he was using her to play on the court's sympathies.

"The night of the murder, was Laurie acting strange?"

"No."

"Was she acting nervous?"

"No."

"Was she acting like a girl who was planning on committing murder that night?"

"Of course not."

"Was she drunk?"

"No."

"Was she on any drugs that you know of and did she have any plans that night that you know of?"

Laurie mentioned that she had planned to go out with a girlfriend from work. She was waiting for the girl to call, but she said that she might not go because she was getting tired.

When Virginia Bembenek finished her testimony, Sean Schultz took the stand. When Laurie saw him sitting behind the microphone, she was suddenly filled with emotion. She missed seeing him and his brother and she wanted to hold him. She knew he must be frightened.

Sean looked over and smiled at her when he got to the witness box. He didn't seem nervous. His version of what happened the night his mother was murdered had not changed and neither had his claim that the murderer was not Lawrencia Bembenek. Numerous times he said that the person he saw on May 28 could not have been Laurie because he was much bigger.

"It couldn't possibly be Laurie," eleven-year-old Sean said. "Even if she had been wearing shoulder pads, like a football player. It still couldn't have been her, because then her body would have to form the shape of a *V*. This body was big and came straight down on the sides."

Sean then moved his hands up and down to show how big and square the body had been.

"Besides, I know Laurie. Laurie always smells good 'cuz she likes to wear perfume and I didn't smell any perfume."

As Sean spoke, remembering the last few moments of his mother's life, the courtroom was totally silent. No one moved. Here was one of two actual witnesses to the murder. A person who saw a man standing over him and running from his mother's room, so close he could reach out and touch the man. He was bright. He was articulate and he remembered.

"He was wearing a green khaki Army jacket," he said firmly. "It wasn't a green jogging suit. I know because when he or she ran down the stairs, I saw the edges of it flap. You know, an Army jacket without the camouflage."

Kramer, a large, somewhat bulky man, jumped out of his seat and asked Sean why he said he or she.

"Is it because you are really not sure if it was a man or woman?"

"Well, I said he or she because those are the only two sexes there are."

"Sean, you know your daddy loves Laurie very much, right?"

"Yes."

"Isn't it a fact that your daddy told you that Laurie didn't do it?"

"No."

"Did your daddy talk to you about it?"

"Yes."

"What did he tell you?"

"He told me to tell the truth."

When Eisenberg talked with Sean, he asked him several times if he was telling the truth. Sean said over and over that yes, he was telling the truth and he knew that it was wrong to lie. He said he was telling the truth when he said that "the man" who killed his mommy was not Laurie Bembenek.

Once, when Sean described seeing his mother lying on her bed, tied up and with a hole in her back, he broke into tears. The judge ordered a brief recess while Sean wiped his eyes. Then Don Eisenberg turned to Sean.

"I have just one question, Sean, I promise. Based upon everything that you saw that night and what happened to you, and the size of the assailant and everything else, do you have any doubt at all that it was or was not Laurie?"

"It wasn't."

Sean's testimony ended the preliminary hearing. Cameras flashed as Laurie rose to leave the room. Everyone wanted her to make some kind of statement. The huge headline in the following morning's *Milwaukee Sentinel* would read BOY SAYS BEMBENEK NOT KILLER. But the headline would not be a good omen.

Eisenberg, Laurie, and her parents left the courtroom without making any statements. Fred said he had to go to a meeting but refused to say where or what it was about. Laurie went out one door and Fred went out another. Eisenberg said he wanted to buy everyone a few drinks and discuss the day's testimony.

"Don't be too cross with Fred because of his emotional performance," Eisenberg told Laurie. "Ex-wives have a unique way of throwing an enormous amount of guilt on men. I should know, I have two of them."

Eisenberg's third and present wife, Sandy, had been a Playboy bunny at the Lake Geneva Playboy Club, the same club where Laurie worked for a few weeks. Occasionally he would actually show a picture of her in her bunny suit to an unbelieving buddy. His three marriages had only heightened his reputation as a ladies' man.

Eisenberg told the Bembeneks that the judge wanted additional time to decide on whether to bind the case over for trial. He had also asked both attorneys to write briefs for him.

"Remember, the only thing the state had to prove at the hearing was probable cause for arrest," Laurie's lawyer said. "It's a probability issue. It's nowhere as tough to prove as in a jury trial, where the state has to prove guilt beyond a reasonable doubt. The burden of proof is different at the prelim. Here all they had to prove was that it would be reasonable to assume that the defendant probably did it."

Laurie gulped down some scotch. She had a feeling Eisenberg was trying to tell her she was going to stand trial for murder.

"I think we did a hell of a job," he said. "We exposed a number of different suspects. The children insisted it wasn't you."

Virginia was more interested in what was not talked about on the witness stand.

"The suspect that lives across the street from

the house on Ramsey ... whatever happened to him?"

Ray Kujawa had been a prime suspect in everyone's mind. He fit Sean's description and was the man who reported a gun and green jogging suit missing from his garage. Virginia couldn't believe he wasn't at least a witness or suspect or some damn thing.

"He refused to testify," Eisenberg said. "What could we do?"

After a few more drinks Eisenberg said what Laurie thought he had been trying to say for thirty minutes.

"Do you think it will be dismissed?" Laurie asked.

"Don't be devastated if it's not. Of course, I wish it would be. It should be. But a lot of judges allow politics to influence their decisions. They have to worry about reelection. You've had an enormous amount of publicity. Fine may just play Pontius Pilate and bind you over, to let a jury decide."

Laurie would have to wait another six weeks before Judge Fine would reach a decision on whether she would stand trial for the murder of Christine Schultz.

During those weeks Laurie would come to know more about the man she had married and about the murder of Christine Schultz. Many secrets were still waiting to be uncovered.

CHAPTER 17

Dog Days

What was left of Laurie Bembenek's self-confidence and hope vanished after the preliminary hearing. She was left with the feeling that she was going to have to stand trial for murder. She not only insisted she did not commit the murder, but she didn't know anything at all about it.

Although she had serious doubts about her relationship with Fred Schultz, Laurie was not able to do anything about it. She had heard him say "everything will be just fine" so many times that she didn't know if she could stand it anymore. She could barely manage to be in the same room with him.

Claiming that he suffered other "trauma," Fred told the police department that he could not continue to work as a detective. He said the death of one wife and the charges of murder against the second were just too much for him to handle.

The Milwaukee Police Department said that if Fred ever wanted to return to regular police work he would have to take a mental examination to prove that he had recovered from the psychological trauma. He kept his desk job but complained that he was being harassed. He said his phone calls were monitored. He couldn't leave the room he worked in and he had no access to police files. He had to ask permission to go to the bathroom.

144 / Kris Radish

It seemed as if the Milwaukee Police Department didn't want him around anymore. Perhaps the department knew something about Fred Schultz that no one else knew.

With Fred still gone all day, Laurie was left to fill up the seconds and minutes of the long days by herself. She still could not go out because news of the preliminary hearing had brought her picture back to the front pages and everyone recognized her.

Four days following the preliminary hearing, *The Milwaukee Journal* ran a huge story on the front page of the local news section.

BEAUTIFUL PEOPLE—BIZARRE CASE MURDER TALE READS LIKE A NOVEL

The story focused on the physical beauty of all the main characters in the Christine Schultz murder case.

"So much for women's rights, the justice system, and beauty only being skin deep," she said out loud as she threw down the paper and walked outside to mail some letters on the corner.

Laurie's depression following the preliminary hearing continued. She lost weight and stopped jogging and working out at the gym, two things that had once been very important to her. Most days she thought she was simply going crazy. Then Fred Schultz did something nice and she was flabbergasted.

One afternoon Laurie and Fred were sitting at the kitchen table, just after Fred had come home from work. He had his tie loosened and was busily eating a cold beef sandwich. Laurie suddenly heard a funny noise in the hallway and sat up in her chair.

When she looked up she saw a German shepherd puppy come around the corner. Laurie loved animals, and the puppy, which she named Sergeant, quickly became the center of her life. She spent hours each day training him, taking him for walks, and playing with him in the backyard.

Although the dog helped cheer her up, Laurie was still depressed. Some days she just rambled round the house in her pajamas and bathrobe. She didn't have a reason to get dressed. She had terrible trouble sleeping and would wake up in the middle of the night and spend hours sitting at her mother's kitchen table.

Eventually she called a women's counseling center in Milwaukee. She was terrified that someone would find out she was getting help and call the police or notify the newspapers. But that never happened. Her counselor was a professional and never told anyone that Lawrencia Bembenek was seeing her.

"My God," the counselor said. "Look what has happened to your life in less than one year. You got sucked into a whirlwind romance because everything else in your life was a mess at the time. Your marriage is one that Fred's family won't accept, and now you've been forced to live in your family's home. Before that you had to move from apartment to apartment."

Laurie listened and took mental notes. No one had ever talked to her like this before. No one had seemed to understand how terrible things really were for her.

"You got two small children dumped in your

lap, and everyone expected you to welcome them with open arms. There were estate problems, custody problems, and then you get arrested for a murder you didn't commit. You've had best friends turn on you, lie about you, and stab you in the back. Laurie! Give yourself a break." The counselor urged Laurie to let Fred share some of her burdens. She said Fred had a responsibility to help the relationship, too. She said that Laurie had to talk to Fred about her feelings.

"When you first met Fred, you admired him and now that the illusion has worn off, you're pretty disappointed, aren't you?"

"Yeah. It's like that book by Marilyn French. She says you think some guy is out of this world, and then you get married and find out that he snores and farts in his sleep."

"You still love him?"

"I think so. But I don't like him very much."

Fred didn't make it easy for Laurie to like him. He admitted one night that he had stopped making payments on the Ramsey Street house and that there might be a foreclosure. Then something happened that helped solidify her negative feelings about Elfred O. Schultz, Jr. She would never be able to say the word *love* in reference to him again.

On October 6, following a football game in which Fred participated, they went to a Milwaukee bar to play pool with his brother Billy and Laurie's friend Marylisa. Marylisa was the woman Laurie was supposed to have gone out with the night of the murder. Since then, she had started dating Fred's younger brother.

The two couples started to play pool and Fred

became irritated when Laurie won two games in a row. As a joke, Fred bumped her pool cue just as she started to shoot. The first time it was funny, but the third time was too much for Laurie to handle.

"You don't know when to quit. Cheater."

"So what?" Fred said. "Let's just play."

"No, it's almost midnight. Let's go."

Half drunk, Laurie and Fred continued their shoving match on the way to the car. Suddenly, things got out of hand. Fred hit Laurie with a flying side-kick that knocked her off her feet and into the gutter. Pain shot through her spine. She started to cry.

"Come on, get up before someone sees you," Fred yelled at her.

"Wait. Are you nuts!"

"You must have slipped. The sidewalks are wet."

"Leave me alone. You kicked me way too hard. Fred, I hurt."

Fred then tried to pick Laurie up and shove her into his van.

"Shut the fuck up and get in the goddamn van," he screamed. "You'll wake up the whole neighborhood."

Someone who witnessed the fight ran to call the West Allis police. Laurie refused to get in the van with Fred. She was frightened and angry. She sat in the backseat of the police car while Fred talked to the cops. When they came to talk to Laurie, they asked her if she was seeing a psychiatrist.

"No," she said, lying.

Laurie felt totally betrayed by Fred Schultz. She knew he was trying to get out of the mess by telling the police officers that she had mental problems.

"Take a deep breath and try to stop crying," one cop told her. "Do you want to file a battery complaint?"

"No. But I want to go to a women's shelter."

In the morning Laurie was confused about whether she should return to her home. With the passing of the night she thought she should consider the confrontation a drunken scuffle that had gotten out of hand. But she also wondered if Fred's violent temper had just carried him away.

Laurie had promised herself long ago not to succumb to any sort of violence or physical dominance. She wasn't afraid of him, but now she knew that he was capable of hurting another woman. Laurie also knew that if they split up, the newspapers and the prosecution would have a field day with the news.

Laurie stepped inside the phone booth at the shelter and decided to call her mom, who was still in Oregon. My mom will tell me what to do, Laurie thought. She's always been there for me, calm and cool and knowing what is best. Suddenly Laurie missed her mother so much, she started to cry. She dialed the number and heard her mother's voice. Laurie was overcome with emotion. She would give anything just to have her mother hold her for a few minutes.

"Where are you, baby?" her mother asked.

Later, Laurie's dad drove over to pick her up and bring her home. He told Laurie that Fred said Laurie was so drunk, she passed out and fell down.

Fred was in a panic and tearfully asked for her forgiveness. Her father wouldn't leave her side.

"I may be sixty-one years old, but I'll be the equalizer the next time you pull this," her father said. "I have two other daughters that had abusive husbands, and I won't stand for it a third time."

Fred nodded in silence.

That night the story about their fight was in the newspapers and Don Eisenberg called to see if Laurie needed to tell him anything about the incident.

"You had an altercation with Fred? Anything I should know about?"

"Boy, you don't miss a thing in Madison. No. It's just about settled now." Her lawyer then asked her if she had anything else to tell him. Laurie said no.

Eisenberg said he had just received a phone call from Judge Fine and the judge wanted to see them as soon as possible.

Laurie had no idea what the judge wanted to talk about. She hoped that just once something good would happen to her.

CHAPTER 18

Guns and Roses

Judge Fine looked serious as Laurie, Eisenberg, and Assistant District Attorney Kramer walked into his chambers.

It was the first week of October and Laurie still ached from her "battle" with Fred. Judge Fine said he had received a letter in the mail concerning the case and he was going to have a quick hearing in his courtroom to discuss it. Laurie turned, looked at Eisenberg, and without speaking asked him what was going on. Eisenberg shrugged his shoulders and they all walked into the courtroom.

Judge Fine began by saying he had received an unsolicited letter in the mail the previous Friday. Then he started to read it.

After he had read just a few sentences, Eisenberg cut him off and asked if he could read the letter first. Judge Fine agreed and Eisenberg and Laurie read the letter together. Laurie's eyes grew wide. It had been written by John Schultz, the brother who hated Fred Schultz and his new wife, Laurie Bembenek.

John had written that "to the best of his knowledge" Laurie had killed Christine Schultz and had tried to kill Sean. To support his idea John Schultz said that he thought Sean and Shannon had been influenced by their father to talk favorably about Laurie Bembenek.

The rambling letter mentioned that Fred had the boys sign a card to Laurie and that Fred asked his sons to write to Laurie. John also said that Laurie promised the boys that she would buy them whatever they wanted once she and their father were working again.

Toward the end of the letter John said that Sean's life was complicated because he was conceived before Fred and Christine were married. As a result John said that Fred always resented Sean and was extremely hard on him. He said that Fred only married Christine because she had been pregnant.

John wrote, "Fred never accepted Sean, and Sean cried out for acceptance, approval, love, like a puppy who runs to meet a stern master wagging his tail between his legs as Sean was to Fred."

When Eisenberg finished reading, he objected to the letter becoming part of the permanent court record. It was hearsay and had nothing to do with the murder or Laurie's guilt. There was absolutely nothing in the letter, he added, that even pointed a finger at Bembenek—at Fred Schultz, maybe—but not at Laurie Bembenek.

Laurie tried to figure out why her brother-in-law had written the letter. He had been close to Christine and had never really accepted Fred's second marriage. He had fought openly with Fred and in one recent incident involving the boys, the Pewaukee police had been called in to settle the dispute.

Eisenberg told Laurie not to worry about the letter, and Judge Fine ordered that it be impounded and not released publicly. But Laurie knew that the judge would most likely remember the letter in two weeks when he had to decide whether she should stand trial for murder. It was just one more thing to be concerned about.

Before she had time to think about what the letter really meant, Eisenberg called her again and asked her to drive to Madison. There was something else he wanted to discuss with her.

Laurie drove the seventy-five miles from Milwaukee to Madison wondering what was going to happen next. Eisenberg looked nervous when she got to his office. There wasn't the usual kidding and jokes about how wonderful she looked and smelled.

"Kramer from the district attorney's office doesn't want to try this case," he told her. "He thinks that either Fred hired someone to kill Christine, or that you and Fred conspired in some way to do it."

Laurie started to rise off her chair. She was furious. Eisenberg stopped her and went on. "They are willing to knock your charge down if you will give them a statement telling them what you know."

"Are they crazy? Why should I make up some ridiculous story? Why should I admit to something I didn't do? Do you actually think I would cover up something for Fred?"

"Obviously Kramer can't figure this case out and would be delighted to have an explanation from you."

"Don, no way would I be stupid enough to be a party to murder. If Fred hired someone to do it, don't you think he would have the murderer use a different gun? Or don't you think Fred would have gotten rid of it? He had over two weeks to lose it or report it stolen! Whatever!"

"I'm in the process of talking to my own ballistics expert about this whole thing," Eisenberg replied. "A gunshot wound like the one that killed Christine was so close to the skin that the muzzle of the barrel actually penetrated the tissue. According to my expert, both blood and tissue would definitely have blown back into the barrel of the gun. You would have had to clean that gun before Durfee and Fred looked at it, and if you would have cleaned it . . ."

"There would not have been the presence of dust," Laurie said.

Her lawyer replied, "Especially since the gun was placed in a holster, back into a closed duffel bag. It doesn't make sense. Well, this all may be premature. Meanwhile, should I tell Kramer no plea bargain?"

"No plea bargain," Laurie said. "I'm not pleading guilty to something I didn't do."

Driving back to Milwaukee, Laurie tried to ignore the fact that Fred was being talked about as a possible suspect. Questions nagged at her. Why was there no investigation into his role? What had he done the day of the murder? She had no idea where he had gone or to whom he had talked. She shook her head.

Fred couldn't have been involved in this, she told herself over and over, hoping that she might come to believe her own words.

On October 16 Judge Ralph Adam Fine announced he had made a decision about the preliminary hearing. Laurie wore a dark brown suit with a white blouse and leather pumps to the proceeding. Fred Schultz sat next to her while Judge Fine announced his decision. Laurie held her breath, prepared for the worst.

As the judge started to read his prepared statement, the courtroom noise stopped. No one moved. He began by saying that the evidence he had reviewed was both "questionable" and "contradictory" and that this was the "most circumstantial case" he had ever seen.

"Much of it is speculative. Much of it is contradictory. Some of it is not credible," Judge Fine said. "Yet, there is, for the purpose of this preliminary examination, a link of probable cause between defendant and the death of Christine Schultz. That link is, of course, Exhibit number two, Fred Schultz's off-duty gun. According to the ballistics report, Exhibit eight, the Regional Crime Laboratory analyst concluded that the bullet recovered from the body of Christine Schultz was fired from that gun."

Laurie somehow maintained a quiet, reserved composure as Judge Fine continued, but then began to shake uncontrollably. Her head was exploding. She turned to stare at Donald Eisenberg.

The judge continued. "The testimony of Officers Durfee and Elfred Schultz does not, for the purposes of probable cause, destroy that link. According to the evidence adduced during the course of the preliminary examination, the only person who had access to that weapon during the relevant time period the night of the murder was the defendant, Lawrencia Bembenek. That link, taken in conjunction with the other evidence adduced during the course of the preliminary examination, is sufficient for this court to find that there is probable cause to believe that the defendant committed a felony within Milwaukee County. Accordingly, she'll be bound over for trial."

Lawrencia Bembenek turned white. She leaned over and pulled on Eisenberg's sleeve. "That's not true. I'm not the only one who had access to that gun! And how do we know that the gun they have now is even the same gun that was in our apartment the night of the murder?"

"Take it easy," Eisenberg said. "Just take it easy."

Laurie knew that Elfred Schultz had access to the gun. So did Judy Zess, Thomas Gaertner, and the landlord.

The judge had decided to bind her over for trial because of the gun, yet there were several people, including some sitting in Judge Fine's courtroom, who already knew the off-duty .38 special was not the gun that had killed Christine Jean Schultz.

CHAPTER 19

To Have and to Hold

The last few weeks of fall burned out quickly, and, had Laurie Bembenek known what was to come, she would have enjoyed those brilliant orange, yellow, and gold days. In the back of her mind Laurie could not help but wonder if this was the last fall she would ever be able to kick through the leaves without running into a huge metal fence topped with rounds of barbed wire.

On November 9, 1981, she appeared before Milwaukee Circuit Court Judge Michael Skwierawski for arraignment on first-degree murder charges. Arraignments are always brief; the accused usually stands before the judge and charges are read. The person then has a chance to plead guilty or innocent. But the Lawrencia Bembenek case was far from normal.

The reporters who lined up in back of the courtroom were disappointed when the beautiful blond ex-cop stood up before the judge and refused to answer the charges. Eisenberg had told her not to say anything. He was protesting the proceeding. He didn't think his client should even be in the courtroom.

So the scruffy-bearded, red-haired Skwierawski entered a not guilty plea on her behalf. A deliberate, quiet man who wore square, wire-rimmed glasses, Skwierawski also gave Laurie and Eisenberg a chance to ask for another judge.

Skwierawski told Eisenberg and the assistant district attorney, Kramer, that he had once represented Thomas D. Gaertner. Although Laurie and Eisenberg knew that Gaertner was an integral part of her case, Eisenberg decided not to ask for another judge. In fact, he said he wouldn't even bother calling Gaertner to the stand despite the fact that Laurie had allegedly asked him if he knew anyone who could kill Christine Schultz.

"There's nothing he can do for me," Eisenberg said about Gaertner.

Laurie was ordered to stand trial on February 22, 1982, and motions for the case were scheduled to be heard on February 8. Despite the deluge of press coverage, Eisenberg said he wasn't going to ask for the trial to be moved out of Milwaukee County. He did not believe it mattered.

Laurie's story had already appeared in some of the sleaziest tabloids and magazines across the country. It was obvious to everyone, including Laurie, that the case was more than interesting but for all the wrong reasons.

Her Playboy bunny image was unfair, she thought, and no one had bothered to investigate the murder. The cameras were always focused on her, and Laurie thought someone should be looking for the person who had murdered Christine Schultz.

The day following her arraignment, Laurie received a notice from the Department of Labor, Industry and Human Relations informing her that her sex discrimination claim against the City of Milwaukee was unfounded. Laurie wasn't surprised by the ruling and she sent the letter to one of Eisenberg's partners because she wanted to pursue the matter. There was also another matter that needed pursuing.

Eisenberg phoned her the same day and told her she was not legally married to Elfred Schultz, Jr. "Where did you get married to Fred?" he asked.

"Before a judge. It must have been Waukegan County, I think. Anyway, it was in Illinois. Why do you want to know?"

"What was the date?"

"January 31, 1981."

"I think we have a problem," Eisenberg said. "Why did you get married there?"

"Because Fred suggested it, I don't know. We eloped. It seemed romantic, I guess. Why all the questions?"

"I'll have to do a little more checking, but I don't think you two are legally married."

Once again Laurie couldn't believe what she was hearing. Eisenberg told her that the marriage might be legal in Illinois but probably not in Wisconsin. He said the State of Wisconsin prohibits people from remarrying less than six months after their final divorce hearing and Fred had not been divorced for six months when they married.

"If your marriage hasn't been legal, the D.A. will swoop right down on that fact and accuse you of cohabiting. I don't want your credibility attacked."

"What on earth do we do if it's not legal?"

"Get remarried in Wisconsin."

"I don't believe this," Laurie said. "Fred could get fired for cohabitation. If we go downtown and apply for a marriage license, the newspapers will have a field day again."

When Laurie talked to Fred about the marriage in Illinois, he came up with an explanation that made absolutely no sense to her. Elfred Schultz had failed to check a box on his new marriage certificate that asked him if he had a former wife. Fred said he hadn't lied, it had just been an oversight.

Despite her uncertainty about her relationship with Fred and the results of a psychological exam that said the marriage had severe problems, Eisenberg helped them plan a new wedding ceremony. They would remarry in his Madison office the last week of November.

The marriage problems didn't get much better. Laurie was listless and bored all day at home. She had decided to register for classes at the University of Wisconsin at Milwaukee, but it would be several months before classes started. In the meantime she defrosted the refrigerator and dusted the house—jobs she hated.

Laurie had also developed a "repulsion" to Fred. She wasn't interested in sex and Fred wasn't happy about that. One night, when Laurie rolled over and tried to fall asleep, Fred flew into a rage. "Are you going to sleep?" he asked. "This is the third night in a row."

"So? I'm falling asleep."

"You don't love me anymore."

"Don't be ridiculous. I just don't feel like making love. That doesn't mean that I don't love you. Go to sleep."

"No, damn it. Sex was the first thing that went

to hell in my last marriage, and I'm not going to let it happen again!"

"Why must you constantly compare me to Chris? You are overreacting to this."

"No, I'm not," Fred started to yell at her. "You've been so callous these past few months, I don't think you even love me anymore. And now this."

Laurie sat up in bed and told Fred to be quiet because her father was sleeping in the next room, but he refused and started yelling louder. Fred began to dress. He said he was leaving. Laurie's father woke up and tried to intercede.

"Let him go, Dad," Laurie said. "You can't talk to that man."

Fred then returned, hoping that Laurie would ask him to stay. She didn't. But he called a few minutes later.

"What do you want?" she asked him.

"Do you know what would be just great? If you'd beg me to come home right now."

"Are you nuts!" Laurie said. "For one thing, I am so disgusted that you didn't even have the decency to refrain from getting my poor dad involved in our argument. He had nothing to do with it, yet you insisted on making all that damn noise until you woke him up. No consideration! Then you have the audacity to accuse me of not doing any more around here. I can't believe that. You're unreal. Three days without sex and you act like it's a federal case. You can stay wherever you are."

Fred never did tell Laurie where he spent the night and she didn't much care. The next morning, just after she put *The Milwaukee Journal* on the floor to help train her puppy, she picked up the mail. There was a letter from Eisenberg. It was a statement from a witness who claimed that Judy Zess had committed perjury.

The letter had been written by a man named Frederick Horenberger on October 27, 1981. It was six pages of interesting and revealing information about Judy Zess.

According to Horenberger, he had met Judy in the last two weeks of June of 1981 when he went over to her apartment to look at a car Tom Gaertner was trying to sell. Horenberger said that while he was visiting Zess, Gaertner called from prison and he listened as Judy told him she had been to the police department to look at evidence from the Christine Schultz murder.

Judy told Horenberger that she was going to be a witness against Laurie Bembenek at the Christine Schultz murder trial. Horenberger said that Judy had a tap on her phone line that had been installed by the Milwaukee Police Department just in case Laurie called her.

Horenberger said in his letter that Judy told him she had been working on a deal with the Milwaukee police to cooperate with them in exchange for some favors. Judy told him that she was having sex with Frank Cole, a Milwaukee detective assigned to the Christine Schultz murder case, and Cole was setting up some deals for her.

Horenberger said he spent the night with Judy Zess and learned that Judy would do anything to help Gaertner.

When Laurie finished reading the letter, a tiny light went on. For just a few minutes everything made sense and fell into place. She understood why Judy had done an about-face on the witness stand and she shuddered to think that Judy had been waiting for her to call or send a note so the information could be used against her.

Horenberger had also attached a memo to his letter describing a run-in he had with Frank Cole on the way out of Judy's apartment. Judy Zess's revolving sexual door bumped Horenberger in the rear end that day. Cole was not pleased to see him and told him he would be in big trouble if he was ever over there again. Horenberger had a criminal record and he knew Cole could raise havoc with his parole officer.

Laurie reread the letter and wondered how much of it was truth and how much of it was fiction. Judy had lied to Horenberger about making a pass at her because they had never slept in the same bed.

She remembered the comments made by Judy's New York friend in Florida. She also recalled Judy's anger when she learned about Laurie's marriage to Fred. Judy loved wearing Laurie's clothes and was always taking pictures of her. If it was true and Judy Zess was attracted to her, everything did make much more sense.

Eisenberg told Laurie he planned to use Horenberger as a witness and for days Laurie felt confident, relieved to know that maybe she wasn't losing her mind after all. But the day she remarried Fred Schultz in Donald Eisenberg's office, she was suddenly right back where she had started.

The wedding was quick. A judge performed the ceremony, Laurie wore a simple pair of black wool slacks, and Fred suggested that they drive to the

Playboy Club at Lake Geneva for a celebration lunch. Laurie wasn't thrilled with the idea because she hated going out in public and being recognized, but she thought it was important to try to salvage her relationship with Fred Schultz. She knew that without Fred a jury would be hard pressed to look at her kindly.

When they got to the club, they discovered a convention was in progress and all the dining rooms were crowded. They waited at the bar for a table. Laurie ordered scotch and watched as Fred quickly drained his whiskey. Glancing around, Laurie thought about the police having been there, questioning her former coworkers.

Halfway through lunch, Fred started to act like he had too much to drink. Then he mentioned to the waitress that Laurie had worked at the club.

"I wish you wouldn't have said anything about me working here," Laurie told him.

"Then you should have said something before we got here."

"What do I have to do? Screen you before we go anywhere? I thought you'd have more common sense."

"Do you have something to be ashamed of?"

"No! I'm not ashamed that I worked here, although I wouldn't put it on my resumé. It was something that I had to resort to for a few weeks. I'm ashamed that the police were here, questioning everyone about me."

Laurie ended up running from the table and locking herself in a bathroom stall.

This is crazy, she told herself. Fred is crazy. He plays mind games. He argues in circles. I can't stand this any longer.

Laurie composed herself and walked back toward the table. She had to put up with whatever Fred Schultz did and said. She felt trapped.

Driving back to Milwaukee in total silence, she glanced over at her husband and realized that their marriage a few hours earlier meant absolutely nothing to her.

CHAPTER 20

Troubling Transcripts

The weeks before the Christmas of 1981 were the best weeks Lawrencia Ann Bembenek had spent in months. She felt good about the approaching holidays and started exercising at the gym again.

Eisenberg kept telling her he was busy working on the case and for a few weeks she talked herself into believing that everything would be just fine. But her optimistic feelings didn't last long.

First, she had another argument with Fred. He bought Shannon and Sean expensive Christmas gifts, radios with earphones, even though they had agreed not to buy things that cost more than $20 because they didn't have enough money. Fred made it clear that when it came to "his" children, Laurie was not allowed to express an opinion. He told her Christine's parents had purchased an Atari home computer game for the boys.

"We don't have the money to play that game," Laurie told Fred. "You can't outbuy them. I think you should return those expensive radios and buy them something more practical."

"These are my children," he replied, "and you are not going to tell me what to spend on them."

"It's not really the money. It's what you choose to buy."

"You're not complaining about money when I

spend it on you," Fred said, "so don't tell me what I can or can't buy for those kids."

Then Laurie's father decided to fly to Oregon and spend some time with his wife, who was still visiting Laurie's sister. As Laurie drove him to the airport, she felt as if she were losing her best friend. With both her parents gone she would be alone with her husband. The thought suddenly frightened her.

Standing at the airport gate, waving good-bye to her dad, Laurie started to cry. She felt she would never see her father again.

After her father left, Laurie experienced a series of recurring dreams that totally obliterated her festive mood. In one dream she was in Florida moving boxes and furniture into a beach house with several friends. She was embarrassed because several of the chairs were tattered and shabby. Then she joined a crowd of people who had gathered at a picnic area by the shoreline, when suddenly the tide rapidly began to advance on everyone with great speed and frightening power. The crowd ran up the hill, away from the water, and Laurie ran after them, because she couldn't swim. When she reached the top of the hill, she was stopped by a cyclone fence. Just as she was about to throw herself over the top, she realized it was an electric fence. Her hands were thrown off by a shock. She looked over her left shoulder, horrified at the thought of her only means of escape cut off. The waves swept closer and closer. Just before they would reach her, Laurie would wake up, drenched in sweat, gasping for breath.

Her other nightmare was even more bizarre and

horrifying. Laurie dreamed she was in a city, applying for jobs and climbing dirty stairways that led into small old offices. After a brief time she became confused and lost. She walked down the street searching for a phone when she suddenly heard an ugly mechanical noise behind her. It was a terrifying grinding of gears and a horrid, rhythmic clicking.

She turned to see a robotlike creature following her. It had the head of a skull and wore an Uncle Sam's hat. Its jaw opened and closed with jerky, machinelike movements. She ran and found a telephone in a hallway of a building. Before she could attempt to call Fred, strange people were strapping her onto a stretcher and injecting something into her arm to make her unconscious. Laurie struggled with them, begging and pleading to let them call her husband. At that point she would always wake up.

Laurie's dreams continued to turn into nightmares. On December 10 Fred came home from work and said that he wanted to talk about something important. He sat at the kitchen table facing Laurie and held out his hand.

Fred told Laurie he wanted to quit working for the police department. He said he hated working at the desk and he was also tired of putting up with all the questions about the murder.

Fred also mentioned quickly that department officials told him they were going to charge him with several department rule violations because of the circumstances surrounding his marriage to Laurie in Illinois.

Laurie told him to do what he thought was best. He immediately applied for a job on the Wauwatosa Police Department and was discouraged when he was ranked fourteenth out of fifteen candidates.

"It's going to take a lot of guts for someone to hire me, even though my qualifications are higher than anyone else they could get," he said.

The newspapers immediately wrote a story about Fred quitting. Laurie laughed when she read what a local columnist had to say about them:

> However it made news. Because they're part of one of the most bizarre murder cases in recent years, this young, good-looking married couple. In the kitchen, talking. A dog playing on the floor.

In reality, Laurie thought they were about as abnormal as a couple could get.

"How many wives on this block are getting ready to go to a murder trial for supposedly killing their husband's first wife?" she asked Fred. Whatever was left of her once normal life faded away.

Laurie wasn't surprised either when a friend called her and said she had seen Judy Zess and Stu Honeck out on a date. Laurie told Eisenberg about Judy and Honeck. She had no idea what their date meant or what was going on, but she knew Don Eisenberg would find out. It seemed odd, but when she thought about it, even strange events and occurrences now seemed normal.

Laurie's Christmas at home would be a lasting memory. Instead of sticking around the house and feeling sorry for herself, she decided to share her

Christmas with a Milwaukee Laotian family she had read about in the newspaper. The family of fourteen had been left homeless by a pre-Christmas fire.

Buying Christmas presents for the family helped her forget her own problems. When she visited them in their new, tiny apartment, she was moved to tears by their gratefulness. Laurie handed out presents to each of the twelve children and was touched by their sincerity. The visit to the family made her realize that no matter how bad things were for her, someone else was always worse off.

Laurie registered for classes at the University of Wisconsin in Milwaukee and occasionally had meetings to discuss her defense with Eisenberg when he was in Milwaukee on business. Fred always went with her. The meetings were often held at local restaurants and bars and Eisenberg would always drink, usually too much, while they ate and talked.

Laurie didn't think it was odd that Eisenberg never took notes during the meetings. She had a superman image of him and had decided months ago that he needed her complete trust. One Milwaukee meeting with Eisenberg, though, proved particularly disturbing.

Laurie had been introduced to his wife, Sandy, and was taken aback when she met Eisenberg at a restaurant with another woman. The woman was a waitress, and the owner of the restaurant had presented her to Eisenberg as a "blind date gift." Eisenberg and the waitress acted like new lovers. They were french-kissing, holding hands, and making sexual comments. Laurie, who liked

Sandy, was totally embarrassed by Eisenberg's behavior. Her image of the hardworking, dedicated, professional attorney was shattered, but Laurie couldn't turn back. Her murder trial would take place in less than two months.

During the last week of December Fred suggested that they spend New Year's Eve in Las Vegas. He had just received money from some carpentry jobs and he said they deserved it. Laurie wasn't sure traveling alone with Fred was a good idea, but she needed to get away. They actually managed to get through the trip without any major fights. Once they came close. Laurie mentioned that she had been to Las Vegas once before with an old boyfriend, and Fred became upset.

"You don't have to brag about your former boyfriends."

"What's wrong? You can't be jealous!"

"I shouldn't be . . . It's just that I finally found a true love. I can't help myself."

"Fred, what's going to happen to us in February? I'm scared to death."

"Don't worry about it. Everything's going to be all right. It has to be. You'll see."

Fred and Laurie were sitting around the swimming pool at their hotel. For a minute neither of them said anything. Then Fred looked up and said something Laurie thought was peculiar.

"But I wouldn't care even if you did kill Chris."

Laurie was about to protest her innocence when a waitress asked them if they wanted another drink. Fred started to talk to her as if nothing had happened.

When Fred and Laurie left Las Vegas, they went to Florida to stay with some friends so Fred could apply for police jobs. Fred was gone all day, but Laurie wasn't really sure what he was doing. As far as she knew, he could have been at the beach. He said he was applying to become a policeman so they could move to Florida when the trial was over.

What bothered Laurie most while they were in Florida was the realization that she was depressed no matter where she was. With the trial hanging over her head, there was a constant feeling of dread.

Laurie had pretty much worked full-time since she was sixteen years old, and the days and weeks of idle time contributed to her unhappiness and depression. When she returned to Milwaukee, she spent her time washing and waxing the floors, doing the laundry, and cleaning up after Fred. It was hardly the existence she had dreamed of. Laurie described her feelings to a close friend.

I was Joan Crawford reincarnated, cleaning like an anal-compulsive Freudian case study, only to watch my efforts destroyed in less than fifteen minutes after Fred walked in the door. He would undress piecemeal after work, draping his coat, jacket, and vest and tie on various doorknobs and chairs. Socks were abandoned in small navy blue lumps on the rug, and piles of keys, sunglasses, and memo books littered the countertops.

Laurie started classes at the university just after the holidays. She would eventually drop out of school because she was unable to concentrate.

During the second week of January Laurie discovered in the *Milwaukee Sentinel* an article about Frederick Horenberger, the same man who had sent Eisenberg the revealing letter about Judy Zess. He had been convicted of armed robbery, and his victim had been Judy Zess. Laurie immediately sensed that something was wrong. Because of Judy's testimony saying that Horenberger was the man who had beaten and robbed her, he had been convicted. Judy had also said things about her that were not true. Laurie clipped out the article and her mind raced.

She said out loud, "Tied into the robbery and convicted! My God. There goes my witness. He knew too much. That's why he's gone. He saw Frank Cole at Judy's. She told him about the deal she and Tom were making with the cops. She told him about her plans to lie on the witness stand. She told him about her affair with Cole. Now Horenberger is gone."

When Laurie showed the article to Fred, he said that Horenberger could still testify for her but his credibility would be nonexistent. Laurie knew that Eisenberg had been counting on Horenberger and his letter to help in her defense. Now he most likely wouldn't be able to call him to testify.

Then her counselor's husband had a heart attack and she quickly canceled Laurie's weekly sessions. When her mother called to tell her that she was going to have an emergency hysterectomy, Laurie felt what was left of her world crumble. That meant her mother would be unable to attend the trial. Laurie wasn't sure she could make it without her.

Laurie then found out that Fred had been ordered

to pay his sons $6,600 from his police pension fund. She made that discovery by reading about it in the newspaper. At a hearing that Fred hadn't bothered to attend, Circuit Judge Robert M. Curley had ordered him to split with his children the $13,219 pension fund he had received when he quit the police department.

Judge Curley said that Fred had signed a stipulation in December of 1980 that guaranteed Christine Schultz or her estate would receive half of his pension fund. Fred had never bothered to tell Laurie about that, either.

Laurie didn't understand why Fred was so secretive about anything that had to do with his boys or with Christine. She told him it would be easier if she found out what was going on from him and not from the newspaper. Fred just shrugged.

During the third week of January, Laurie lost her gold wedding band. She didn't feel right not wearing it, and when she looked down at her bare ring finger she wondered if the loss was a bad omen.

Laurie Bembenek and Fred Schultz spent their first wedding anniversary shopping on the east side of Milwaukee and touring an art gallery. It was an uneventful, unromantic day. Laurie tried hard not to think about everything that had happened to her during the past year.

Then just ten days before her trial was to begin on February 24, 1981, Laurie had a final meeting with Eisenberg. What he had to tell her was more of a bad omen than anything Lawrencia Bembenek had imagined.

Laurie met him at a Milwaukee restaurant and

they sat alone in a quiet, dark booth. Somehow Laurie had convinced Fred not to come along.

"What I have to show you is very important," Eisenberg said.

"What is it?" Laurie asked.

Eisenberg didn't want to talk in front of the waitress. They both ordered drinks and when the waitress left, Laurie had a moment to study the man who was about to defend her life. He wore a dark, expensive suit and stylish silk tie. Diamonds glistened on his cufflinks, on his rings, and on his tie tack. Today Donald Eisenberg appeared solemn.

"This is serious. I've been investigating this case for about nine months now. In the beginning I made you realize how important it is for you to be completely honest with me, because I defend you. I know you have been. Like I told you before, I don't care what you've done. I wouldn't care if you did commit the murder, because it's not my job to pass moral judgment on you. I've defended people for every crime you can imagine."

Eisenberg maintained his seriousness. Laurie had never seen him this way. Usually he was flirting with her or with one of the waitresses.

"So what do you want to show me?" she asked.

"First, I want to ask you something. This is very important. Is there anything you are not telling me?"

"No! What do you mean?"

"About Fred. Are you covering up for him any way?"

"No!"

"Are you afraid of Fred?"

"No!"

"You've told me everything?"

"Yes. Why?"

Eisenberg quickly shuffled through some papers and looked at Laurie. He told her his investigator had talked to someone who claimed that Fred hired a hit man out of Chicago to kill Christine Schultz.

"A lot of what he says jibes with the case," Eisenberg said. "But then again, he may have been able to piece it together from the newspapers. He says one thing that makes a lot of sense. That there were actually two guys in the house that night. I've always wondered how one person could tie up Christine and hold a gun on her at the same time or why she didn't resist at all against only one man. There were no signs of a struggle. She was a good-sized woman, not some weak female."

Eisenberg told her that the source said the boys, Shannon and Sean, were awakened on purpose the night of the murder. They wanted Sean to see that the man who killed his mother wasn't his father.

Laurie grabbed the transcript from Eisenberg and started reading it as fast as she could. "The guy who gave you this is a convict?"

"Yes."

"But I thought someone incarcerated has little or no credibility in court."

Eisenberg cut her off and never answered her question. She was thinking about Frederick Horenberger.

"Do you have any idea what this could be about?" her lawyer asked. "If you do, please tell me right now. We are talking about a life sentence now. We are not talking about going away for a few months."

"I don't have any idea," Laurie answered honestly. "I don't know what this is all about, honest to God. I would never cover up for a murder."

Don Eisenberg told her that if the statement from the convict was true, then Fred Schultz was using her.

Laurie could barely comprehend what Eisenberg was saying. The waitress brought a huge red menu, but Laurie couldn't even read it. Her head was spinning.

Why did Fred tell them I had a key to that house, when I didn't even know he had a key, Laurie asked herself. How did blood get on his duty revolver? Why did he burst into tears at the preliminary hearing? He didn't write about all the times he called me the night of the murder in his police reports, either. Why did he want to move into that house? Why?

"I don't know what to do," Laurie finally told Eisenberg. "I have to think about this. If we had better proof that Fred hired someone . . . but it's such a big risk to take."

Laurie was hoping Eisenberg would tell her what to do. But he was certain they would win the case. He said she would have to make this decision on her own. He did tell her that the convict's statement could be false.

"Speaking of flimsy evidence, I don't see how we can lose this case," Eisenberg said. "It's nothing but a collection of contradictory facts and speculative theory."

When lunch was over, Eisenberg drove off in his new Jaguar and left Laurie standing near her mother's old car. She had already sold her new flame-orange Camaro to help pay Eisenberg's fee. She stood there watching him disappear.

She didn't want to believe that her husband had hired someone to kill Christine Schultz and then make it appear that she had committed the murder.

"That's the bottom line," Laurie said out loud as Eisenberg's car turned the corner and vanished. "I don't want to believe that Fred Schultz had anything to do with this."

CHAPTER 21

Choices of Chance

Laurie knew that Fred had the perfect alibi the night of the murder. He was on duty as a detective for the Milwaukee Police Department. She also knew that anything was possible when a Milwaukee cop was on duty. She knew that the police officers were not always where they said they were. She had seen everything from cops drinking on duty to selling pornography from the trunks of city police cars.

Laurie simply couldn't believe that Fred had plotted against her. She had been trained her entire life to think the best of people, especially people who said they loved you and wanted to spend the rest of their life with you.

When Laurie came home from her meeting with Eisenberg, she fell asleep on the living-room couch. When she woke up, with a slight hangover from too many drinks with Eisenberg, she knew she had to make a decision on whether to go after Fred at the trial.

Fred has stuck by me through this whole thing, she thought to herself. He lost his house, his job, his children. I should be ashamed of myself for having doubted his love for even one second. That statement can't be true. I've had my doubts, but no, I couldn't turn on him once we got him on the stand. If I did, I wouldn't be able to live with myself.

Laurie called Don Eisenberg. She told him not to use the convict's statement that said Elfred Schultz had plotted to kill his first wife. Eisenberg did not object to Laurie's decision.

She started running at an indoor track every day. It was the only time she could feel free from her anxiety. She accompanied Fred on every carpentry assignment that he had, often working late into the night. He had contracted to do several commercial jobs and they could only get in to work after hours when the businesses had closed.

Back home there was one tiny bit of good news. It was a letter from Laurie's mom asking to be picked up at the airport. Laurie's parents would be there in time for the trial. Fred drove with her to the airport but he wouldn't get out of the car, and Laurie went in to get her parents by herself.

As soon as Laurie spotted her mother and father, she began to cry and ran right into her mother's arms.

"Don't cry. We're home now," her mother said softly.

Just a week before the trial, Eisenberg called her to say that he had filed a motion for discovery. That motion asked the judge to order the state to release any and all information that they planned on using in court to Eisenberg. He received copies of all the police reports.

The reports filled up four huge boxes. Laurie read through them all and found that most of them seemed totally irrelevant. There was a report from a member of her police academy class saying that Laurie had told him she could do anything a man could do. There were interviews from friends of Laurie, her family, and people she had worked with. She saw mug shots of twenty different suspects, all of them male.

Laurie couldn't believe all the reports from people who lived near Christine's home. There was a stack of police interviews from people who had seen a man with a green jogging suit and a long reddish pony tail jogging near the scene of the murder. There was also an unusually large number of statements from Judy Zess.

Then Don pulled out a report involving a woman named Kathryn Morgan.

"Where was your mother on June eighteenth?" Don asked her.

Laurie flipped through her calendar and tried to remember if her mother had been on vacation that day.

"I hope so. The state has a witness named Mrs. Morgan who claims that she saw your mother going through the garbage at your old apartment complex. She says your mother took something home with her in a garbage bag."

"What?"

"Morgan says that, on June eighteenth, she was sitting outside of her apartment across the yard from your old place, when a woman pulled up in a car. She said the woman was about five-foot-seven. She was wearing shorts and a tank top. Morgan claims the woman got out of her car and approached her to inquire if the green bins were the trash containers for the apartments."

Eisenberg said that according to the report the woman then went over to the bin, pulled out a bag, put it in her car, and left.

Laurie said her mother didn't even fit the description. She told Eisenberg that on that date her mother would have been baby-sitting for Shannon and Sean because she would have been at work. She also said that her father would have had the car at work and that her mother would never have been tall enough to reach into the bin and pick out garbage.

"The state is probably trying to prove that you threw out some evidence and had your mother retrieve it for you," Eisenberg said. "Is there any way we can prove your dad had the car that day?"

Laurie said that his boss would remember and then she stopped and recalled, "Remember when my mother testified at the preliminary? Something happened that was strange. Just before Kramer finished with his cross-examination, he asked my mom to remove her glasses. Obviously, she complied, and then he told her to put them back on. Let me see the report again."

The report said that Mrs. Morgan identified Virginia Bembenek on September 2, 1981, the second day of the preliminary hearing as the same woman she had seen removing the bag from the garbage. Morgan identified her after her mother removed her glasses.

"My mom can't drive without them," Laurie said "She can barely see without them. Her eyes are so bad, she doesn't drive at night or on the freeway anymore."

Eisenberg told Laurie her information would help. Laurie couldn't believe all these people were saying things that were not true. "I find it so incredible that all these crazy people come forward with all this bullshit!"

Eisenberg agreed. "It always happens with a widely publicized case such as yours. People are thrill seekers. They want to get in on the act. Bored housewife plays detective." Eisenberg said that even though the information from Mrs. Morgan was false, it would hurt them. He said circumstantial evidence was like little building blocks. "You have this witness, and that statement, and pretty soon you build yourself a case," he said.

"But none of it is true. Can you picture my mother conspiring to cover up a murder? She wouldn't even let me play hooky from school."

Laurie flipped through more reports and read several from friends of Christine who told police that Fred had physically abused her. One report from Christine's attorney, Eugene Kershek, said that Fred had threatened Christine just weeks before the murder.

"Don," Laurie said, "most of these reports were taken in July, after my arrest. It's like they arrested me and then decided they better prove I did it."

Another report from Christine's baby-sitter said that Fred had given Laurie a tour of the house in front of her. Laurie said that wasn't true, either. Laurie said she had never been farther than the entrance to the front door. The first time she had been in the Ramsey Street home was the day following the murder.

Laurie took all the reports home and was instructed to read through them and then report back to Don.

"This is just another example of how I am guilty until proven innocent instead of innocent until proven guilty," Laurie told Eisenberg.

Back home, Laurie piled the reports on the living room coffee table and started to read. The report by Fred said that when he arrived with his partner Michael Durfee at their apartment, he immediately felt the hood of her car to see if it was warm. He wanted to see if she had used it recently. Laurie thought that was an odd thing to do. Fred said the car was cold but he was wondering if she had gone out without telling him.

The next report was written by Fred's lieutenant, Carl Ruscitti. Ruscitti said that Fred approached him to say that they had found some of his bullets out of place in his holster in May.

In the report Fred claimed to have questioned Laurie about the bullets, but she denied knowing anything about them. It seemed as if Laurie had been tampering with Fred's bullets. When Laurie read that, she flew off the couch and ran into the kitchen where Fred was reading the newspaper. She threw the report down in front of him.

"What?" he asked.

"What on earth did you tell your lieutenant?"

"I didn't tell Ruscitti anything. I mean, what I told him isn't written down here. I was misconstrued . . ."

"Why would you tell him something like that? It's not true. I feel so betrayed. What are you trying to do to me?"

"Laurie, I was telling him about the time when I found that bullet on the floor by my clothes tree."

"By your clothes tree in your corner of the bedroom, where you used to hang your ammo belt and gun and everything else. I remember the incident. We already had the boys, Fred. Sean and Shannon were right there. And you accused them of playing with your bullets, when the damn bullet probably just fell out of your pouch onto the floor. That happened in June."

"So?"

"So the reports says May. And it says you claimed to have questioned me about it? This report wouldn't exist if you hadn't gone to Ruscitti with it in the first place. A bullet falls out of your ammo pouch, amidst all of your junk in the corner, and the next thing I know, my husband runs to his commanding officer about it!"

"What I told Ruscitti was that it would have been possible for Judy Zess to have been looking at my ammunition. That's why I told him. I don't know why he wrote that other shit."

"You turned an innocent incident into a condemning one!"

"You of all people should know how the police misconstrue reports."

"And you felt the hood of my car that night?"

"I did that in front of Durfee on purpose. I did it to show him that it was cold. That way they couldn't turn around and . . ."

"But, Fred, why would you do that? Why would you even do something like that, unless you were suspicious? How could you?"

Then Laurie mentioned all the reports that said Fred had abused Christine.

"Those people have as much credibility as Mrs. Morgan. They're lies. Just like the report about your mother is a lie. Just like the reports about you are lies. Did I ever doubt you for even one second? I don't believe any of the lies about you. Why do you believe the reports about me?"

Laurie was trapped. She had to back off. What

Fred was telling her did make sense. He told her that the police reports written about her could be a lie. The reports might all be lies, but they existed and the prosecution was going to use them against her. She knew they could be—and most likely would be—very damaging.

Laurie spent the final days before her trial reading through the rest of the reports and trying to ready herself psychologically for the trial. She tried to relax and rest, but there really wasn't anything that Lawrencia Ann Bembenek could do to prepare herself for the days to come.

CHAPTER 22

A Jury of Peers

The City of Milwaukee eagerly awaited the opening of Lawrencia Bembenek's trial on February 23, 1982.

Groups of people started gathering outside the courtroom an hour before the trial was scheduled to begin. The crowd was made up of the usual set of trial watchers, grandmothers who bring along their knitting and a few friends, young men and women who want to be lawyers when they grow up, friends of the defendant, friends of the deceased, various witnesses, and lots of gawkers.

The group attending Laurie's trial included all of the above and then some. There was a curious mix of average American citizens who wanted to see this trial. Lots of people in the Milwaukee area thought something was not quite right about the charges against Lawrencia Bembenek. After all, no one had found anything that would directly tie Laurie to the murder.

When the doors were opened, there was a rush of people trying to grab a seat. About a hundred were turned away. They would have to settle for what the newspaper had to say about the trial that evening.

Laurie tried to ignore all the stares as she walked into the courtroom. She was with Eisenberg. He wore a somewhat conservative-looking dark suit and dark tie. Laurie wore a dark dress. She knew it would be described in detail in all the news accounts.

The lengthy process of jury selection was the first order of business. Jurors are picked randomly by computer and before being selected for a particular jury, each juror must answer several questions and be screened by both the defense and prosecuting attorneys.

Laurie knew that it was unlikely they would find someone who had not heard about her case. She also wondered about the possibility of ending up with a jury composed almost entirely of older women.

The prospective jurors were told that the trial could last as long as three weeks and they would have to be sequestered. That meant they would have to stay at a motel, be away from their families, and could not listen to or watch any news reports about the case.

The majority of the men said they had important jobs and could not be away from work. Most of the women interviewed seemed more than eager to serve the court. Laurie didn't take that as a good sign. If they had been minority women, maybe, but not the kind of women who would look with disgust at anyone with blond hair, a great figure, and a divorced husband.

Finally, seven women and five men were selected. Included in the group were several housewives, a part-time truck driver, a floral designer, a clerk, and a health inspector. They would decide how Lawrencia Bembenek would spend the rest of her life. In prison or as a free woman wrongly accused of a crime. When their names were announced, Laurie leaned over and whispered to Eisenberg, "I don't know why, but I have a feeling about this balance," she said. "This really isn't a jury of my peers."

"It disturbs me, too," Eisenberg said. "But there's not much we can do. We went through the original list of twenty-five names. Kramer was allowed to strike some and so were we until we got down to the twelve jurors and two alternates."

Eisenberg had filed a motion to have the case dismissed because of lack of probable cause. He was also trying to suppress evidence that he thought had been obtained illegally from Laurie's locker at Marquette University.

A hairbrush that was taken from Laurie's locker had been sent to the crime lab and at least one strand of hair on the brush was consistent with the strand of hair that had supposedly been found on the gag used on Christine.

That strand of hair was allegedly discovered by crime lab employees when they unfolded the gag.

Eisenberg and Laurie sat right next to each other so they could pass notes and discuss the proceedings. Eisenberg underlined the sentence that said "one color-processed blond hair" that was found "consistent in characteristics" with the hairs from the hairbrush and "could be from the same source."

"This is the sloppiest police work I've seen," Eisenberg whispered. " 'Could be'? 'Could be'? You might be convicted on could bes or could not bes? Jesus Christ! To top it off, it was an unconstitutional search."

The judge, Michael Skwierawski, wanted to hear some testimony before he ruled on the motions and before the actual trial started and the jury was brought back into the courtroom.

Tom Conway, a man who had been Laurie's sergeant at Marquette, but who had since lost his job, took the stand. He said after Laurie's arrest she gave him her locker combination so he could get her extra uniforms.

Just after he opened her locker, he said a pair of Milwaukee detectives showed up and asked if they could be present when he looked through her locker. Suddenly, the detectives snapped up her purse and told Conway, "We'll need this."

Laurie was surprised when Eisenberg asked her to testify about what happened. She took the stand and said she gave Conway permission to get out her uniforms but none of her personal property. She was only on the stand for a few minutes.

After Laurie's testimony there was a brief recess. She wandered out into the hall and past the television cameras and reporters.

"Ms. Bembenek," one reporter yelled to her. "Care to comment?"

"On what? Your suit?" Laurie teased. "You look like one of the lawyers around here."

"I dress like this intentionally," said the reporter. "That's how I get people around here to talk with me."

"Except this person," Laurie said, walking quickly away.

Back in the courtroom the judge was ready to rule on Eisenberg's motions.

"I am convinced for a variety of reasons that the police actions in this case were not such that they transposed or transformed what was essentially a private action of a private citizen into some governmental action," Skwierawski said.

He then denied the motion to suppress the items taken from Laurie's purse. Laurie wondered if the police who confiscated her purse were not part of a governmental body, then who were they representing?

The police were there acting as a glee club, right? she said to herself.

Skwierawski also denied the motion to dismiss the case due to probable cause. He said probable cause had already been determined at the preliminary hearing and this court didn't want to usurp another judge's decision.

"Why even file a motion if you know it will be denied?" Laurie asked Eisenberg.

"For the record," Don whispered back.

Eisenberg had also subpoenaed Chief of Police Harold Breier and had sent along an order for discovery that included access to department records on Stu Honeck and Judy Zess.

The assistant district attorney objected when Eisenberg asked for the information.

"Your honor!" he said, rising from his chair. "I must object to the defense's request for these records! I also object to Mr. Eisenberg's strategy. His intentions are focused upon pointing the finger at other suspects, and that is not his job. His job is to defend Miss Bembenek, not to identify other possible defendants!"

"Your honor," Eisenberg protested, "may it please the court to understand that the defense's sole purpose in subpoenaing this information is to inform the court that previous testimony by these witnesses was perjury. At the preliminary hearing, Mr. Honeck denied having any problem with alcoholism, and I believe these records will show that he does indeed have a problem, which may be relevant to his recollection of the events on the night of the murder. If he consumed a great deal of alcohol that same night . . ."

"Your honor," Kramer objected. "Whether Mr. Honeck is an alcoholic, or not, bears absolutely no relevance whatsoever to this case, and I see no reason why it should be admissible."

The judge finally interrupted both men. "Gentlemen, if you will stop for a moment, I will tell you that I intend to review the records of both Miss Zess and Mr. Honeck in the privacy of my chambers, and decide whether or not they in fact have any relevance to this case."

Judge Skwierawski did go into his chambers and came back out thirty minutes later to announce that he was denying the motion to use the records of Honeck and Zess. Laurie wasn't surprised.

Then Eisenberg complained that he had not been able to interview the Schultz boys prior to the opening of the trial. He said his repeated attempts to talk with the boys had been rebuffed by the boys' guardians, the Crists.

After questioning Kramer and Eisenberg, Skwierawski ordered that the boys meet with Eisenberg in a room near the courtroom.

Following that, the judge ordered a disruptive spectator thrown into the county jail until the court was finished for the day. It was finally time to bring in the twelve jurors and two alternates and begin the murder trial of Lawrencia Bembenek.

Laurie thought Kramer's opening statement was a theatrical blend of fact and fiction, with an emphasis on fiction. He offered the jury an account of Christine Schultz's murder on May 28, 1981. His theory was that Laurie sneaked into the Ramsey Street house intending to scare Christine so she would want to move from her home. Kramer said that Laurie's plan went astray when Christine struggled and the gun that killed her, the gun that Laurie Bembenek held in her hand, discharged into her back and killed her. According to Kramer, Laurie wanted to make the crime scene look like a robbery had taken place, so that Christine would think that her home was no longer a safe place to live. But, that plan didn't work. Laurie Bembenek quickly turned into a murderer.

Kramer talked about how Fred built the house on Ramsey and had a hard time leaving once his marriage fell apart. He said Fred Schultz was also having extreme financial difficulties because he had to keep paying for the house even though he didn't live there. Then, Kramer said, Fred Schultz met a very young and very attractive woman.

"Ms. Bembenek liked to live in what I would refer to as the fast lane. She wanted, she expected, and she enjoyed the finer things in life. She liked clothes, jewelry. She liked to travel. She had worked as a display person, I believe you would call it, at the Boston Store, where she had access to, obviously, wigs and other decorations that they used to put in their displays in the windows. She had also worked as a bunny at the Playboy Club for a brief period of time, where she also had access to wigs and other makeup."

Kramer talked about Laurie and Fred's quick marriage, their honeymoon, and how Laurie used some plastic clothesline on the trip to Jamaica. He said Fred was hopeful that his ex-wife would move into a home her parents owned in northern Wisconsin so he could move into the house on Ramsey Street, but that hadn't happened.

He said the night of the murder Lawrencia Bembenek donned a wig, put on her black shoes from the police department and a green jogging suit, and jogged to the home of Christine Schultz. He said Laurie was familiar with the house and slipped in the back door with Fred's off-duty revolver tucked under her arm. He said Laurie wore gloves and entered Christine's bedroom, wrapped a bandana around her face, tied her up, and then ran across the hall to check on the boys.

"Well, obviously Sean is startled awake by the feeling of a gloved hand on his face," Kramer said, "and some type of a . . . I guess he described it as a plastic-coated elastic or cord, choking him around his neck. He instinctively starts to scream frantically, flailing and kicking about in the darkened bedroom. Shannon is also awakened from his sleep in the darkened bedroom and begins to kick about at a person he believes is attacking his brother. You can imagine, ladies and gentlemen, the sounds emanating from that bedroom. You can imagine . . ."

After some arguments from Eisenberg protesting what Christine Schultz did and didn't hear, Kramer proceeded to tell the jury that Bembenek ran back into Christine's bedroom. He said the rope was loosening around her wrists and Mrs. Schultz recognized Laurie.

"It became apparent to Mrs. Schultz what was going to happen because she stated something to the effect, 'Oh, God, oh, God,' and at that moment the defendant, Miss Bembenek, fired into her back with the weapon and killed her."

Laurie was just about ready to jump out of her seat as she listened to Kramer. He was making up the entire story. She grabbed her pen and a legal pad of paper and started writing notes to Eisenberg.

"If Kramer says there was no intent to kill, then why was I charged with first-degree murder?"

Laurie continued writing as Kramer described how Sean and Shannon ran to their mother's room and tried to help her. He said the boys called Honeck. He said when the police arrived, Sean told them it was a large man in a green Army jacket, but Shannon said it was a man or woman in a green jogging suit with yellow stripes running down the side.

"This is absurd," Laurie wrote to Eisenberg. "It's idiotic to think that a grown woman could be scared out of her own house. How farfetched! She could change her locks or buy a guard dog or have someone stay with her, but she wouldn't just move out! Christine's boyfriend was a cop! Honeck could have kept an eye on the house if she was scared. It's a stupid theory. Besides, Fred and I had a terrible fight over the issue of moving into that house. I refused to live in it!"

Laurie also wondered how Christine could recognize her if she was disguised in a wig, and whatever else she had "gathered up" from the Playboy

Club. She also thought it was strange that Kramer mentioned Christine turned around and recognized her because she had been tied up and shot in the back. None of it made any sense.

Kramer talked about Fred Schultz arriving at the scene, never mentioning that he had once been a prime suspect. He said Schultz then went with Detective Durfee over to Fred's apartment and woke up his wife. They looked at Fred's off-duty gun and Durfee saw that there was some dust on it.

"He smelled the gun," Kramer said. "He concluded at that time that the gun had not been fired and gave the gun back to Detective Schultz. Either Detective Durfee or Detective Schultz indicated they'd better take the gun downtown. So Detective Durfee, Detective Schultz, and Ms. Bembenek agreed to go from the apartment with the off-duty gun down to the police station."

Later, Kramer said a police officer named Gauger examined the same weapon and compared it with the bullet that was removed from the body of Christine Schultz by Dr. Elaine Samuels, the medical examiner, and with some other bullets received from Mr. Schultz. After that examination, Kramer said it was determined that Fred Schultz's off-duty gun really had been the weapon that killed Christine Schultz.

Kramer talked about the wig that had been found in the plumbing of the apartment next door to Fred and Laurie and about a hair that had been found on the calf of Christine Schultz. That hair, he said, was consistent with the fibers of the wig. According to Kramer, hairs found on the bandana that was used to gag Christine Schultz were also found to be consistent with the hairs removed from Lawrencia's hairbrush.

Laurie had a hard time listening as Kramer told the jury she had been seen around town in a green jogging suit. He said a *Milwaukee Journal* photographer had taken a photo of her in it. Although the photo was black and white, Kramer said the photographer said he thought it was a green jogging suit.

"I've never owned a green jogging suit in my life," Laurie whispered to Eisenberg. "They have a red one as part of the evidence. There must be someone who looks like me running around town in a green jogging suit."

Kramer said the suit disappeared and that most likely Laurie's mother, Virginia Bembenek, removed it from the dumpster outside of Laurie's apartment. He even had a witness, Mrs. Morgan, who had seen her do it.

Kramer was finally finished. He had explained why Laurie Bembenek killed Christine Schultz. She had killed Christine Schultz because she wanted to live in the Ramsey Street home and because she wanted to live a fast life.

"That is why Miss Bembenek shot Christine Schultz," he said. "Those are the reasons why she is sitting there today. And I'm confident that after you listen to all of that testimony you will answer the question, Who killed Christine Schultz? by finding Miss Bembenek guilty."

For just a few seconds Donald Eisenberg didn't move from his chair. Laurie had no idea what would happen next. Everyone in the jury box was looking at him and at her. Finally the judge turned to Eisenberg. "Mr. Eisenberg, do you wish to make an opening statement at the outset?"

"Yes, your honor. I wasn't going to, but I believe I will at this juncture."

Eisenberg stood up, buttoned his suit jacket, and faced the jury. He told the jury he had originally decided not to make an opening statement, but then changed his mind. Eisenberg said he wanted the men and women on the jury to know what he planned for the trial.

"The information that has been filed in this case charging her with first-degree murder also is not proof of evidence of any fact whatsoever. I want you to realize that the only believable evidence is that evidence that is credible and comes from the witness stand. All that Laurie wants from the twelve of you, and I say that in due respect to the two of you [the alternate jurors], is a fair and honest treatment of the credible and believable evidence from the witness stand."

Eisenberg told them to remember that there are always two sides to every story. He told the jurors it wasn't fair to assume that Laurie was guilty just because she was a lovely young lady. He then gave a brief outline of her life.

He talked about her problems with the police department when she was at the police academy. He explained the real reason for her dismissal from the academy was a supposedly falsified police report. But she had not lied on the police report.

He said much of the evidence mentioned by Kramer was not evidence that they actually had. He said the black police oxfords that the killer wore the night of the murder were not in custody.

He said there was no way to prove the wig in the drain was the same wig used the night of the murder. There was no green jogging suit, either, Eisenberg said.

He said that Judy Zess had access to the apartment, and the alleged murder weapon up to the date of the murder. He said there was no way to know for certain if the hair fibers found on the body of Christine Schultz were the same as the fibers on the wig found in the drain.

"The person from the crime lab will testify that it could have been from one hundred fifty million other wigs," he said.

Eisenberg also spent a considerable amount of time talking about the twenty-one days it took for the police department to determine that it really was the off-duty revolver of Fred Schultz that killed his first wife. Then he talked about the Schultz boys.

"We believe that the evidence will show that Sean, who I believe you will find to be a bright, intelligent, caring, loving, super young man, will testify that the assailant, the person who killed his mother, didn't wear a green jogging suit, but he wore an Army-type jacket without camouflage. Not a green jogging suit. An Army-type jacket without camouflage that had—was flapping and was big."

He also explained that it was impossible for Virginia Bembenek to drive without her glasses. He said the license-plate numbers did not even match. She was not the woman who a Mrs. Morgan had seen picking garbage out of a dumpster near Fred and Laurie's 20th Street apartment.

"We, Laurie and I, ladies and gentlemen, are

positive that after all of the evidence, as it unfolds here before you, you will have no doubt in your minds as to Laurie's innocence. A criminal trial, ladies and gentlemen, as you no doubt will see during the next few days, is a search for the truth. Ladies and gentlemen, please help Laurie and help me find that truth."

Laurie listened as Eisenberg finished his opening statement. She glanced over at the jurors, the men and women who literally held her life in their hands.

Are they listening? she thought. Are they really listening or are they just looking?

CHAPTER 23

Innocent Until . . .

Once the trial started, Laurie had a hard time remembering what day it was. She told her mother that she felt totally detached, as if she were merely standing in the wings of a theater, viewing a play that she starred in at the same time. She was like as dreamer, afraid of waking.

"As I watch everyone, Mom," Laurie said, "I am unable to move or cry out against those who are hurting me intentionally, against those who are lying viciously, for reasons unknown to me."

Every morning, Laurie woke long before the alarm was set to go off. Then she would lie in bed and just stare at the digital clock, watching one second after another tick away. Finally she would jump out of bed, rummage through her closet for something clean to wear, and race to get to the courthouse on time.

Every morning during the three-week-long trial Laurie would watch the crowds of excited onlookers jockey for seats in the courtroom. The minute the courtroom doors opened there would be the same rush to find a seat.

"Maybe if I tap my shoes together three times I will wake up from this terrible dream," she whispered to her mother as they walked into the courtroom.

During the testimony Laurie kept an eye on the

jurors. They rarely looked at her and one elderly man constantly dozed off. Then there was a mentally unstable woman who continually disrupted the proceedings, almost on a daily basis, until the judge ordered her held in the Milwaukee County Jail. Once as she was being taken out of the courtroom, she grabbed Laurie's purse and everything inside went flying across the courtroom.

On the third day of the trial Sean Schultz took the stand. His testimony was similar to the testimony he gave during the preliminary hearing, but almost nine months had passed since the murder. His memory wasn't quite as fresh as it had been. He remembered his mother washing dishes after he had gone to bed with his brother, Shannon. He said they were both sleeping in the bottom bunk.

"I'm not sure of the time, but after she was done with the dishes she had come up and we discussed some stuff about—because we went up north without telling my dad, and I was upset about that, and my mom was upset because my dad was mad. And I wanted to see my dad, so I was upset about that," Sean told Kramer.

Sean said he eventually fell asleep and then woke up when he felt a rope or something tugging on his neck. Then a hand came down over his face. He said the person trying to hurt him wore gloves. The gloves were dirty and tan-colored. Sean said he screamed and then he saw the person run out of the room.

"The person had like a baggy green canvas Army jacket without camouflage," he said. "It seemed like, you know, the black police shoes with the cut low top, too."

Sean said then about two seconds later he heard

a bang and saw the man running and jumping down the stairs. He also remembered that when the person was in his room, he, or she, made a low growling sound.

Then Kramer asked him if he thought the person who had been in his room the night of the murder was Laurie Bembenek.

Kramer: Now, do you believe that the person that you saw in your house the night your mother was shot was the defendant, Laurie Bembenek?

Sean: No.

Kramer: Why not?

Sean: Because of the size of the person.

Kramer: Anything other than the size of the person?

Sean: Well, the height, the width of the body. That's all.

When Kramer finished examining Sean, it was Eisenberg's turn. Sean was a key witness for Laurie. Although he did not actually witness the murder, he had seen the person who committed the murder, and he had stuck to his story that the person was a man. It was not Laurie Bembenek.

Sean said he always liked Laurie. He said Laurie was always kind to him and his brother and she never babied them. She treated them like big boys and let them make some of their own decisions.

Eisenberg concentrated on the physical description of the assailant. Sean told him that the man was not wearing a green jogging suit. It was a green Army jacket. He also told Eisenberg, again, that it could not have been Laurie because Laurie was much smaller than the man who attacked him.

Shannon testified next. He recalled looking up the night of the murder while he was in bed and seeing a man with a green jogging suit that had yellow stripes down the sleeves. He saw a reddish-brown ponytail running down the man's back.

Shannon could not be specific about anything else that happened the night his mother was murdered.

Next, Judy Zess was called as a witness. She told Kramer she knew Laurie had at least one short blond wig when she was working as a police officer. Judy said the wig was short, too short to be made into a ponytail. Zess did admit while on the witness stand that she had a shoulder-length brownish wig that she kept at her parents' home in Delafield.

She said Laurie had a traveling laundry kit with a plastic clothesline in it and she stuck to her story from the preliminary hearing that Laurie had talked about having Christine Schultz "blown away." Then Judy Zess said when she lived with Laurie, she knew that Laurie had a green jogging suit.

Laurie thought Judy appeared nervous on the witness stand. She kept her eyes down and didn't look at Laurie during her entire testimony.

When it was Eisenberg's turn to ask her questions, Judy's memory started playing tricks on her. She couldn't remember the exact date or the month she turned in her key to the apartment she had once shared with Fred Schultz and Laurie on

20th Street. She gave Eisenberg three different dates even though she had said in earlier testimony that she turned the key in on June 24, a month following the murder of Christine Schultz.

She said Laurie and Fred did not live "high on the hog" and didn't spend a lot of money on clothes, food, or expensive gifts. She also said Fred and Laurie paid all their bills and didn't appear to have financial problems.

Even though Judy had told Laurie that her now-husband, Tom Gaertner, was furious when he found out that Laurie was married to Fred Schultz, the man who had shot and killed his best friend, she told Eisenberg that Gaertner was only "mildly" upset when he talked to her about it.

She did say that she saw a pair of forest-green baseball pants in one of Fred's boxes that was kept in the storage shed at the 20th Street apartment. Her description of what she actually saw in that box changed several times while Eisenberg questioned her.

Then, when Eisenberg was finished, Kramer asked her if she had ever heard Laurie say anything else about Christine Schultz.

Zess: In May, prior to Tom going to the Mr. USA contest, would have been May 19, 1981, we were packing up some of our belongings and Laurie said to Tom, "Do you know anyone who could take a contract out on Chris?"

Laurie could barely look at Judy Zess by the time Kramer was finished with her. She knew she had to sit through Fred Schultz's testimony, too, and she wondered what other surprises she would hear. She vented her anger throughout the trial by writing notes to Eisenberg with colorful marker pens.

Eugene Kershek, Christine Schultz's divorce attorney, was never asked about statements Christine Schultz made to him concerning her fear of Fred Schultz. The police report Laurie had read stated that Christine told Kershek she was frightened because Fred had told her he would "blow her fucking head off." But that was never brought out in court.

Christine's baby-sitter, Tammy Brumirski, testified that in the early part of May she was babysitting for Shannon and Sean when Fred and Laurie came to pick up the boys. She said Fred showed Laurie through the house just before they left with the boys.

When Eisenberg asked her questions, she couldn't remember exact dates and admitted that she was confused about when Laurie and Fred had actually come to the house.

A *Milwaukee Journal* photographer, Robert Goessner, then told Kramer that he saw Laurie Bembenek in December of 1980 when she came into the photo department to have a photo taken to use with a story the paper was writing about her discrimination suit against the city. He said he remembered that Laurie was wearing a green jogging suit. He remembered, he said, because he thought she was so attractive. His proof of the green jogging suit was a black-and-white photograph.

Laurie grabbed her pen and started writing furiously on the long yellow legal pad. A female friend of hers worked at a photo lab and had once told Laurie about a process that could be used on a black-and-white photo to determine the true colors.

Eisenberg looked at what Laurie wrote and decided to ask the photographer about it. Goessner admitted that such a process did exist and could prove what the real color of the jacket was.

"Of course the police didn't test the negative," Laurie wrote to Don. "Because it only would have proved that the jacket I am wearing in that photograph is red!"

Don nodded and then leaned over to whisper in Laurie's ear. "If I was Kramer, I would be ashamed to introduce such cheap, ridiculous evidence."

Eisenberg asked Goessner, who did not even take the photograph, if anyone had ever attempted to test the negative to determine the color of the jacket Laurie was wearing.

Goessner said no but that the equipment would be available if the district attorney or anyone else wanted to find out for certain if the jacket was green or red.

The district attorney's office had confiscated Laurie's red jogging jacket as evidence. That's the jacket she had on when the photo was taken by the *Journal*.

Laurie felt as if anyone in the world could get up on the stand and say anything they wanted about her and against her. She knew that as a defendant, she had every right to sit back and let the state prove everything. Technically, she was under no obligation to prove anything. She was innocent until proven guilty. Laurie knew that the state had to prove she was guilty, beyond a reasonable doubt. But in reality she had to fight like hell or she would be convicted of a crime she had not committed.

Next, John Schultz, Fred's brother who had written the letter to Judge Fine saying that he thought Laurie killed Christine Schultz, testified for the prosecution. He said that his feelings about Laurie's guilt were just that—his feelings.

Eisenberg got John Schultz to admit that his wife Kathy and Christine had been very close friends. John said that Kathy was upset over her death and there had been problems between the five Schultz brothers because of the murder.

> Eisenberg: Is there one bit of information in your letter to Judge Fine that you can substantiate as evidence to prove that Laurie Bembenek killed Christine Schultz?
> John: No, sir.

John Schultz also admitted that Laurie had never been inappropriate with Sean and Shannon and that she did not tell them what to say before the police questioned them about the murder.

The Milwaukee County assistant medical examiner took the stand and testified that she performed the autopsy on Christine Schultz. Laurie thought Dr. Elaine Samuels was a very precise, intelligent woman. She explained that the bullet—which she called "the missile"—entered the back of the right shoulder, and made a direct, diagonal path to the center of the heart "with astounding accuracy."

Dr. Samuels was an extremely bright woman and Eisenberg wanted to take advantage of her vast amount of knowledge to make other state experts look incompetent. Eisenberg started to ask her about the words "blow-back" when Kramer objected.

"Blow-back is a subject meant for a ballistics expert. I don't think Dr. Samuels is qualified to testify about that subject."

"Your honor, would the court ask Dr. Samuels if she thinks she is qualified, and not depend on Mr. Kramer's assumption that she is not," Eisenberg asked.

"Dr. Samuels?" the judge asked.

"I think it is directly within the realm of forensic pathology," Dr. Samuels said.

Laurie was irritated by the prevailing attitude that Dr. Samuels was "strange" not because she worked in the "morgue," but because of her appearance. Elaine Samuels didn't meet socially defined standards of what doctors are "supposed to" look like. First of all, she was a woman and that was one strike against her. Second, she wore her hair very short and did not use makeup. She was heavy and wore black-rimmed glasses. The glasses gave her a masculine appearance.

Laurie thought that Elaine Samuels was brilliant, and others in the medical field who could

Laurie Bembenek stands in her new raincoat outside her South Taylor Street home in Milwaukee, Wisconsin, just a few days after her second birthday, in August 1961.

On her First Holy Communion Day, in April 1966, Laurie Bembenek was six years old.

Laurie was twelve years old in 1971, when she posed for this photo in the front yard of her Milwaukee home.

Fred Schultz escorts his wife Laurie to her table during a Milwaukee wedding reception, on August 2, 1981, less than three months following the murder of Christine Schultz.

Laurie poses for her bridesmaid pictures at the same wedding. Fred refused to let Laurie stand up in the wedding unless he could also be a member of the wedding party.

Fred Schultz attended this 1978 Tracks party as the official photographer. Similar parties were held at various public parks in Milwaukee County and were heavily attended by Milwaukee police officers.

This photo of Fred, taken at the same 1978 party, was one of dozens turned in to the internal affairs division of the Milwaukee Police Department by Laurie before she met her future husband. Laurie wanted the department to see that police officers, such as Fred, were openly breaking the law by dancing naked in public.

Christine Jean Schultz was murdered at this house on Ramsey Street in Milwaukee, on May 28, 1981. Investigator Ira Robins claims it would have been easy for someone to murder Christine and then escape by jumping over the fence and onto the freeway. (Photo by Greg Gent Studios, Inc.)

This is the apartment building on South Twentieth Street in Milwaukee where Laurie Bembenek and Fred Schultz lived with Judy Zess. Police said Laurie left this apartment, jogged almost two miles to Ramsey Street, murdered Christine Schultz, and then jogged back home. (Photo by Greg Gent Studios, Inc.)

Private investigator Ira B. Robins has spent the last eight years of his life trying to prove that Lawrencia Bembenek did not kill Christine Schultz. (Photo by Greg Gent Studios, Inc.)

In 1983, Laurie had been in prison for one year. Here she is sitting outside her housing unit.

In 1985, Laurie posed outside the prison when her parents came to visit.

Laurie was twenty-six years old in 1985, when she worked on this Christmas poster at the Taycheedah prison.

In 1985, Virginia and Joe Bembenek stand with Laurie following a ceremony at Taycheedah where Laurie received an award for her poetry.

Laurie's best friend at Taycheedah was Kathy Braun, also serving a life sentence for murder. Kathy sat with Laurie during a 1985 meeting at the prison.

In 1986, Laurie and her friend Kathy Braun pose on Santa's lap during a Christmas party at the prison.

In 1984, Laurie was twenty-five years old and had been at
Taycheedah for almost two years. Flower arranging was one of the
classes Laurie was expected to take at the prison.

Laurie stands with her mother and father outside Taycheedah in 1986, when she received an associate degree from the University of Wisconsin.

In 1987, when she was twenty-eight, Laurie had been in prison for six years. Here she is waiting to see a friend in the prison visitors' room.

Laurie in 1987, twenty-eight years old, sitting in the visitors' room at Taycheedah.

When her friends came to see her, Laurie tried to make them feel comfortable in the prison setting by wearing her wild shoelaces and sunglasses.

Laurie in April of 1989, twenty-nine years old, in the visitors' room at Taycheedah.

In 1989, Laurie had been in prison for seven years.

Virginia Bembenek, Melanie Bembenek, and Joseph Bembenek visit with Laurie in 1989.

Laurie and Ira Robins during a Christmas 1990 visit at Taycheedah.

Laurie had just turned thirty-one, in 1990, when she smiled for this photo at Taycheedah.

Virginia and Joseph Bembenek, in August 1981, pose in their
Milwaukee home in front of a photo of Laurie.

Laurie and Nick Gugliatto, shortly after they met at Taycheedah, in August 1990.

Laurie and Nick outside at Taycheedah in October 1990, during one of his visits.

This photo was taken in the visitors' room in late 1990, just after Nick and Laurie decided to get married.

This photo, taken in February 1991, is the last one of Nick and Laurie before she escaped from Taycheedah in July 1991.

During the August 1990 hearing, Laurie wore the same dress she had worn during her trial ten years earlier.

Laurie at Taycheedah Correctional Institute, in September 1989.
(Photo by George Anich)

see beyond her glasses agreed. But because of her appearance her credibility was always under fire.

Dr. Samuels then explained blow-back.

"Blow-back is an event that takes place when a gun is fired at close range to the body. Blood and tissue explode from the missile entering the body, and splash back into the barrel of the gun," she said.

"Did you observe the bullet wound on the body of Christine Schultz?" Eisenberg asked her.

"Yes."

"Would you describe the bullet wound?"

"The wound itself was quite large. The skin around the wound held the impression of the gun's muzzle in a visible, circular pattern."

"Would you say the gun was at close range?"

"Yes. It had to have been touching the skin."

"Dr. Samuels, to a degree of medical, scientific certainty, would it be your opinion that 'blow-back' would have occurred?"

"Yes."

Eisenberg wanted the jury to hear what Dr. Elaine Samuels said because when the off-duty gun of Fred Schultz was checked at the crime lab there were no traces of tissue or of blood inside the muzzle of the gun. There also were no traces of cleaning solvent. Just traces of dust.

Dr. Samuels also testified that several hairs were found on the blue bandana that was wrapped around Christine Schultz's mouth, but the hairs were consistent with the hair of Christine Schultz.

Other crime lab experts would testify that the hairs found on Christine's body were "consistent" with hairs from the wig that had been found in the 20th Street apartment complex and "consistent" with the hairs that were found in Laurie's hairbrush.

Eisenberg tried to let the jury know that hair analysis was far from an exact science and that hair from any one of their heads could also have "similar" characteristics to hair or fibers that were found on Christine's body.

When Eisenberg interviewed the next witness, Milwaukee Police Detective Drew Halvorsen, he was able to point out several things that the detective had not done when he investigated the scene of the murder. Halvorsen admitted that even though blood was found near the walls at the bottom of the steps in Christine's house, the blood was never examined to determine its origin. The detective was also unable to tell Eisenberg if Laurie's black police shoes had been confiscated to see if they matched the shoes Sean and Shannon had seen the night of the murder.

According to the detective, even though traces of blood were found under several of Christine's fingernails, no one checked to see if Laurie had been scraped or marked because of a possible struggle with Christine Schultz.

When Detective Michael Durfee, Fred's partner the night of the murder, arrived to take the witness stand, his testimony, just like the testimony of Judy Zess, had also gone through some changes since the preliminary hearing.

According to Durfee, he was with Fred Schultz investigating a burglary at 2 A.M. on May 28, 1981, just about the time Christine Schultz was murdered. Durfee's remembrances of what happened following that matched other reports of what happened the night of the murder. He went with Fred back to the Fifth District police station, they received a call notifying them of Christine's death, they drove to the scene of the murder, and then they went to check out Fred's off-duty revolver. Then the story changed. He included a part where he said Fred and Laurie talked for a few minutes alone after Durfee and Fred arrived at their apartment. He said he could not hear the conversation.

Laurie knew Durfee was lying. When they had arrived at her apartment, they had almost run into the bedroom to get the gun.

This isn't logical, she thought. If Fred and I had a moment or two alone, like Durfee said, and if I were guilty, I would have told Fred to do anything but examine the gun. Fred could have said it was lost or stolen.

Then Durfee explained how he had examined the gun that was later determined to be the murder weapon.

"I took the gun out of the holster," Durfee explained. "And I rubbed my thumb across the end of the barrel and looked at my thumb and saw that there was no black carbon or residue left on my thumb. I looked at the cylinder from the barrel end, observed that there were five live cartridges in the gun, and that the bullets were all lead bullets as opposed to jacketed or hollow point."

Durfee said he also observed a light coating of dust along the frame of the hammer. He said he could not see any residue inside the barrel and when he smelled the gun, it didn't smell as if it had been fired. He said after the inspection Fred Schultz then put the gun into his brown attaché case and took the case with him when he left the apartment.

Ever since he started on the case Eisenberg had been waiting for this moment to examine Durfee. He knew that Detective Durfee had curiously misplaced a key piece of evidence in the Christine Schultz murder case.

Eisenberg: Where is your logbook from the night of the murder.

Durfee: I don't have it.

Eisenberg: You're required to keep it, though?

Durfee: No, sir.

Eisenberg: You can now throw away your logbooks?

Durfee: Yes, sir.

Eisenberg: Now, when I say a brown logbook, do you have one with you now? Any kind of one?

Durfee: Yes, sir.

Eisenberg: All right. And this is the standard-issue brown logbook we're talking about?

Durfee: Yes.

Eisenberg: And the one you have handed me is January 25, 1982, to the present?

Durfee: Yes, sir.

Eisenberg: Where is your logbook setting forth the events that occurred on May 28 and 29, 1981?

Durfee: I wouldn't know where it turns up after I throw it away, sir.

Eisenberg: And that is the logbook that you wrote down the material facts that occurred in a first-degree murder here in the City of Milwaukee?

Durfee: To the best of my recollection, I made

no entries regarding any of my activities
that day in that book.

Eisenberg: I take it, then, that you would have
made no entries concerning the serial number of the off-duty weapon that was shown
you in the early morning hours of the 28th
or 29th, 1981?

Durfee: That's correct.

Laurie sat listening to Durfee in utter amazement. The minute she heard him say, "To the best
of my recollection," she knew that something was
wrong. That was what police officers were trained
to say when they had screwed up. When they had
made a mistake. When they needed to cover their
ass.

She also knew that Durfee did not just throw
away his notebook. That isn't how the system
works. The cops use the notebooks to make detailed police reports and to protect themselves in
case they become part of a serious crime, including a murder trial. Somebody was hiding something, and Laurie didn't have the faintest idea
what it was.

Eisenberg wasn't finished with Durfee. He asked
Durfee if he had ever written down the serial
number of Fred Schultz's off-duty weapon. Durfee
said no.

Eisenberg: Can you tell this jury right now that
this gun, Exhibit 6, is the exact same gun
that you saw in the early morning hours of
the 28th?

Durfee: No, sir.

Eisenberg asked Durfee if he had ever seen Fred Schultz write down the serial number of the gun and Durfee said no, Fred Schultz didn't write down the number either.

Eisenberg was still stuck on the issue of the brown police notebook. He didn't believe that Durfee could write a detailed police report from his memory. It seemed highly unlikely.

Eisenberg: You did a report on May 28, 1981, right?

Durfee: That's correct.

Eisenberg: Why did you do another report on June 18, 1981, concerning the same facts?

Durfee: Because I was instructed by officers of senior rank to do so in more detail than the May 28 report.

Eisenberg: And in those 21 days, did you write that report in more detail from memory?

Durfee: Yes, sir.

Eisenberg was finished with Durfee, but as he walked back to his chair he gave Laurie a quick smile. Laurie guessed what he was thinking.

He'd love to get his hands on Durfee's little brown notebook, said Laurie to herself, and so would I. I wonder whose safe it's locked up in tonight. Better yet, I wonder what in the world is in it that could be so damaging. I wonder what Fred Schultz and Michael Durfee were doing on May 28, 1981.

CHAPTER 24

Garbage, Guns, and Green

Ten days into the murder trial there was no letup in the media coverage or in the numbers of people interested in the Christine Schultz murder and the woman accused of it. The more people knew about Laurie Bembenek and the trial, the more they wanted to know. Every newspaper and magazine in town prominently displayed a story about Laurie. The murder trial was the lead on the nightly news and if people were talking, they were talking about "the case."

Despite the deluge of press coverage, some good and some bad, Laurie had no way of knowing how the trial was progressing. She had never been to a murder trial before and she could only listen to what Eisenberg had to say and then hope that he was telling her the truth. She wanted to believe him every time he said things were going great and not to worry. But some of her worst fears had already become reality. She was on trial for first-degree murder.

Her only sanctuary during those weeks was behind the locked door of her parents' home. Once she got back from the trial, usually before six in the evening, she would kick off her shoes, have a drink, and then try to relax. She would play cards or Scrabble, watch a movie, and play with her dog.

Everything would be okay until the evening news came on.

Laurie continued to feel that the media people were biased. They mentioned what she wore to court every day and she knew that would never happen if a man were on trial for murder. There was also a prevailing attitude in Milwaukee that if the police arrested someone, that person must be guilty. After all, the police seemed almost above the law and the idea of their making a mistake seemed impossible to most people. But Lawrencia Bembenek knew differently.

She had seen the Milwaukee Police Department up close and she knew the department was full of ordinary men and women who made ordinary mistakes. Laurie had also seen how easy it was for them to cover their own errors and to plot out a case against someone else. The fact that she had been dismissed from the department for writing a false police report, which the department later admitted was not falsified, was just one example.

So, Laurie watched each day, not in utter amazement but still with some disbelief, as the prosecuting attorney's witnesses continued to take the stand and say things that she knew were not true.

An example of the prosecution's selective witnesses and their selective testimony occurred when a member of Laurie's police recruit class, Keith Faubel, took the witness stand. Faubel said that he had seen Laurie at the police academy wearing a green jogging suit. Eisenberg grilled Faubel about the color of the suit and Faubel said it was forest green, not even close to the color described by Sean and Shannon.

Then Eisenberg started reading a list of names. "Well, let me read some names for you. How about Darlene Anderson, Patricia Lipsey, Linda Reaves, Jackie Warren, Willie Bradford, Jeffrey Eastern, LaMont McGlown, Jerry Gedig, Marge Lipschultz . . ."

The list continued. Eisenberg was reading off all the names of the officers who had been in Laurie's recruit class. Out of the fifty people on the list, Faubel was the only one who had ever seen Lawrencia Bembenek in a green jogging suit.

Again, Laurie wondered what had compelled this man to testify against her. Did the Milwaukee Police Department have something on him? Did they threaten him with the loss of his job? Laurie wished she had the answers. She wished she had access to the police personnel files. It would probably be like opening Pandora's box.

Elfred O. Schultz's turn to sit in the wooden witness chair came on Saturday, February 27. He wore a three-piece suit and occasionally looked over at his wife and smiled. Fred was calm throughout the questioning and, unlike at the preliminary hearing, he kept his composure when he talked about Christine Schultz. This time he didn't cry on the witness stand.

Kramer ran through the standard questions about his job, his family, his actions the night of the murder. When Kramer pressed him and tried to get him to admit that he knew his marriage to Laurie in Illinois was not legal, Eisenberg stepped in. Eisenberg didn't think that his marriage to Laurie had anything to do with the murder of Christine Schultz.

Schultz admitted that he had two keys to the

house on Ramsey Street. He said he made the keys from a key that Sean had. He said he kept one key with him all the time and another one in his leather jewelry box.

A large portion of Fred's testimony then centered on his off-duty revolver that was allegedly used to kill Christine Schultz. Kramer wanted to show that Laurie had access to the gun.

Kramer: Do you know whether or not Miss Bembenek ever had that off-duty weapon or had access to it?

Fred: To my knowledge, no.

Kramer: Did she ever have the bullets or the bullet container that would be the container on the belt of the holster?

Fred: To my knowledge, no.

Fred also stuck by his story that he had an argument with Laurie about his bullet pouch. He said that he never really determined if Laurie had been playing with his bullets. He said he told her they needed to be in the bullet pouch in a specific way so he could get at them quickly in a life-and-death situation.

Laurie knew when the jury heard that information it would still look as if she had played with his bullets. She wished, again, that Fred had not even bothered to mention that incident, which happened after the murder, to Officer Ruscitti.

Fred recounted the early morning hours following the murder when he went back to his own apartment to check the off-duty gun with Detective Durfee. He said they both decided the gun had not been fired.

When Kramer finished, Eisenberg asked Schultz about the importance of using the small brown police notebooks for recording events while an officer is on duty. Unlike his partner, Durfee, Schultz said he kept his notebooks because they were valuable tools. He said without them his reports would not be accurate.

Eisenberg looked through some of Schultz's notebooks and commented that his writing stopped just after he was informed of Christine Schultz's death. "And the reason I take it you wrote nothing is, number one, this was a real touching, serious, deadly thing to you and you were more concerned personally than you were as an officer?" Eisenberg asked.

"Yes," Fred responded.

Then Eisenberg had Schultz pull out a briefcase that was filled with police notebooks. Schultz said that he had every notebook he had ever used as a Milwaukee police officer. He said the books went back to the first day he was sworn in as a police officer.

> Eisenberg: Why didn't you destroy these?
> Schultz: We're required to keep them as records.

Fred Schultz had just made Michael Durfee look like a fool. Eisenberg hoped the jury would wonder why one cop would save all his records and the other would throw them away. He wanted the jury to wonder how Michael Durfee could write detailed police records from memory. Especially police records that had to do with the murder of a young woman.

Eisenberg got Fred Schultz to say that Laurie's designer clothes consisted of a pair or two of forty-dollar jeans. He said she didn't have a mink coat, or diamonds or fancy cars. He said they didn't go out a lot or eat in fancy restaurants. He also said that Laurie was totally opposed to moving into the house on Ramsey Street.

Schultz identified a red jogging suit jacket as belonging to Laurie but said he had never seen her in a green jogging suit and was certain she did not own one.

Eisenberg asked Fred if he thought his wife had killed Christine Schultz. Fred said no. Fred said he asked her and he said he would know if she was lying. He said his wife was not lying when she told him on numerous occasions that she had not killed Christine.

The testimony of Fred Schultz was not spectacular or revealing. Newspaper accounts in the evening paper would say the testimony was favorable to Laurie. The most memorable moment of Fred's testimony was actually orchestrated by Eisenberg. The lawyer surprised everyone when he presented his own snub-nosed revolver. Eisenberg wanted the jury to know that it is easy for guns to look the same. Later, when he was seated at the defense table, behind Kramer, Eisenberg held the gun and was absentmindedly clicking the barrel release over and over again. Kramer was irritated by the sound.

"Stop playing with that gun behind my back," he yelled.

Eisenberg laughed but finally put the revolver away when Judge Skwierawski told him to.

* * *

On March 1, Laurie thought the testimony of Kathryn Morgan, the woman who had identified her mother as the woman who was picking garbage out of the dumpster, was rather bizarre. Mrs. Morgan told the same story that Laurie had read in the police report. She had caught Mrs. Virginia Bembenek digging through the trash bin near Laurie and Fred's apartment shortly after the murder.

Don Eisenberg lashed into Mrs. Morgan because he thought her testimony was totally unbelievable.

"Isn't it a fact that you identified Mrs. Bembenek at Lawrencia Bembenek's preliminary hearing?"

"Yes."

"After requesting that Mrs. Bembenek remove her glasses?"

"Yes."

"The woman you saw on June 18 going through the dumpster was not wearing glasses?"

"No."

"Are you aware of the fact that Virginia Bembenek is almost blind without her glasses?"

"No."

"Are you aware of the fact that Virginia Bembenek cannot drive without her glasses?"

"No."

Eisenberg grilled her. He said Mrs. Bembenek did not wear shorts and had not done so for years because she was embarrassed by the veins in her legs. Mrs. Morgan said the woman going through the dumpster was wearing shorts.

"Do you really expect this court to believe, Mrs. Morgan, that a woman who was allegedly trying to recover murder evidence from a large trash container would come up to a perfect stranger in broad daylight, ask you about the trash containers, and then take a bag out of them and then drive away?"

Eisenberg then wanted to know how Mrs. Morgan had come to identify the car she saw the woman drive.

"A detective came to my house and asked me if I would go with him to identify the car," she said.

Mrs. Morgan said she got in his car and the police officer drove her to a house on Ramsey Street where she saw a brown automobile in the driveway.

"Mrs. Morgan," Eisenberg said, "it says in this report that your exact words were, 'It looks similar to the car I saw on June 18.' Now, I hope you're not getting confused in the excitement of the trial and the TV cameras and everything. Didn't you say the car looked similar?"

"Yes."

"Not that it was the same car?"

"No."

Laurie thought the next trick that the prosecution tried to pull was a fast one. Kramer claimed to have four witnesses, two cops and their wives, who said they remembered bumping into her and Fred at a movie theater in the winter of 1981. They said Laurie was wearing the green jogging suit.

All four of the witnesses were on the witness list but when it came time to call them to the stand, Kramer said that one couple was in Colorado and would not be able to testify. The cop who did testify, Gary Shaw, had somehow managed to get a promotion to detective.

"This is so they don't have to corroborate their damn story," Don whispered to Laurie. "What the hell is this one about? You were at some movie with Fred?"

"Yeah, it was a cop movie, too. Good grief, *Fort Apache: The Bronx*, with Paul Newman in uniform. Was he handsome!"

"Forget Paul Newman, Laurie," Eisenberg said. "What were you wearing?"

"Probably jeans and my ski jacket, as usual. I remember Fred talking to two couples in the lobby. Isn't winter a cold time of year to be wearing a jogging suit?"

"They've already covered that argument," Don said. "This report says that's the reason why they remember the green jogging suit, because it was too cold to wear something like that."

"Tricky."

Laurie and Fred's neighbor at the 20th Street apartments, Sharon Niswonger, told the court that Judy Zess would often ask her to let her into the apartment complex so she could get into Fred and Laurie's apartment. Niswonger also said she didn't think it was possible to tell if the wig that was pulled from the drain of her apartment came from her bathroom or from the bathroom in Laurie and Fred's apartment.

In the preliminary hearing when Judge Fine bound Laurie over to stand trial, he said her access to the gun was a key element in his decision. Yet here was another witness claiming that Judy Zess had equal access to the gun. And try as she might, Laurie could not ignore the fact that the alleged murder weapon belonged to Fred Schultz.

Half the time she didn't even know where the gun was kept. Fred kept moving it.

Several police officers who assisted in Laurie's arrest were called as witnesses and Eisenberg told her their list of witnesses was just about over. Then he could call a few witnesses of his own. During the final hours of the prosecuting attorney's examinations, Eisenberg felt he was able to make several good points, including the accepted notion that hair analysis is not an exact science and one of the more controversial areas of police investigation.

The state called Arthur J. Varriale, the head of the serology and microserology and microanalytical department at the State Crime Lab, located in New Berlin, Wisconsin, as a witness. Varriale's job was to analyze hairs, textile fibers, blood, and body fluids. But Varriale had come to court just to testify about hair and textile fibers. Varriale said his work was a science.

Varriale said that he looked at several fibers that were given to him by Diane Hanson, also a crime lab employee who examined blood, body fluids, and hair in the Schultz murder case. His job was to compare three fibers sent to him by Hanson with the fibers from the wig that was recovered in the drain at the 20th Street apartment. He said he was able to determine that the hair found on Christine's leg was similar to the hairs from the wig that was pulled from the plumbing.

Eisenberg was able to get Varriale to say that what he did might be a science but it wasn't an exact science. "So what you are now telling the jury is that the fiber you examined, found on the leg of Christine Schultz, could be the same, or they could not be the same. Isn't that correct?" Eisenberg asked Varriale.

"Would you repeat the question?"

"The two fibers you examined. You cannot tell this jury that, beyond a reasonable doubt, with a degree of scientific certainty, those fibers are identical, can you?"

"No."

Diane Hanson, the hair analysis expert from the state crime lab, took the stand. Eisenberg had worked with her before, and he told Laurie she had a terrible reputation. When he asked her questions, she became visibly angry. He persuaded her to admit that her bachelor's degree was in the field of bacteriology, totally removed from the study of hair analysis. Her knowledge of hair was gained piecemeal, in a smattering of six weeks at various seminars.

Hanson admitted that hair analysis was even less accurate than fiber analysis. Then Hanson lost her temper and admitted that she had ignored a court order not to discuss the case. She had talked about her testimony with Varriale. The judge decided he should excuse the jury while he looked into the matter. The judge determined after questioning Hanson that she had indeed violated the sequestration order. But he denied Eisenberg's motion to strike Hanson's testimony. He also would not allow Eisenberg to question Hanson or Varriale on their testimonies.

Laurie sat at the defense table remembering the right-wing opinions and attitudes of the instructors at the police academy. They were always saying that the law protects the criminal. They acted as if all a police officer had to do was conduct a search or seizure in an incorrect way, or violate a tiny legal technicality, and a court of law would throw the case out.

They talked as if law-enforcement officers had infinite potential for error that would ultimately lead to charges being dropped. They stressed procedure to the extent that would make one think that civil libertarians were hovering over the criminal justice system, just waiting to pounce on a violation of rights to point out to a liberal appellate court.

Laurie leaned over and said not so quietly to Eisenberg, "Now, my eyes are open. I can see that the state, with all its power, is allowed to proceed as if no Bill of Rights or U.S. Constitution exists."

The last person to testify for the prosecution was Monty Lutz, the state crime lab ballistics expert. It was no surprise when Lutz said that the bullet removed from Christine Schultz came from Fred's off-duty gun. Despite Lutz's testimony, Eisenberg thought he could disprove that Fred Schultz's off-duty gun had killed Christine. He asked Lutz if the revolver was made of aluminum.

"No, just the frame is aluminum. The barrel, and the other parts of the gun are not. I don't know how detailed you would like me to get."

"Thank you, Mr. Lutz. If soap and water were used to clean the gun, would rust appear over a period of time?"

"Definitely."

"If cleaning fluid or solvent was used, would dust be present?"

"I suppose over a period of time . . ."

"Over a period of a few hours?"

"It depends on where the gun was stored."

"If it was in a holster, stored in a closed compartment, like a gym bag with a zipper?"

"Oh. Then I'd have to say no. Dust would not be present if the gun had been cleaned and then put away."

Eisenberg emphasized this line of questioning because Fred's off-duty gun had not been cleaned. That totally contradicted the absence of blood or carbon in the gun.

Knowing that the prosecution wasn't planning on calling any more witnesses, Laurie really didn't rest any easier. It was Eisenberg's turn to present character witnesses. Laurie knew they didn't have any surprises planned for Kramer. Kramer knew it, too.

Laurie was going to testify. That was usually a signal that there was nothing to hide. That the defendant was innocent. Lawrencia Bembenek was going to be a determining factor in how the jury looked at this murder case. Her main worry about testifying wasn't telling the truth or letting the jury make a decision about what she said. She told Eisenberg she was worried about how Kramer would twist whatever she had to say.

"No matter what I say, it won't be right," she told Eisenberg. "These people already think I'm guilty of committing a crime I didn't commit."

"Don't worry," Eisenberg told her, patting her on the back. "You'll do just fine."

CHAPTER 25

Truth, Tears, and Tales

Because they were scheduled to testify in her behalf, Laurie's parents had not been allowed in the courtroom during the trial. The judge didn't want any witnesses listening to what other witnesses had to say. Day after day they sat on a small wooden bench outside the courtroom, talking quietly, watching other people walk in and out of the courtroom, and offering up prayers for their daughter.

On Wednesday, March 4, when Laurie's trial was nearing its end, it was finally the Bembeneks' turn in the courtroom. Eisenberg had already called six witnesses for the defense. They were former members of her police academy class. None of them had ever seen Laurie in a green jogging suit.

Laurie knew that her mother was anxious about testifying. Mrs. Bembenek wanted to make every word count. She was terrified that her daughter was going to end up in prison.

Mrs. Bembenek testified that she had to wear glasses and was unable to wear contact lenses. She said that she did not go rummaging through a dumpster behind her daughter's apartment complex.

She explained how she helped Laurie pack up the apartment the night of the murder. She said she was the one who packed Fred Schultz's leather jewelry box. She told Eisenberg that she had heard at least one heated argument between Laurie and Fred because Laurie did not want to move into the house on Ramsey Street.

Mrs. Bembenek said Laurie had her faults but that she had always been a good daughter. She said her daughter "absolutely did not" kill Christine Schultz.

Laurie's father also testified, and then Elfred O. Schultz, Sr., Fred's father, took the stand.

Schultz told Eisenberg about a series of phone calls that he received between March 29 and April 5 of 1981. Schultz said the caller would always say something like, "You bastard, you bastard. I'll get you. You son-of-a-bitch."

Finally, Schultz said he realized the calls were probably aimed at his son. He said when he received the next phone call he told the caller that he was calling a Pewaukee address and he was Elfred Schultz, Sr. He said after that the calls stopped.

Schultz broke into tears when he talked about his five sons and the problems that had been created by Christine's murder. He said his son John had been close to Christine and because of that John felt Laurie had been involved in the murder. He said no one else in the family felt that way.

He said he liked Laurie Bembenek and he couldn't believe that she was the killer of Christine Schultz.

The court went into recess after Schultz's testimony and Laurie rushed into the hall to find her parents. Her mother was standing against the wall, crying.

"Don't, Mom," Laurie said, hugging her close. "You were fine. It's over."

"I was just so scared that I'd say something wrong! You know how those police can confuse a person who is just trying to tell the truth! So much depended on my testimony today! I'm so afraid for you!"

"I know," Laurie said, afraid to let go of her mother. "Don't worry. Please don't worry."

The following day, March 4, would be the last day of testimony. It would be the day Lawrencia Bembenek testified.

Laurie wore a white peasant blouse to court with a black tie wrapped around the collar. Her new gold wedding band was the only piece of jewelry she wore.

Before Laurie testified, three friends of hers were called as character witnesses. They all said that Laurie was the last person on earth who would kill somebody.

Just as Laurie rose to walk to the witness stand, Kramer stood up, too.

"Just a minute," Kramer said. "There is another matter, your honor. There are names on the defense list that I object to, and I move that they be stricken from testifying based on their relevance to the case. One of these names is Frederick Horenberger."

Laurie froze when she heard Horenberger's name. She realized the district attorney was attempting to prohibit the testimony of the only person who could discredit the statements of Judy Zess, the prosecution's star witness. During her testimony Judy had verified everything the state wanted her to verify. She had put Kramer's whole case together for him. Now her testimony would go unchallenged.

"If Mr. Eisenberg insists on calling this witness to the stand, as I understand Mr. Horenberger has been transported from the Waupun Correctional Institution to the Milwaukee County Jail, then the court feels that the defense should be willing to tell us why his testimony is relevant. Mr. Eisenberg, would you care to give me an offer of proof?"

"Your honor," Eisenberg said, "I cannot tell you the relevance of Horenberger's testimony, without giving away my whole defense to Mr. Kramer."

There were several more minutes of argument and finally Judge Skwierawski decided that Horenberger's testimony was hearsay evidence. The judge said Horenberger would not be allowed to testify.

"Even if it's evidence of perjury?" Laurie wrote in big, bold letters on her legal pad.

Eisenberg just shrugged and Laurie felt her last speck of optimism disappear.

"Are you ready?" Eisenberg asked her.

"Yes. But I'm a bit scared of Kramer."

"Don't be, Laurie. You are smarter than he is. Laurie, if you are scared, don't be afraid to show it. You usually appear a bit too calm. Probably your police training."

"I'm not an actress."

"Then be yourself."

Laurie spent a total of five hours on the witness stand. Beads of sweat dripped down her back. She tried to be precise in answering all the questions.

Every time she looked up she saw a bevy of cameras leveled at her. The jurors stared at her, too, emotionless, judging her every move, her every word.

Eisenberg spread out Laurie's entire life for the jury. Her schooling, religious beliefs, police training, and how she met and married Fred. He asked her about the complaint she had filed against the department and her reasons for wanting to become a police officer in the first place.

Laurie appeared calm but in fact she was so frightened, she thought she was going to be sick every time she answered a question. For some reason, Laurie started to cry when Eisenberg asked her about the diamond ring she had bought for Fred.

"I understand that in May of last year, you took your tax refund and bought your husband an expensive diamond ring, did you not?"

"Yes."

"Why did you buy that for him?"

"Because he never had anything like that . . ."

Laurie couldn't continue and the bailiff brought her a cup of water. She took out her handkerchief and ran it across her eyes.

"How do you feel right now?" Eisenberg asked her.

"Scared to death."

She recounted the days before the murder of Christine Schultz and detailed her actions the night of the murder. There was nothing revealing or damaging about her testimony. She said the same things she had been saying over and over for months.

During the lunch recess Laurie drank three

quick glasses of wine. She was trying to get ready for Kramer's cross-examination. During Eisenberg's examination Kramer had been smiling and shaking his head constantly. Laurie kept reminding herself not to lose her temper with him or to be sarcastic or flippant. She thought he was a very easy man to dislike.

Kramer immediately attacked what she had said about her work and problems with the police department.

Kramer: Miss Bembenek, does the alleged harassment you encountered from the Milwaukee Police Department have anything to do with this trial?

Laurie: I don't know.

Kramer: And do any of the things you have just spent the entire morning telling this jury, have anything at all to do with this trial?

Laurie: I don't know.

Kramer: Miss Bembenek, let's go into the reason why you were dismissed from the police department. Isn't it a fact that you were seen by Milwaukee vice squad officers smoking a marijuana cigarette at a Milwaukee concert?

Eisenberg jumped up to object but Skwierawski told him he had opened the door for questioning by bringing the subject up when he examined Laurie. Even without a response from Laurie, Kramer had made his point. He wanted the jury to think that she had been smoking marijuana. He asked her one or two more questions and then totally changed the subject to her January 31 wedding.

Kramer tried to get Laurie to admit that she knew it was illegal for Fred to marry in Wisconsin because his divorce had not been final for six months.

"I went to Waukegan to get married because Fred suggested it. We eloped."

"That was the only reason."

"And I though it was romantic."

"Oh. You thought it was romantic. But, isn't it a fact that you signed that marriage license, knowing that you two were not free and clear by law to marry?"

"No! I was free to marry."

"You didn't know Fred wasn't?"

"No. How could I know?"

"Didn't you discuss the divorce?"

"No."

"Oh. Okay. Did you discuss money?"

"In regards to what?"

"Money. You know, what his salary was, what his alimony payments were, his child support, his house payments. Did you discuss that?"

"No."

"Before you were married, you had no discussions about money?"

"No. We were in love. We talked about what we had in common. We didn't discuss money."

Kramer's questions went on and on. He asked Laurie if she hated Christine. Laurie said no, she did not hate Christine Schultz. He wanted to know if she owned diamond rings. Laurie said all her rings were fake. She never owned a real diamond ring. He wanted to know if she owned designer clothes.

"Not originals," Laurie said.

"Originals?"

"Nancy Reagan wears originals."

"You don't own any originals?"

"Your honor," Eisenberg interrupted. "Would the court please instruct Mr. Kramer to ask the defendant to explain what 'originals' are?"

The judge nodded for Laurie to go on.

"Originals are in the neighborhood of $5,000 apiece. But take designer jeans. Everyone wears those nowadays."

At one point Kramer had Laurie step down from the witness stand so she could hold up the red jogging suit. Then he made her stand next to him so the jury could see how tall she was. He told the jury it would be easy for a woman this tall to look like a man.

When Laurie finally stepped down from the witness stand, everyone thought Kramer was finished. Then Kramer informed the judge that he wanted to call two additional witnesses.

Eisenberg and Laurie didn't recognize the names of the two women who were going to testify against her.

The first witness was Marilyn Gehrt. She owned a wig store on 27th Street in Milwaukee called "Olde Wig World." She told Kramer Laurie Bembenek had purchased a wig from her the previous spring.

Laurie wondered where this woman had come from. She had never even driven by the wig shop.

"Can you believe this cheap shot?" Eisenberg asked Laurie as he started to get up. "Watch this."

"Miss Gehrt," he said. "When did you come forward with this information."

"Yesterday," she replied.

"Yesterday?" Eisenberg shouted. "Yesterday? The day before the last day of the trial. This highly publicized case has continuously hit the media for the last nine months! Just what inspired you to come forward?"

"It just dawned on me."

"It just dawned on you. How convenient. Do you deny that you've read about this case in the paper or have heard it on the television or radio?"

"I've read about it."

"You said the defendant walked into your shop last spring and bought a wig from you?"

"Yes."

"Do you know the date when this occurred?"

"One afternoon."

"Do you recall what day it was?"

"No."

"Can you at least tell what month it was?"

"I don't recall."

"How is it, then, that you can come into this courtroom and identify this young girl as the one who allegedly bought a wig from you?"

"When she paid for the wig, I noticed her name on the check."

"Are you aware of the fact that the defendant has not had a checking account since 1977?"

"Umm, no."

The next witness was even worse. Her name was Annette Wilson. She was a security guard who worked at Boston Store. Laurie saw Annette walk into the courtroom and she was stunned. She remembered a conversation she had had with the woman before she left her job at Boston Store to enter the police academy.

Annette scoffed when Laurie told her she was entering the academy. She told Laurie her father was a police officer and he told her that women didn't belong in the department.

Miss Wilson came to court to tell everyone that Laurie had stolen a green jogging suit from Boston Store. She couldn't remember when or what the exact color of it was, though. Eisenberg went for broke.

"Isn't it a fact that you never liked Laurie?"

"On the contrary, we got along well."

Laurie wanted to jump and yell, "Liar, liar, liar!" Annette Wilson had been openly hostile toward her.

Eisenberg asked for shoplifting records or anything that would indicate Laurie had stolen the outfit. Wilson had nothing.

"Isn't a fact, Miss Wilson, that you don't like Laurie because she's prettier than you?"

Eisenberg had gone over the edge. Spectators booed and the judge even stifled a laugh.

Finally, the state rested its case and the judge said he would hear closing arguments on the following day.

The murder trial of Lawrencia Bembenek had lasted over two weeks. A total of forty-nine witnesses had testified and 134 different pieces of evidence had been looked at.

The courtroom was still packed when the judge talked to the jurors about making their decisions on Lawrencia Bembenek's innocence or guilt. The jurors' instructions included details on what they should and should not consider when deciding Laurie's innocence or guilt. Their primary purpose, he said, was to determine if the defendant intended to kill Christine Schultz and, secondly, that she actually did cause the death of Christine Schultz.

"If you are satisfied beyond a reasonable doubt from the evidence in this case that the defendant, Lawrencia Bembenek, did commit an act of shooting which caused the death of Christine Schultz at the time and place charged in the information and that at any time before doing such an act the defendant had formed in her mind the purpose to take the life of Christine Schultz and that act of shooting was done by the defendant in the pursuance of such mental purpose, then you should find the defendant guilty of murder in the first degree as charged in this information. If you are not so satisfied, then you must find the defendant not guilty of murder in the first degree."

The judge talked at great length about reasonable doubt. He told the jurors if they had reasonable doubt—a doubt based upon reason and common sense—then they had to find her not guilty.

Skwierawski's lengthy jury instructions covered witness credibility, stricken testimony, and attorney comments. He told them to take their time and to weigh all the information that had been presented to them.

The jury then listened for the next six hours as Kramer and Eisenberg took turns presenting their final arguments, basically a summary of everything that had taken place during the trial.

Kramer asserted that Laurie killed Christine Schultz so that she and Fred could sell the house and get the money. He said his witnesses were all good, hardworking people who came forward to testify against Laurie because they felt an obligation to do so. He tried to discredit Sean Schultz's testimony by saying the room was too dark and Sean was frightened and a young boy. He said there was no doubt that Christine Schultz recognized Laurie and screamed for help. He mentioned the testimony of Judy Zess and talked about threats that Laurie had made against Christine Schultz.

According to Kramer, Laurie Bembenek's motive for killing Christine Schultz was one of greed. He said that Laurie had the false conception that Christine Schultz was not being fair and that she was not woman enough to accept the fact that she had lost her husband, Elfred Schultz. With Christine out of the way, Kramer said, Laurie and Fred could sell the house or move into it and they would no longer have to pay alimony. They could have more money, he said, and it was the thought of that money that drove Laurie Bembenek to murder Christine Schultz.

Kramer surmised that Laurie drove part of the way to Christine's house and then walked the rest of the way. That's why her car wasn't warm when Fred Schultz touched the hood the night of the murder. After all, Kramer said, the bullet in Christine Schultz's body matched the barrel of Fred's off-duty revolver.

He said that Laurie brainwashed Shannon and Sean Schultz into thinking and saying that the person they saw in their house the night of the murder was not Laurie Bembenek.

"If you believe Lawrencia Bembenek, she is not guilty. You are going to have to be the judges of that. But let me say this. Based upon my presentation of evidence, based upon evidence in the case, all of the evidence in the case, if Miss Bembenek convinces you of that, she not only would have killed Christine Schultz, but she will have gotten away with it. Don't let that happen."

Donald Eisenberg spent almost five hours on his closing arguments. He went through the evidence presented by Kramer piece by piece. He pointed out that reasonable doubt existed in every single thing presented by the prosecution.

Eisenberg said there was no way Kramer proved Laurie was at the scene of the crime or had ever even held the alleged murder weapon. He said everything was circumstantial. They did not even have one fingerprint of hers from the weapon or the crime scene.

He talked about missing notebooks and about the key to Christine Schultz's house that Fred kept on his key chain. He wanted to know why the off-duty weapon was cleared by two detectives and then later determined to be the murder weapon.

Eisenberg wanted the jurors to remember that Sean and Shannon Schultz both said the person who killed their mother was not Laurie Bembenek. He reminded them that much of what Kramer had said was speculation. No one ever produced a green jogging suit or the clothesline that Laurie Bembenek was supposed to have used to tie up Christine. No one had seen her jogging down the street, or flushing a wig down a toilet, or scrubbing the dirt off her black police shoes.

"Laurie Bembenek's hope, ladies and gentlemen, is in your hands," Eisenberg told the jurors. "If you have reason to doubt, then you cannot say beyond a reasonable doubt. And if you cannot say beyond a reasonable doubt, you must not say guilty."

He reminded the jurors that they could not convict someone because she was beautiful. He told them to look at the facts of the case and nothing else. He said that Laurie Bembenek was not a killer and the state had not even come close to proving that she had killed Christine Schultz.

The jury got up to leave the room and begin deliberations. There was nothing left for Lawrencia Bembenek to do but wait.

CHAPTER 26

The Name of the Game

The weekend of March 6, 1982, was a devastating combination of anxious speculation and pessimistic expectation for Lawrencia Bembenek. Every time the phone rang her heart pounded so hard, she thought she was having a heart attack.

Laurie actually found it impossible to think about being convicted of murder. She couldn't believe it was possible because she knew she was not the one who had killed Christine Schultz. Yet she had a nagging fear that kept her on edge. She grabbed a bottle of scotch and tried to drink herself into a more relaxed state.

When she was able to sleep, her dreams were invaded by voices and echoes from the trial and the preliminary hearing. "I don't love her anymore." "She married Fred for his vasectomy." "They're both sure it was you. But I know it wasn't. Because it was me. Ha, ha, ha, ha!"

On Saturday night Fred and Laurie drove to the east side of Milwaukee to meet with Eisenberg and his wife for dinner. Laurie was barely seated when a man walked into the bar and asked, "Did anybody hear if Bembenek got burned yet?"

Laurie looked over at him and his mouth dropped open.

"It was indeed a witch hunt," she said. "You look like you could be the father of someone my age. Would you say such a thing if I was your daughter?"

"Bartender?" the man said, motioning toward Laurie's table. "A round of drinks here, on me."

When it was time to leave, Fred volunteered to get the car so Laurie wouldn't have to walk through the snow-filled streets. As she stood and waited for him, a couple came into the restaurant and stopped near her. "Good luck," they said. It felt strange to have total strangers recognize her and she was still surprised every time it happened.

When Laurie and Fred got home, her mother came to meet them at the door. "I'm so proud of you, Laurie," her mom said, hugging her. "You're so brave. My God, I don't know how you can stand it."

Fred went upstairs and fell asleep. Laurie sat up and talked with her parents.

"I've been thinking," said her father. "You may not want to talk about the trial. But I keep thinking about the ballistics report. It just doesn't make any sense. What would stop the police from switching the original slug that the coroner removed from the body, with a slug from Fred's gun?"

"Isn't that a bit farfetched," Laurie asked.

"Not really. What happens when the body gets taken to the morgue? Step by step. The doctor removes the bullet, marks it with her initials, puts it in a little bag, and who does she hand it over to? The cops. Who are the cops? Someone like Cole or Ruscitti. Then the cops confiscate Fred's gun. Do they test-fire it before taking it to the crime lab? It would be simple enough, once it's in their hands. They could initial one of the slugs from Fred's gun, just like the coroner marked the murderer's bullet, take it to the crime lab, and bingo! They match. Who takes it to the crime lab? Frank Cole. Who's hot on your tail? Frank Cole."

Laurie was quiet for a moment. It was true that Judy Zess was the prosecution's star witness and Frank Cole was in Judy's bed.

"I don't know, Dad," she said. "I don't know who took the bullet to the crime lab from the morgue. There must be a signature on some report that would tell us."

"Are you naïve enough to think that's not possible? Without the gun they don't have a case!"

"I'm not saying it's impossible," Laurie said. "We already know that Cole was in cahoots with Zess, but we weren't allowed to even try to prove it. Can you imagine trying to prove something like you just suggested?"

Laurie's mother said that was enough trial talk for one night. Laurie went upstairs and Fred was snoring loudly. Here I am waiting to find out how I am going to spend the rest of my life and he can't even stay awake in case I need him, Laurie thought as she walked over to the bedroom window.

Fred and Laurie slept in the same bedroom where she had spent her childhood years. Laurie turned away from the frosty window and looked at Fred. Never in her wildest dreams did she ever think she would be living in her parents' house with her husband.

The jury had not reached a verdict the next morning when Eisenberg phoned and asked Fred and Laurie to meet him for brunch at a downtown Milwaukee restaurant. Fred's brother Bob joined them, and Laurie immediately sensed that Eisenberg was unusually tense. Eisenberg began the breakfast conversation by saying the long jury deliberations could be a good sign. "I've seen juries take less than twenty minutes to return a verdict of guilty," he said. "We may have a hung jury."

"Then what happens?" Laurie asked.

"Then it's like Judy Zess's trial, remember? She had a hung jury and they dropped the charges."

"They would do that with a murder charge, too?" Bob asked. "Just drop it if the jury can't reach a decision?"

"Well, they could retry the case, but I doubt that."

While they were eating, Eisenberg received a phone call. Laurie found it hard to breathe while he was gone. She was certain that the verdict had come in.

But when Eisenberg came back he told them that the jury had requested to see the apartment complex where Fred and Laurie lived on 20th Street. Don had no objection, but Kramer refused. Since both counsel had to agree, the judge had to deny the jury's request. Eisenberg said the judge didn't tell the jurors it was Kramer and not Eisenberg who opposed the visit.

"But that's not fair," Laurie said. "The jury might think that we didn't want them to see the apartment. They might think we have something to hide."

"I wonder why they wanted to see the place," Don said. "Damn! I wish I knew what was going through their heads."

"So do I," Laurie said. "I wish they could see the size of those garbage bins my mother was accused of digging through. We should have taken a photograph of them, with a person as tall as my mother standing next to them."

For some reason Laurie was already thinking of things they should have done to help prove she was innocent.

By Sunday night the judge announced that he would no longer accept a verdict that day. He refused to declare a hung jury. Laurie stayed up late that night and watched television with her mom and dad. She didn't want to talk about what might be happening with the jury. She was slipping back into the same depression that had been her constant companion since she had been charged with murder.

The next morning she was told to meet Don at the courthouse because the jury had requested that portions of the transcripts be read back to them. They had been deliberating almost four days.

"They want to hear Durfee's testimony again, part of yours, and part of Fred's," Eisenberg explained. "Obviously I'm going to object. It's not even fair to take testimony out of context."

"Well, if Kramer didn't want the jury to see the apartments, then we should be able to refuse this request," Laurie said.

But Judge Skwierawski had other ideas. Despite Eisenberg's objections, the judge said that even though he would normally deny such a request, this time he would allow portions of the transcripts to be read back to the jury.

Monday dragged on and on. By the end of the day the jury still had not reached a verdict.

On Tuesday, March 9, 1982, Laurie was so depressed, she could hardly get out of bed. It was close to zero outside and everything looked gray. When she peered out of her bedroom window, all she could see was black and white.

Finally, about 11:30 A.M. Laurie took a long hot shower and then she wrapped her hair in a towel and sat at the kitchen table playing Scrabble with her mother. Just before noon, the telephone rang. Laurie held her breath and picked up the receiver.

"The jury has reached a verdict," Eisenberg said. "Cross your fingers and see you downtown."

The color had drained from Laurie's face and she turned to face her mother. A feeling of dread flooded through her. Laurie knew that in Wisconsin a life sentence meant that a prisoner would spend between fifteen and twenty years in prison before becoming eligible for parole.

"It's going to be all right," her mother said, holding her by the shoulders. "It has to be."

"But we thought it would be a hung jury."

"No jury in its right mind could find you guilty."

"Mom! You just don't know. You weren't there for all of it, because you were sequestered. It was so unfair! I have this awful feeling. . . ."

"No," her mother said, cutting her off. "Here, take this and wear it for good luck."

Laurie's mother gave her her thin gold wedding band.

Upstairs, Laurie raced to get dressed. She

grabbed a white sweater and a plaid skirt. Her whole body was trembling. Laurie could barely make it to the front door.

When Laurie, her parents, and Fred arrived, the courtroom seemed strangely silent. The reporters and photographers were there. Everyone was waiting.

"How are you?" Eisenberg asked her.

Laurie told him she felt as if she had been suffering from a terminal illness for a very long time and was just about to die. "I feel like I'm at my own funeral. Why is everyone so quiet in here?"

"A better question is why there are so many sheriff's deputies in here? Do they expect a riot?" said Eisenberg.

Deputies were lined up against all three sides of the courtroom.

Eisenberg said he had talked with the bailiffs and they told him the jury took several different votes. They kept coming up with different answers.

"I'll tell you one thing, Laurie. When the jury comes in, if they are looking at you, you are safe. If none of them look at you, it's time to appeal."

Then the judge showed up. Laurie sat down next to Eisenberg and put her hands in front of her face. Then the jurors walked in one by one.

The heavy woman with the long brown hair wouldn't look at Laurie.

The black man watched his feet as he entered the jury box.

"Oh, no," Eisenberg groaned. "God, no."

None of the jurors looked at Laurie Bembenek.

"Ladies and gentlemen of the jury, have you reached a verdict?" the judge asked.

"We have, your honor."

The jury foreman, a short, dark-haired woman who wore half glasses, handed the verdict to Judge Skwierawski.

He opened it slowly. Read it to himself and then, without changing the expression on his face, said, "We find the defendant, Lawrencia Bembenek, guilty of first-degree murder."

For a moment Laurie actually thought she was dead. She couldn't move. She stopped breathing. Somehow she managed to get up and she found herself standing in front of the judge. Tears were running down her face. Eisenberg stood off to her right. Laurie thought her head was going to explode.

The judge asked her if she wanted to say anything. Laurie heard a no and assumed it must have come out of her own mouth.

The judge had something to say, though. He declared that although the case could have gone either way, he saw enough evidence to convict Laurie of first-degree murder. He said again that this was the most circumstantial case he had ever seen.

"Accordingly, based on the conviction for first-degree murder, it is the sentence of this court that you, Lawrencia Bembenek, are to serve a term of life imprisonment in the Wisconsin State Prison at Taycheedah designated as the reception center to which you shall be delivered by the sheriff."

Laurie heard loud, terrible sobs behind her. She knew the noise was coming from her mother.

Don't turn around and look at them or you will die, she told herself.

Eisenberg wanted Laurie released on bail because he planned to file an appeal of the conviction. Kramer said he objected to bail. He said she was a threat. Judge Skwierawski agreed with Kramer. He said Laurie had just been found guilty of a very serious crime and he could not release her on bail.

There was nothing else anyone could do for her. The jurors still refused to look at her. They filed out of the courtroom as quickly as possible. Eisenberg put his arm around Laurie's shoulder for just a moment and ushered her toward a group of deputies.

She was immediately surrounded by the guards. A huge chain was wrapped around her waist and her hands were handcuffed to it. Laurie never got a chance to say good-bye to her parents or to Fred. She never even saw them.

Suddenly she was in a room, alone, sitting on a chair. "Oh," she heard a male voice say, "the new prisoner is here! I didn't recognize her with clothes on!"

Laurie was then taken to another room, where she signed some papers she didn't even read. Then she changed into a thin jail gown and was walked into the Milwaukee County Jail.

A deputy told her to make any phone call she wanted to because in the morning she would be taken to the medium-security women's prison at Taycheedah near Fond du Lac, Wisconsin, a small community about sixty-five miles north of Milwaukee.

A door opened and Laurie was pointed toward the cellblock. She was standing right in front of the phone but she couldn't even see it. Other prisoners sat around a table and stared at her.

Laurie was escorted to her cell block, where she started sobbing uncontrollably. A jail matron walked in and put a supper tray on the shelf attached to the wall. Laurie thought it looked like dog food with a spoon in it.

She got up and walked out of her open cell door and back to the phone that was in the cell block, dialed her parents' phone number, and Fred answered. She told him she needed a coat and the case for her contact lenses. She was back in her cell, crying, when another matron walked in and told her channel 4 wanted an interview.

"No," Laurie said. She was crying so hard, her whole body was shaking.

Then a sheriff's deputy came in to get her. "Get dressed," she said.

"Excuse me?"

"Come with me. I'll get your clothes. You are going to Taycheedah right now."

Laurie had no idea why she was being rushed to the prison. She had not been allowed to get her coat and she sat shivering in the back of a sheriff's department squad car with three other officers. Without her contact lenses, everything looked blurry. When the car pulled into Taycheedah she could barely see. Just before she got out of the car one of the female deputies turned to her and said, "Good luck, Lawrencia."

Inside she was taken to a small room with two shower stalls. A large male lieutenant told her she would be kept in receiving and orientation until she had been medically cleared. She heard keys jingling everywhere.

"It's up to you how you want to do your time," the man barked at her. "You can keep your mouth shut, and have it pretty easy, or you can do hard time. It's all up to you."

"Hard time," Laurie said quietly to herself. Just hours ago she had been sitting at her mother's kitchen table playing Scrabble and warming her feet under her dog.

Laurie stood alone inside a small cell. The metal door in front of her locked automatically with a loud, scraping sound. Within seconds she heard the sound of walkie-talkies and two female prison guards came into her cell and ordered her to remove all her clothes.

Humiliated and still frightened, Laurie stood in front of them, naked and crying. She stared at the tile floor.

"Turn around, bend over, and spread your cheeks."

The guards then stood and watched as Laurie showered with a lice shampoo. She was then given another thin gown and a cotton robe that smelled like body odor. She wondered who had worn the robe before her.

Laurie Bembenek sat on the edge of her metal cot and looked at a brick wall. She had no idea what time it was. But she knew the date. It was March 9, 1982. It was the day she had been convicted of first-degree murder.

CHAPTER 27

Survival of the Fittest

Back in Milwaukee the city was divided about the verdict the twelve-member jury had delivered to Judge Skwierawski. Bars, restaurants, and living rooms were filled with people debating the innocence or guilt of Lawrencia Bembenek. The newspaper editors were busy laying out large headlines for the morning editions that said, BEMBENEK GETS LIFE. Both Milwaukee newspapers were quick to say that justice had been done and that Lawrencia Bembenek had gotten what she deserved.

But, one *Milwaukee Journal* satirical columnist hinted that her crime had been her beauty. Joel McNally wrote that the trial of Lawrencia Bembenek was primarily a visual story. He said that reporters who covered the story would quickly discover that their lives had been drastically altered. McNally said that after covering the sensational Bembenek murder trial writers would now have to describe every article of clothing everyone was wearing. He joked that even stories about local fires would have to include detailed descriptions about the color of boots and rain slickers. He also said that from then on everyone would have to identify the person he was writing about by mentioning every job the subject had ever held, such as former police officer, security guard, model, Playboy bunny, and aerobic dance and fitness instructor.

The general public was equally critical of the press coverage and the outcome of the trial. Letters to the editor and people who called radio talk shows said that Laurie Bembenek had not been given a fair trial. Several female writers who had been keeping track of Judge Skwierawski's trials suggested he made his ruling on the basis of sex.

Comments from city officials, including the mayor and police chief, were absent from the newspapers. But the people who voted them in office would not let them forget the trial of Lawrencia Bembenek.

Kramer shook hands with his assistants. Eisenberg gathered up all his papers and left to have a drink. He said he would appeal the conviction as soon as possible. Laurie's parents went home and locked all the doors.

Fred Schultz was sitting in front of Joseph and Virginia Bembenek's house talking to a newspaper reporter.

"Who did it? Who knows . . . who knows? I don't know," he told the reporter.

Fred also complained about the amount of money spent defending his wife. More than $50,000. "Everything I've worked for. Everything her father and mother have. That's where it comes from."

He told the reporter he was mad, disappointed, and hurt over the verdict. "If it takes a year, two years, whatever, I'll be there. I'll just be a little older when she gets out."

The jurors started talking about the verdict, too. Five of the women had immediately decided she was guilty. They knew right away. They argued. They disagreed and they couldn't stop thinking about that gun. That's what got to them. Laurie had access to the gun. They also said the testimony of Detective Durfee helped them decide. Especially when he said Laurie and Fred had talked alone for a few minutes when the two detectives first arrived at the 20th Street apartment just after the murder had been committed.

The jurors also commented on what Laurie wore to the trial. They said it really bothered them when she wore the conservative blouse on the day she testified. Some also made comments about Laurie's desire not to have children. What kind of woman must she be.

The day after her arrival at the Women's Correctional Institute at Taycheedah, Laurie thought that she had been transported to hell. Perhaps I died, and this is hell, she thought. Except hell holds no innocent souls.

Her head ached from crying, and Laurie felt as if she had no control of her own body or any other aspect of her life.

Laurie's first hours in her locked cell were filled with doubts about the existence of God. She couldn't believe that a Supreme Being would allow such a merciless, senseless devastation to occur.

Sometimes during the early morning hours of her first day in prison Lawrencia Bembenek also considered committing suicide. She looked at the large old water pipe that jutted from the wall and ran parallel with the ceiling. She realized it would be easy to tear strips from her bed sheets and fashion a rope long enough to tie to the pipe. She thought death would be a relief. But then she also thought of her parents, especially her mother. She knew they would want her to fight. Laurie knew that they had been hurt by everything that had happened to her and she couldn't hurt them anymore.

Laurie's days quickly slipped into a predictable routine. There was nothing to do and no one to talk to. She had plenty of time to think about how miserable she was. Every morning at six she heard a set of keys open the lock to her cell door. Then she would hear the sergeant on duty ask, "Six A.M. Do you want a breakfast tray, Bembenek?"

"No, thank you," Laurie would call from her bunk.

Twenty minutes later the door would open a second time and another officer would ask, "Tray, please."

"I don't have a tray. I refused breakfast."

Then about thirty minutes later she would hear the keys a third time. "Shower."

Day after day there was never any hot or warm water.

Next on the daily agenda came cleaning. Each cell received a mop and bucket. Laurie would dress in her state-issue clothing—baggy denim pants, a gray sweatshirt, white socks, and old white tennis shoes—and mop her floor. Then she had the rest of the day to look forward to.

During her first few days in prison, dozens of different prison guards opened her door just so they could look at her. She also heard inmates talking outside her window. "Is that the police in that one?" they asked each other.

From the beginning Laurie noticed inconsistencies between the officers at the prison. Some would enforce the rules very strictly and others would overlook minor discrepancies. Some were human beings and others treated the prisoners like animals.

Anxious to have some kind of contact with her family, Laurie was also quickly introduced to the world of prison paperwork. There were forms for everything. There was a form for canteen privileges, for phone calls, for visitors, for medical attention.

One guard told her that new arrivals could see their family after seventy-two hours. Laurie quickly wrote to her parents, to Fred, and to Eisenberg. She stopped writing when her pencil wore down. She slipped it under the door and had to wait for a guard to notice it and sharpen it before she could write any more letters.

Taycheedah is the only women's prison in Wisconsin and houses everyone from housewives who have written bad checks to convicted murderers. In 1982, the prison was overcrowded and did not meet some federal and state standards. More than two hundred women were staying at the 126-bed facility.

Peering out the tiny window in her cell, Laurie could see a farmhouse and a barn far past the fence that surrounded the prison. Laurie would stand by the window for hours, staring at the house and wondering about the people who lived in it. She also watched the blinking lights of Fond du Lac. She felt claustrophobic. There was no place to go. Nothing to do and what, she wondered, could she look forward to?

Laurie's questions and doubts about God continued to occupy her mind during those first days and weeks in prison. She had fallen away from her Catholic beliefs several years before after realizing how male-dominated and money-oriented the church could be. She kept remembering a priest from grade school who hated women and constantly picked on all the girls. Laurie often challenged him, especially when he taught catechism. Her challenges so angered him that he would swear at her. Once, when she had her feet on the gym wall, he called her a slut.

This was the priest who heard our confessions, gave us penance for our childish sins? This was a man of the cloth, taking the Lord's name in vain and interpreting the actions of a seventh-grade girl as sexual? Laurie thought.

The priest was eventually caught in homosexual activities with young boys at a retreat house. Laurie remembered him, looked at her present life, and she became more certain that there could not be a God.

Laurie found out quickly how arbitrary prison rules are. When she bit into a sandwich and her front tooth broke off, she asked a guard for a dental request form. She also wanted to talk to someone. It had been days since she had had a conversation.

"I can't wait until I can see my family," she told him. "They'll be here tomorrow."

"You can't have any visitors until you are medically cleared," he told her. "That probably won't be for another week or so."

"But the female guard that has been here at night said they could see me after seventy-two hours," Laurie said, starting to cry.

"I'm sorry. That's an old policy. She gave you the wrong info."

"I wrote home and told my mom and dad they could visit. Now they'll drive all the way from Milwaukee for nothing!"

The rules changed so quickly in prison, the guards often didn't know what was going on.

After she had been in prison about a week, Laurie started receiving hundreds of letters from people throughout Wisconsin, and the entire United States, who supported her claim of innocence. Fred wrote and said that a defense fund had been established to help pay for legal bills. He also told her he was going to hold a fund-raiser called "Run for Bambi" and jog from Milwaukee to Taycheedah, about sixty-five miles, to help raise money for the fund.

Fred raised about $2,800 on his Bambi run but was unable to jog the entire sixty-five miles because his ankle "gave out" after nineteen miles. A few friends, including two of his brothers, accompanied him on the run. When they got to Taycheedah Fred was allowed to see Laurie for two hours.

He told reporters who waited outside that he was allowed one kiss and one hug for hello and one kiss and one hug for good-bye. "The worst part, as you can see, is that I can't take her home," he said.

Laurie was desperate for contact with her family and when she finally started receiving mail from her mother and father, she broke down again. Her mother explained how they rushed back to the jail the day she was sentenced to bring her a coat and to say good-bye but she had already been transported to Taycheedah.

"They couldn't wait to take you from us, my darling daughter," her mother wrote.

Laurie clutched her parents' letters to her chest while she slept each night. Thoughts of her parents kept her alive.

If people really died from a broken heart, Laurie thought, I would have surrendered months ago. Alive, there is no relief from this pain. I would gladly welcome death, but I hold on, because of you, Mom and Dad, because of you.

Finally, Laurie received her medical clearance and was moved to another floor in the same prison building. She also heard that her parents and Eisenberg were waiting to see her in the visitors room. Before she saw her family she was taken to see the prison warden, Nona Switala. It was their first meeting.

"Well, is it as bad as you thought it would be?" the warden asked Laurie.

"Yes," Laurie said.

"You're still adjusting."

Switala told Laurie that the prison had been receiving dozens of phone requests from television and newspaper reporters who wanted to interview her.

"They're anxious to interview you, Laurie," Switala said. "If you don't wish to be bothered, I will do everything in my power to see to it that they leave you alone—if that's what you want."

She told Laurie the reporters had been asking

questions about every aspect of Laurie's prison life.

Laurie told the warden she didn't want to talk to anyone, and she was then allowed to see her family. Fred was there, too, and he grabbed Laurie and tried to give her a passionate kiss. Laurie was embarrassed and pushed him away.

Eisenberg said he had been able to interview the jury forewoman and he found out that the jury was initially divided about the verdict.

"Apparently, the forewoman was extremely aggressive in arguing her viewpoint, while the jury was deliberating, and swayed many to the guilty side. She really wanted to hang you," Eisenberg said.

He told Laurie that he had filed a notice of appeal with the state appellate court. But, he added, it could take at least six months for them to look at the appeal. It would also take at least six weeks to get the trial transcripts typed.

Judge Skwierawski had already denied an appeal bond to let Laurie out on bail while she appealed her guilty verdict.

"If I can just hang on for six months," Laurie told him.

"Guess what," Eisenberg said. "There is a God! Annette Wilson, the woman who testified that you stole a green jogging suit, was fired from her job at Boston Store. Her supervisor, Scott Nicholson, called me and said she was lying. He offered to give us an affidavit."

When Laurie's family left, she rushed to the window to wave good-bye, but a guard stopped her and said waving good-bye was unauthorized communication. She stood alone and watched the taillights disappear.

When Laurie was finally allowed to mingle with the rest of the prison population, she had to learn a whole new set of rules. Her first meal out of her cell was at a table with three black women, and Laurie had difficulty understanding what they were saying.

"You ear hustling?" one woman asked her.

"Excuse me?" Laurie asked her back.

"Dippin'?"

"No," Laurie answered, still not sure what the woman was talking about.

"You gone to A 'n' E yet?"

"No," Laurie said. She knew the woman was talking about an assessment and evaluation review.

"What are you in for?" Laurie asked, feeling as if she was in the middle of a late night movie.

"Aggravatin' a battery."

"You mean aggravated battery?" Laurie asked, trying not to laugh out loud. She could just picture this large woman with the hood of her car thrown open, aggravating a battery.

Laurie quickly learned about the inside workings of the prison. M.R. meant mandatory release date. Kites were illegal letters passed from inmate to inmate. "Seg" was short for adjustment segregation. It was a strange world.

Her new 137-square-foot cell on the third floor of the Addams housing unit had a desk and a metal bed. There was a bulletin board on the wall. There was a switch that allowed inmates to listen to one radio station—country-western.

The guards were strict about enforcing a rule that didn't allow inmates to sit on the bed with the bedspread on it. If Laurie wanted to sit on her bed she had to undo it. But there was also another rule that prevented inmates from leaving the cell with the bed unmade.

Laurie's cell bathroom was a small porcelain pot with a lid on it that the inmates called a jitney. Legally the women should not have been locked into their cells without a regular toilet, but the housing units were old and there was never any money for remodeling.

The widespread acceptance of lesbian activity at the prison quickly became obvious. Even though there was a rule against sexual conduct, the rule was rarely enforced. Most likely, Laurie thought, because many of the guards were lesbians, too. Even women who had husbands on the outside often took a female partner in the prison, mostly out of loneliness. Laurie made it clear that she wasn't a lesbian and that she wasn't looking for a partner. She was part of a small minority.

The population at Taycheedah included one of everything. There were masculine, muscular women and others who looked like little lost girls. Laurie was surprised at the number of mentally handicapped women there. Others were physically handicapped, on crutches, in wheelchairs, or had missing limbs.

Most inmates that Laurie talked with were serving short sentences for forgery or theft or for drug-related crimes. There were other lifers, like Laurie. Some had killed husbands or their own children. What impressed Laurie, though, was the disparity of the sentences. One woman would be in for five years and another woman, convicted of the same crime, had received a twenty-five-year sentence. Nothing seemed to make sense.

Drug use in prison was also prevalent. The women would smuggle in drugs using every available body cavity. The guards were always giving random urine checks and the penalty for a bad analysis or "dirty urine" was 365 days in program segregation. That meant 365 days alone, in your cell.

Laurie spent much of her time during the first few months in prison writing letters. She wrote constantly to Eisenberg and her letters were filled with much hope. She attached stickers to the letters that said, "Good humor makes all things tolerable" and "There hasn't been a prison built that can hold me."

She was still confident that Eisenberg would get her out of jail. Eisenberg wrote back, via his secretary, and often signed his letters, "Love and Kisses." He also sent dozens of bills to her family and to Fred. He kept detailed records of mileage, conference meetings that often included meals, travel time, and costs, and phone calls. The costs were staggering, and when Laurie received copies of the bills, she wondered how in the world they would be able to pay for them. Eisenberg had already received about $30,000 and Laurie Bembenek was still in prison.

One letter Laurie wrote, just three weeks after she was sent to Taycheedah, was an interesting mix of sarcasm, hope, and despondence.

Mon. 3/22/82

Dear Don,

I saw the article in yesterday's Milwaukee Urinal [*Milwaukee Journal*] about you—you flamboyant devil! It was a rather inadequate article, but I suppose it could have been worse. I get a kick out of the precise manner in which you were quoted saying that Sandy would "kill" you if she knew you were proudly displaying photos of her in the bunny costume. Was it intentional? All of my friends and family picked up on that right away—as if it was a typical example of how it's impossible to quote sarcasm. That was a good picture of you, too.

Yesterday they had some shit in the Journal because of the way a reporter described Taycheedah. They had the appalling audacity to refer to it as a country club, a private college and resort, too! So naturally, a barrage of idiots wrote the Journal complaining that their taxes were affording us murderers and armed robbers such luxurious surroundings! A few girls wrote, explaining that they were working their way through Marquette U., and sarcastically inquired how they could rent a dorm room here at TCI so they could go to school free of charge. The whole thing REALLY pissed me off! It never ceases to amaze me how the Journal consistently continues to misrepresent everything about me! Oh, well. There were some good letters, people recognizing Skwierawski's bias towards women. A girl who used to be his court reporter wanted to start a petition to oust him. How I wish! I wonder what his mother did to him?

I told Fred to send you a letter from Horenberger—a bit of sour grapes, I'd say. Who in their right mind would change horses in midstream? We have got to win that appeal! Nothing was fair! Not a damn thing! Having evidence of perjury and not being allowed to use it is not right! I hope it will be obvious to the next judge that Skwierawski did everything in his power to prevent us from getting a fair trial. We have to emphasize the gun issue more—access, identification, etc., because apparently that's what the jury convicted me on—despite the obvious explanation! I know all those women were no good!

A guy named Clay Lampe from Waupun has written me and for what it's worth I'll pass on the information. He knows and hates Tom and Judy and he thinks he's telling me something new when all he does is repeat Horenberger's story, only with a few names. I'll send you what he wrote me. The first letter that he wrote to me explained that my husband Freddy gave him a break once long ago. The only thing that he says is incorrect is that he claims he met me but I think he might have me confused with Judy's other friend Laurie who is also blond.

What's the use of having a law against perjury if it's something you can't prove anyway?

Does an appeal mean another whole trial all over again in front of a new jury and judge?

Hey! Did you hear what happened to that hog from Boston Store security who testified against me as the surprise witness! Ha! She got fired! The other security guard, Scott, was super pissed at her and called her a liar—he said I was never under suspicion.

My cousin Maria Bembenek also said her girlfriend who owns the wig shop first began asking about me after seeing my name in the paper. She would have never even come forward but an off-duty cop was in her shop (the night before she was subpoenaed) and overheard her gossiping about me, and notified the authorities.

I'm adjusting a lot better since I've been able to see my family, and can be allowed out of my cell for meals and the library and stuff, but I still hate it here. After 30 days I'll be assigned to either a work program or school so hopefully that will keep me a lot more busy and make the time go faster. It's the boredom that is aggravating.

My parents had to go back to Oregon to get their things and bring them back to Milwaukee. They had some things in a safety deposit box, etc.

Barbara Hoffman [a convicted murderer and former client of Eisenberg's] got put in lock up for punishment. I wonder what happened. I haven't seen her since you introduced her to me.

As soon as I get some stamps I'll be able to mail this.

Love,

Bambi

P.S. I was given a series of tests but I kept trying to stuff the square peg into the round hole! Ha!!

In April, a month after she moved into the prison, Laurie was assigned a roommate and was moved into the maximum security unit in the Neprud Housing Unit. Her roommate, Laura, was straight. She had been sentenced to three years for theft by fraud, taking money from an employer. The women discovered they had grown up in the same neighborhood. Their cell was eight by fourteen feet and had a toilet. A prison luxury that was being forced on the inmates because a group of women had filed a lawsuit against the state.

The view from Laurie's window was of two apple trees, and because her cell was directly above the kitchen, the room often filled with smoke.

Guards would perform random contraband checks on all the cells, too. Laurie and Laura would come back from lunch and find their entire room ripped apart, pencils broken, and clothes scattered across the floor.

When Laurie finally appeared before the Program Review Committee and requested entrance into a two-year schooling program, her request was rejected. "Based on your sentence structure, you are not an appropriate candidate for educational rehabilitation," she was told.

The committee members said it seemed useless for her to attend school for two years and then "sit around for ten years" because she would not be eligible for parole until 1993. She would either be assigned to work in the prison kitchen, laundry, or cleaning services. Laurie went into the kitchen, where she scrubbed pots and peeled potatoes. She had a feeling the prison supervisors didn't want anyone thinking she was getting special treatment.

Laurie made fifteen cents an hour and worked from 5 A.M. to 1 P.M. every day.

One night, toward the end of May, Laurie and Laura lay awake in their bunk beds talking. It was dark and they had the window pushed open about one inch to let in a bit of fresh air.

"It's the strangest thing," Laurie said. "But I was peeling potatoes today over some newspapers and the smell suddenly reminded me of home so much. Does that happen to you?"

"Of course," Laura said. "I miss the simple things so much. Being able to answer a telephone."

"Driving a car."

"Raiding a refrigerator!"

"Or sitting outside at night," Laurie said. "I used to love sitting on the front porch on a fragrant summer night . . . lilacs . . . the wind chimes singing in the breeze . . . the crickets. . . ."

"Or the feel of money in your hand!"

"What are we talking about, Laura?"

"What?"

"What is the important thing we miss? And don't say men!"

"What?"

"Why didn't either of us say that it's privacy that we miss? To have our love letters read, our every movement authorized! Our property and our very bodies open to inspection and scrutinization—God! A world without strip searches, walkie-talkies blaring, and the heavy footsteps of the guards with the hourly flash of lights in our eyes at night!"

"You're right," Laura said.

"Privacy!" Laurie shouted. "I could scream it from the rooftop. Privacy is what I miss the most."

CHAPTER 28

True Colors

Once in prison what was left of Laurie's relationship with Fred quickly disappeared. Fred would grant interviews to various news reporters and tell them how much he still loved Lawrencia Bembenek and that he would wait for her forever. Forever for Fred Schultz apparently meant three months.

Laurie's friends hinted that although Fred might appear to be a devoted husband, he was seeing other women. But Laurie didn't want to believe what people began telling her. When her parents refused to visit her in prison when Fred was there, Laurie knew something was going on.

Her mother finally told her that Fred was spending excessive amounts of money and staying out all night—with their car. Laurie had decided to wear prison-issue clothing instead of her own clothes so she and Fred could save money for legal fees. Then her mother told her Fred was buying stereo speakers, personalized stationery, and all kinds of new clothes.

Her father was more blunt. He was working with Fred and said he didn't know how much longer he could keep doing it. "This guy does not want to work," her father said during one of his visits. "He drives me nuts. We'll agree to start a job at eight. So I get up, shower, and get dressed while Fred's having breakfast. Then he'll start to read the morning paper, so I'll leave the house and start loading the van."

Two hours later, Fred would still not be ready to go to work.

"Most days he shows up at the job about two and the day is already shot. I don't want to insult him, but I've been doing this kind of work for thirty-five years. I've tried talking with him but it does no good."

Laurie's mother said she didn't think she could stand being around him much longer. "He's a manipulator. If I tell Fred anything more than once, he gets real strange. He resents it and then refuses to do it."

Her father said now that Laurie was gone, Fred was a different man. He told Laurie they could now understand how Fred had fooled her for so long. They said they had liked him at first but now couldn't stand the sight of him.

"After all," Mrs. Bembenek said, "if you had never met Fred, you wouldn't be in prison."

Despite his inconsistent behavior, Fred sent Eisenberg a letter on April 19, 1982, proclaiming his love for Laurie and begging Eisenberg to find the real killer of Christine Schultz. Fred thanked Eisenberg for his friendship and tenacity. He also called himself "a rather simple man" whose main desire was to love a woman and live the rest of his life with her. Fred said he did not want to be rich or famous, but cash reserves would come in handy. He also promised that he would give or do anything to free Laurie.

As he continued writing, Fred said, "It gets harder and harder every day to live without Bambi." Fred also said that although he was not a deeply religious person, he prayed often for God's forgiveness for the many mistakes he had made in his life. He said he was so in love with Bambi, he could wait eleven years until she was eligible for parole, but he was not sure Bambi could handle all those years in prison.

Fred ended his letter by telling Eisenberg to give him a call when he visited Milwaukee so both of them could go "whoop it up a little." His last line was "Damn it! Get those bastards."

When Fred came to see her, Laurie confronted him with the information she had been receiving from her family and friends. Fred claimed he couldn't even afford to send her money for shampoo and stamps. When she asked him to make a copy of a photo of them together, he told her week after week that he had forgotten to do it.

Laurie had also discovered that Fred was running up huge phone bills by calling Florida and that he was charging all of his carpentry lumber to her father's account. When Laurie asked him about the bills and the personal items he was buying, he became very angry. "I need something for myself once in a while," he told her. "I have to think of myself. After all, I'm in prison, too."

Laurie could barely bring herself to look at him. He had been charging items like expensive dinners and clothing to her VISA account, and she was receiving the bills in prison.

"Don't you ever say anything so stupid to me again," she told him. "You just got through telling me that you went water-skiing this week with your buddy George Marks, you went to a birthday party and a nightclub, and you have the audacity to say you are in prison too? I wish to God I was in a prison like yours!"

Several of Laurie's friends also told her that Fred had been seen around Milwaukee with a young woman who was eighteen, worked at a downtown dime store, and "looked like Lady Diana." When he came to visit and Laurie noticed a new gold bracelet on his wrist, he told Laurie it had been "a gift."

The first week of June Fred was quiet when he came to see Laurie. He looked down when he told her he was going to move to Florida and try to get a job on the Miami police force. He said he would work in construction until he could get back into police work.

"What about your children?" Laurie asked.

"I'll just get an extension on the joint custody and worry about it later," he said.

Laurie was actually relieved when he said he was moving. He wanted to take her waterbed, clothes, luggage, and dog with him. Her parents tried to stop him, but he managed to take lots of Laurie's personal belongings.

Just before he left, Fred talked with a *Milwaukee Sentinel* reporter. He refused to say where in Florida he was moving. Laurie didn't even have his address.

"I certainly hope the Miami Police Department will realize I am a good police officer, regardless of who my wife is," he said. "I'm going to be a hermit for a while."

Fred also said he had to continue on with his life, "not only for me, but for us."

When Fred finally contacted Laurie from Florida, he told her he was spending his time swimming and playing tennis. He said the job he had lined up fell through and he was terribly bored and running out of money.

But the following week he suddenly showed up to see her during visiting hours. Laurie just stared at him as he walked across the room toward her. Fred was wearing a red muscle T-shirt and a pair of tiny red satin shorts. He was tan and he had let his hair grow. He told Laurie he had flown home. Laurie wondered how he got the money.

"I would have spent just as much money if I would have stayed in Florida," he said.

"How do you figure?"

"On food and gas."

"You would have spent three hundred dollars on food and gas?"

"I suckered my mother out of a hundred dollars when I got in anyway. So really, I only spent two hundred. Besides, I have four jobs waiting for me at the end of the week."

Laurie wondered why he didn't just stay in Florida and work. She also wondered if her parents even knew he was in town.

"This is a waste of money," Laurie said.

"I don't think you love me anymore."

"I write to you every single day. Isn't that enough?"

"It's the quality, not the quantity."

"You mean the context?"

"Stop using big words with me," Fred yelled. "I'm not a little kid."

"What are you talking about? I write to you every day on my break. Still you're not satisfied. What do you want, a sonnet?"

"Don't be sarcastic. You don't give a shit!"

"You're insecure and demanding."

"Don't use that cop-out."

"It's not a cop-out. I just don't know what you want of me."

"It's tough out there without you," Fred said.

Then Fred said he would have divorced her the day she was charged if he didn't love her. "Sometimes you make me feel as if you are just using me to pay your attorney's bills. I lost everything because of you, my house, my kids, my job. . . ."

"Shut up, Fred. Just shut up. Stop throwing that all up to me. I am through buying it! My parents had to mortgage their house to pay my lawyer. I owe them thirty thousand dollars. You haven't shelled out a penny, so what the hell are you talking about? When I met you, you had already lost your house and your kids, and you were in the process of losing your damn job—so stop it!"

The arguing continued and then Fred stood up and kissed the side of her head. "It's too bad because I could have loved you so much."

He turned and walked out of the visiting room. Within three days he called and apologized but then Laurie caught him in another lie. She asked him to send her parents some money because they were having problems paying their phone bills. Fred said he didn't have any money even though her father had seen thousands of dollars in checks from work they had done together. Fred had also told Laurie he had received $12,000 from a life insurance policy.

"What about the insurance policy you told me about? You said you were going to get twelve thousand dollars from that."

"Oh, that! It was all a big mistake. That was my father's policy. It was just a mistake."

Laurie's parents told her all of the checks Fred

had given them to pay his bills had bounced. She also found out that he had forged her signature on her $2,500 income tax refund check.

Then, in July of 1982, just five months after she had been sent to prison, she received a three-word letter from her husband.

"Good luck. Good-bye."

Laurie would never see or hear from him again. But he would show up in Milwaukee occasionally, without calling his sons or any family members. Laurie wrote to Eisenberg and asked him what she had to do to divorce him.

Eisenberg told her to wait for a while. He said it would look better if the divorce came after her appeal. Laurie thought Fred might end up serving her divorce papers but he never did.

Later in July Eisenberg filed an appeal on her conviction with the state appeals court. Eisenberg said that Circuit Judge Michael J. Skwierawski failed to maintain his composure and repeatedly sided with the prosecution during the trial. He also said that the prosecutor, Robert Kramer, "overstepped the boundaries of permissible conduct" in the trial by alluding to facts not in evidence. He also said that improper evidence had been admitted at the trial and that the murder conviction should be overturned.

Laurie remained optimistic about her chances of winning the appeal. She still believed everything Donald Eisenberg told her. She had nothing else to go on and no one else to believe. Clinging to the idea that she might be set free helped her from one day to the next.

In October she wrote Eisenberg a letter and said

she was ready to divorce Fred. Her friends had run into Fred in Milwaukee, with his young girlfriend. He told them he wasn't going to try and get custody of his children. He would visit them whenever he could. She also told Eisenberg he should be in prison and not her.

"I want a divorce, but you say I must wait till after my appeal—meanwhile he's using my credit cards to buy her dinner and clothes!" she wrote. "And he's totally whitewashing himself to my friends and others, saying that I ruined his life! I wish I could talk to that radio station again and tell the whole WORLD what he's doing to me! What can I do? I've always taken your advice. I feel so helpless while he's cavorting out there, making enemies for me. But I guess the majority of people still suspect him, anyway, not me. What can I do? Can't I seek adultery charges or something? I'm so hurt and frustrated. I wish he was here instead of me. He should be!"

In October, after repeatedly petitioning prison officials, Laurie was accepted into the two-year associate of arts program, run through a local university. She was the first lifer at Taycheedah allowed to take college courses. She also spent hours in the library of the prison looking up the answers to all her legal questions.

Laurie was moved to a medium-security area of the prison and started attending classes. She was also assigned various prison jobs. She cleaned, continued to work in the kitchen, and tried not to think about spending the next ten or twenty years locked up in prison for a crime she had not committed.

CHAPTER 29

A Sense of Injustice

During the second week of February in 1983, the Wisconsin Court of Appeals upheld Lawrencia Bembenek's murder conviction. The court ruled that the pretrial and trial procedures had been properly followed. The court also said that the search of Laurie's locker at Marquette University just after her arrest for the murder of Christine Schultz was not unconstitutional.

Eisenberg had also claimed that the complaint filed against Laurie was not properly written and that the judge and prosecutor were prejudicial to Bembenek. But the appeals court disagreed.

Laurie was devastated by the news. Eisenberg had all but promised her she would win on appeal and be granted a new trial. She thought she would be getting out of prison. So far Donald Eisenberg's promises of freedom had not been met.

Life inside Taycheedah was an emotional roller coaster for Laurie, and the news of her lost appeal only made things worse. Her endless days and nights held no future. She told herself over and over again that none of this would have happened to her if she had never met and married Fred Schultz.

When news of Laurie's appeal reached him in Florida, Fred took the opportunity to tell the world that Laurie was right where she was supposed to be. After pledging his devotion and loyalty to her, Fred Schultz had suddenly changed his mind. Fred said he finally put "two and two" together and realized that it really was Laurie Bembenek who had killed Christine Schultz.

"She murdered a person I loved and still love a little bit and probably will always love, and tried to strangle one of my sons," he said.

When Fred called a Milwaukee radio station following the appeal denial, he said that Laurie had never really confessed to the murder but had hinted at certain things before and after her arrest. He also told the radio station he had sent Laurie a Dear John letter. When the radio announcer asked Schultz if he had a young girlfriend, Schultz laughed. But then later he said, well, maybe there had been some nineteen-year-old girls in one or two taverns that he went to when he visited Milwaukee.

Fred told the announcer that he was broke and living in an apartment without a radio, television, or furniture. He said he had a job as a superintendent of a construction firm.

Laurie admitted that she would divorce Elfred Schultz and she began wondering privately and publicly if Fred knew more about the murder than he had said. She was also starting to question the abilities of her defense attorney.

"If Fred did have something to do with the murder and he worked closely with Eisenberg on my defense, who is to know what was hidden, what was covered up," she told her mother.

Laurie decided it was time to start doing some

more legal research on her own. It seemed that appeals and anything associated with the criminal justice system took forever. In March of 1983, after researching her case in the prison library, she sent Eisenberg a list of questions that she wanted answered as soon as possible.

Laurie wanted to know why he hadn't called some important witnesses during the preliminary hearing. She wanted to know why Eisenberg wasn't checking into Fred's $12,000 life insurance policy, why Horenberger hadn't been used to expose the perjury of Judy Zess, and if anyone had ever really checked out Fred's alibi the night of the murder. She was also worried about getting some of her money back from Fred. Laurie had also heard that Fred had called Eisenberg, and she wanted to know what was going on.

While Laurie waited for Eisenberg's answers, she continued her course work, wrote poetry, did drawings for the visiting-room walls, and answered her mail. Milwaukee had not forgotten about the ex-cop who was losing the best years of her life at a state prison. Whenever there would be news of her case on the television or in the newspapers, Laurie would receive a flood of mail in support of her claim of innocence. Small donations to her defense fund continued to trickle in and she still received dozens of letters each week from people throughout the country who had heard about her case.

Many of those people also wrote letters to District Attorney E. Michael McCann in support of Lawrencia Bembenek. Many of the letters were from average citizens who were concerned about the justice system. They told McCann, "If this can happen to her, who is to say it can't happen to me?"

On April 20 Laurie's mother wrote to Don Eisenberg to let him know how disappointed everyone had become in the work he was doing. The Bembeneks were emotionally and financially ruined. Mrs. Bembenek told Eisenberg that everything he did took too long. She said it was close to impossible to get in touch with him and that it took him days to answer their phone calls.

"We are torn each time we see Laurie," she wrote. "Underneath that shell of composure and self-assurance, she is soft, sensitive, and vulnerable."

She told Eisenberg that Laurie believed in him so completely, he could "walk on water." Mrs. Bembenek pleaded with him to do something because she didn't think her daughter could handle another ten years in prison. "There must be something more we can do, besides what is being done, right now," she said.

Two months following the court of appeals denial Laurie received word that the state supreme court had refused to review her murder conviction and would not even comment on her case, but it wasn't Eisenberg who called to tell her. The bad news came from someone in the prison.

Just days after the latest rejection Laurie passed the stress analysis test that Eisenberg had asked her to take. Eisenberg knew that the results of polygraph tests were not allowed in United States courts, but he had said a stress analysis test might be acceptable. The test is similar to a polygraph but the test examiner uses voice sounds to reach his conclusions. A certified examiner, hired by Eisenberg, asked Laurie if she had killed Christine Schultz or if she knew anything about the murder.

The results of the test showed that Lawrencia Bembenek did not kill Christine Schultz and knew nothing about the murder. She was telling the truth.

Laurie had lost two appeals, but she could still go to the United States Supreme Court if some legal problem in her trial merited its attention. She told Eisenberg that some friends of hers at Boston Store had seen Judy Zess and Tom Gaertner there.

"That means Tom has been paroled already, then their alleged deal with the D.A. worked and here I sit," she told Eisenberg in a letter.

The following month Laurie wrote Eisenberg again and told him she was trying to get approval to work during the summer on the outdoor maintenance crew. She told him that if she could get some fresh air and be outside, she might not be continually depressed.

Laurie said that she had been told by her psychologist at the prison not to get her hopes up. He told her that the prison had received a letter from someone who worked for Milwaukee County stating that Laurie would most likely be a security risk because her appeal had been denied. She was certain Fred had something to do with the letter and she wanted Eisenberg to find out if someone not connected with the prison could try to control her actions now that she was in prison.

Eisenberg's next idea was to approach E. Michael McCann with everything that he had developed on the case since the end of the trial. According to Eisenberg, McCann was "a very sincere, professional, and thoughtful prosecutor" who was terribly concerned about the possibility that an innocent person had been convicted of a crime.

During his meeting with McCann, Eisenberg was promised by McCann that he would have an investigator look into any new evidence or allegations. But Eisenberg didn't get anything in writing. All he had was McCann's word.

Bill Watson, Eisenberg's investigator, continued to follow leads that might offer some new evidence in the case. When he talked with Elaine Samuels, the associate medical examiner who had testified at Laurie's trial, he excitedly told Eisenberg she had some information that could break the case. She wrote a three-page affidavit on August 10, 1983, that everyone was certain would help get Lawrencia Bembenek out of prison.

In the affidavit Samuels said that she had been disturbed by certain irregularities in the murder investigation of Christine Schultz. She said that the medical examiner's office was not called to the scene until two hours following the murder and by the time the examiner arrived the body had been wrapped in plastic, which should not have happened. Samuels said that when the body was wrapped Christine's hands were partially untied and evidence could have been destroyed.

When Samuels called to have a police witness attend the autopsy, she said the Milwaukee Police Department chose not to send anyone. "This is unheard of," she wrote. She said that during the unwitnessed autopsy she recovered many brown hairs along with lots of textile fibers, but she never recovered any blond or red hairs. All the hairs she did recover were identical to the hair of Christine Schultz. Samuels said that during Laurie's trial she felt that District Attorney McCann was attributing the collection of incriminating blond hairs to her. She said that that was misleading information.

"I can find no logical explanation of what amounts to a mysterious appearance of blond hair in an envelope which contained no such hair at the time that it was sealed by me," Samuels said.

Samuels had testified at 350 other murder trials over the years. She said while she had questioned other guilty verdicts, she had never had the doubts she had with the Bembenek conviction. "I'm not sure who did it," she wrote. "But I do believe somebody else did it. I have so believed all along."

When news of Samuels' affidavit hit the newspapers, angry citizens said they wanted something done about it. Over sixteen hundred people signed a petition asking McCann to reopen the Bembenek case. The petition was drafted by Laurie's family and close friends and was circulated on street corners, in grocery stores, and door to door.

McCann, busy running for public office when the citizens made their request, said reopening the case was not a high-priority item but that he would look into it as soon as possible. He said the case had been fairly tried by competent attorneys.

In September Laurie decided to ask McCann herself why nothing was happening with the case. Her three-page, single-spaced letter was full of questions and personal feelings about the case. Laurie said the trial was unfair and from the beginning Judge Skwierawski had allowed the prosecution to use evidence and present a case that would not otherwise be allowed. She said using a black-and-white photograph of her in a jogging suit to prove she owned a green jogging suit was one example of evidence that should never have been allowed. The person who identified her in the green jogging suit was not the photographer who had taken her photo or the reporter who had interviewed her. It was another photographer who had merely passed her in the hall.

Laurie thought the rules of evidence in her trial had been ignored many times. She said Kramer often had been allowed to refer to items that were not in evidence. She said he had talked about a friend of Judy Zess who allegedly had seen photos from Laurie's honeymoon and claimed to have seen a traveling clothesline. But the woman wasn't called to testify and the photos were never introduced as evidence.

Judge Skwierawski had also allowed a search of Laurie's Marquette locker without a warrant to remain in evidence and Laurie had been held in jail for three days without a warrant.

While she waited for some kind of reply to her letter, Laurie was allowed to visit her father, who had been rushed to the hospital to have emergency stomach surgery for cancer. During his recovery, Laurie, accompanied by several guards, visited her father and talked to him for several hours before being taken back to Taycheedah. Her early Christmas present in 1983 was from

Judy Zess. In a ninety-minute deposition taken by Eisenberg on December 23, Zess admitted that she had been coerced by the Milwaukee Police Department into making certain statements against Lawrencia Bembenek. Eisenberg contacted Zess after Laurie told him she had received a cartoon from Judy in the mail. The cartoon showed the character Ziggy standing with a hammer in his hand next to a rock. Judy had written the word YOU above Ziggy, meaning that Laurie was between a rock and a hard place. She never offered Laurie an explanation for her testimony during the trial.

Zess told Eisenberg that she had been pressured by Milwaukee detectives and police officers to say certain things about Laurie. She said many of those things had been taken out of context. Judy said the police had promised her information that could help her husband, Tom Gaertner, who was facing drug charges, if she would cooperate with them. During the deposition, Zess said, the police had isolated sentences and phrases that she used and then blown them out of proportion.

"Let me think of an example," Judy said. "This refers more to the preliminary when he questioned me. If they asked me if I thought Laurie was kidding when she made the comment about having Christine Schultz blown away, they wanted a yes or no answer, and I could not say, yes, she was kidding. I thought I wanted to say no, she probably meant it a little but I don't think she seriously ever was intending or committing to killing the woman. That part was left out. They just wanted to hear, 'No, I don't think she was kidding.' "

She said most of the questioning had been by Lieutenant Ruscitti and that she had felt pressured to say things like, "Yes, that's similar to the cord I saw in my kitchen." Judy said she never got a chance to say there was no way she could tell for sure it was the same clothesline that was used to tie up Christine. She said she had been led to believe that the word *similar* is as good as "the same thing."

"It's like when you had me identify Freddy's gun. I knew it was a .38 Smith & Wesson with a two-inch barrel, but you could have put another Smith & Wesson gun in there. There were no distinctive marks."

Judy also told Eisenberg that the police only wrote down what they wanted when they questioned her. She said a stenographer was never present to record her conversations.

She said she had never seen a green jogging suit, either. Laurie Bembenek never wore nor owned a green jogging suit, she added.

According to Judy, Tom Gaertner also had access to the 20th Street apartment where the alleged murder weapon was kept. She said she kept a key ring with a key to the apartment on it and Tom could have used it whenever he wanted to or "he could have given it to someone."

Judy said the police told her that Laurie was trying to pin the murder on her. She said it was the old "divide and conquer" police tactic, but she never really had any other reason to think or believe that Laurie would try to blame her for the murder.

Because Judy had a sister who had been murdered and the murder was never solved, Judy said the cops played to that side of her also. They said without her testimony and help they couldn't get Laurie Bembenek. They said if she told them what they wanted to know, they would let her know, for Tom's sake, when something was going to happen, like a drug bust, so he could stay away from it.

"I think they were truthful statements that I made but they were totally taken out of context and blown out of proportion to make it look like Laurie seriously wanted to kill that woman, rather than just say, 'I wish her alimony would be reduced.'"

Judy also said she thought Durfee had lied when he said that Laurie and Fred talked alone for a few minutes the night of the murder.

She said that her theory from the beginning was that Fred had the gun and switched it. Judy said Fred Schultz had the puzzle piece that was missing.

"Freddy somehow was involved," she said. "If you look at it, he got rid of his wife, his kids, and his present wife."

Then Judy admitted that she knew one of the jurors, a friend from high school—someone she had grown up with and partied with. Judy said it was probably wrong that neither of them had mentioned they knew each other.

When Laurie heard about Judy Zess's testimony, she began to hope again. May 1984 would be the year she finally got out of prison. Maybe the truth would finally come out.

CHAPTER 30

The Waiting Game

While Laurie's close friends, her family, and her attorney felt as though things were finally coming together, Laurie wasn't quite as confident. Her life was a waiting game, a game she was not very good at.

To help her get through the days, weeks, and months, Laurie divided her daily routine into three segments.

First she would simply get out of bed in the morning. That meant she had made it through one more day. The first part of her day took her to lunch. Then there was the time from lunch to supper and finally, the last part of the day, from supper to the time she went back to sleep—or tried to.

"It's too dangerous to think about time as a lump sum," she said. "To think of ten years is too devastating. We just plod through each day, each second, and we don't think about anything past that point."

At the end of 1983 and during the beginning of 1984, Laurie's depression was consuming her. She had been in prison almost twenty-one months and she had stopped taking care of herself physically. She often didn't even bother to comb her hair. She never looked in a mirror. She told anyone who asked that she was "just a zombie," staggering around.

Her salvation during those months was a prison psychologist, Mike Levine. When Laurie began crying uncontrollably and babbling, she went to see him. He began meeting with her just as she was about to lose her mind.

Laurie had never been the kind of person who shared her deep thoughts and feelings. No one, not even her parents, knew how close she was to having a total breakdown. If she didn't get help, Laurie knew that it was very possible she would end up like dozens of other inmates who walked around all day in a daze because they couldn't deal with the reality of everyday prison life.

Levine told Laurie that she was like a soda bottle, full of carbonation, that had been shaken and shaken. "It has to come out," he told Laurie. "You have to share your feelings and talk about this. On the surface you appear to be so brave, but that's not what is really happening at all. You are ready to explode."

Laurie talked to Levine. She trusted him and he helped her learn how to deal with her feelings.

Once Laurie learned how to cope and that it was just fine to fall apart, considering what had happened to her life, she began writing again. Her poetry became an outlet for her anger, sorrow, and frustrations. One poem, *Sense Memories*, won a first-place award in a statewide prison writing contest.

SENSE MEMORIES

Thoughts of home
born with smell

of freshly cut grass on the wind
fading faces, summer nights
jazz festivals and crowded beer gardens
sun-drenched warm wood floors
How the mind fights reality
with memories.
Ideas, meaningless
without the freedom to use them
Still, I hope
afraid to become withdrawn
into conditioned hopelessness.
Sadness—incessant like
the ocean consuming the shoreline.

Laurie again told Eisenberg, who was working on a motion for a new trial, that she finally wanted to divorce Fred. Eisenberg suggested she let Robert M. Weidenbaum, a good attorney and a personal friend, handle the divorce. Laurie agreed and said that she wanted to be done with Fred Schultz as soon as possible.

The first week of March, almost two years after Laurie had been found guilty of murdering Christine, McCann said that he was not going to reopen the Bembenek case. He thought the jury's verdict was correct. To reopen the case, McCann said, would impeach the jury's integrity. McCann had read the report filed by Elaine Samuels, the assistant medical examiner, and had decided that while some things related to the handling of Christine Schultz's body were atypical, they were not improper.

The up-and-down status of Laurie's case continued. Just as quickly as McCann denied the request to reopen the case, there was also a positive break. A Milwaukee police officer, Michael Brophy, who was interviewed by Bill Watson, said he had seen Durfee and Fred in a Milwaukee bar between 2 and 2:30 A.M. on May 28, 1981, the morning Christine Schultz was murdered.

Durfee and Schultz had both testified that they were investigating a burglary during that time. But Brophy said he had gone into Monreal's, a restaurant and bar on the east side of Milwaukee, close to 2 A.M. on May 28, and that Schultz and Durfee were sitting at a table, talking with a waitress. He said Fred Schultz had made a phone call. Brophy said he was pretty sure they were still sitting there when he left about two-thirty.

Eisenberg told Laurie he was going to use the statements from Brophy, Elaine Samuels, and Judy Zess in his motion for a new trial. Laurie assumed he was working to use all the information he had been given. But Eisenberg was busy trying to save his professional life. He received notice in late March that the state supreme court was considering suspending his license because of a conflict-of-interest complaint.

The complaint centered around the well-publicized murder trial in 1980 of Barbara Hoffman of Madison, Wisconsin. Eisenberg had represented Hoffman, who was convicted of one cyanide poisoning charge and acquitted of another. At the same time Eisenberg was also representing Samuel Cerro on drug charges. Eisenberg knew that Cerro had information about one of the alleged Hoffman murders. Ethically, Eisenberg should not have been representing both Cerro and Hoffman at the same time, but apparently he made no attempt to avoid the conflict of interest.

Ironically, Laurie knew Barbara Hoffman, who was also at Taycheedah, and had written to Eisenberg about her several times. Laurie was concerned about Barbara's mental health.

On April 1, Eisenberg received notice that his license had been suspended for six months. That meant he could not practice law or handle any of his ongoing cases. Laurie panicked when she heard the news. He was supposed to represent her in court in just a few days to present evidence in support of a motion for a new trial. With limited phone privileges, she could only make phone calls during specific hours.

Weidenbaum happened to be at Taycheedah that day to talk with her about her divorce case and she asked him if he would represent her in court for some preliminary motions. Weidenbaum agreed and when he arrived in court, the case was continued for at least another thirty days.

During the delay, Laurie's parents contacted James Morrison, the attorney who earlier had helped Laurie to file her discrimination suit against the Milwaukee Police Department. Morrison was now in private practice in Washington, D.C., but he agreed to work on the case and do what he could. He told the Bembeneks he had not forgotten about their daughter. He said the case against her was weak and he was positive she was innocent and that someone else had committed the murder.

Eisenberg suggested that Laurie also work with Thomas Halloran, a Milwaukee attorney, who did occasional work for him and who was in private practice in Milwaukee. Halloran agreed to take the case and Morrison agreed to work with him, as a backup.

Both men said they needed more time to prepare, and the motion for a new trial was temporarily withdrawn until they could put everything together. By then Laurie had seen the materials Eisenberg had prepared for the motion and she was shocked. It looked as if Eisenberg had thrown everything together in just a few minutes. The pages didn't even match. Some were on legal-size paper, some on regular size. It was the first time she was grateful that the case had been continued.

On June 29, 1984, when she was twenty-four years old and had been in prison twenty-five months, Laurie filed for divorce from Fred Schultz. He was thirty-five, working in the construction business, and he had a new life in Bokeelia, Florida. Laurie was relieved that her marriage would soon be over. She had more important things to worry about.

During the summer of 1984 she met occasionally with Halloran. He told her he hoped to file the motion for a new trial by the end of August. Laurie wondered constantly if she would ever get out of prison. She wondered if there was anyone in the entire world who could or would do what had to be done to prove she was an innocent victim.

In Milwaukee, less than a hundred miles away, there was someone willing to risk everything to help free an innocent victim. Ira B. Robins, a private investigator, was about to get involved with the Lawrencia Ann Bembenek murder case.

CHAPTER 31

Factory Air

The car mechanic squinted when Ira Robins walked into the dimly lit garage and stood at the edge of the car pit. Robins was so large, he blocked out most of the light that had been streaming in through the half-open door. At six-one and two hundred fifty-five pounds, Robins was the kind of guy who would make anyone stop and squint. His body, his mannerisms, and his booming voice commanded attention. He looked like a big, dangerous teddy bear.

"Hey," Robins bellowed in a half greeting, half salute. "That muffler you put on last month fell off. Can you fix it so I can get another month out of it?" The mechanic laughed. Robins was always in and out of the shop with his junkers.

It was September 1984. The air was light. Winter was already lashing out against the warm fall days. Robins was a man who liked extremes. The cold September mornings and hot afternoons appealed to him. He figured it was the best of both worlds.

Moments before, Robins, a private investigator, had been en route to a stakeout in his barely breathing 1971 Thunderbird when he heard his muffler hit the street. He pulled over and threw what was left of the rusty muffler into the back of the car. It landed on the backseat and nestled there among empty white Styrofoam coffee cups and lots of old newspapers. The last thing he needed was a car that sounded like a Boeing 747.

"Bring it in," the mechanic said. "You probably did it on purpose so you could talk to me."

Robins felt at home inside the dark garage. As a former police officer, he knew the place was also a hangout for guys who stepped around the law. He was also aware that if he hung around while his car was put back together, he might get a tip about one of his many cases. Anything could happen in a place like this. Robins thrived on his underworld contacts, and even the bad guys understood that Robins was someone they could count on if they got a bum rap. He knew how to talk to the drug dealers, the pimps, the robbers, and the guys who ran them and owned them.

That day his tip came from the mechanic who wired his beat-up car back together. Standing directly under the car, where no one could hear, the mechanic asked Robins one simple question. "Do you know anything about the Bembenek case?"

"Hell, everyone knows about the Bembenek case," Robins replied, wondering what his friend was getting at. "What do you have?"

Robins knew as much as everyone else did about Lawrencia Ann Bembenek, the former Milwaukee police officer and ex-Playboy Club waitress who had been the talk of the town. He was aware she had already been in prison for over two years. But he also knew that Bembenek had hundreds of supporters, including everyone from police officers to suburban housewives who had claimed from the beginning that she was set up, framed, and was totally innocent of the crime. Robins himself had occasionally wondered about the murder.

None of it made much sense to him, and police friends had been telling him the wrong person was in jail. As the mechanic talked, something began to hum inside Robins' analytical mind. The mechanic started to get nervous when Robins pressed him for information. The detective knew there had to be more to the story. He knew the guy knew something.

"I heard the wig was planted so they would get Bembenek," the mechanic said as he tried to move away from Robins. "That's all, I just heard something about the wig."

For a while the two men went back and forth. Robins thought the mechanic knew more, the mechanic thought Robins knew more. Robins was pretending, but the mechanic wasn't. When the mechanic broke out in a sweat, Robins decided to lay off. He wasn't working on the case anyway, and he knew he could always come back and get more information later.

Once the muffler was wired to the car, Robins returned to his stakeout. It was late afternoon. He parked his wreck away from the streetlights near a huge warehouse. Robins watched a couple dozen workers shuffle into what was left of the day and lunge for their car doors. He said a quick prayer of thanks that he didn't have to live like that. "Those poor guys," he whispered into his luke-warm coffee.

For an hour, and another and then another, Robins waited and he watched. He knew it would be just a matter of time. Someone coming out late with something he shouldn't have. The air that came into the window was heavy and foul. Milwaukee factory smell.

While he waited, Robins tried to think about yesterday and the day before, but he couldn't shake his conversation with the mechanic. He started thinking about Lawrencia Ann Bembenek.

Robins was the kind of guy who hated to see someone get a bum rap. He had been brought up to believe that justice was important and that the little guy really did count. Robins also knew the inner workings of police departments. He knew that cops could pretty much do whatever they wanted and often that included fabricating evidence. He had seen it happen before, and he wondered if it had happened in the Bembenek case.

When he closed his eyes, he could barely picture Lawrencia Bembenek's face, although it was a face he had seen over and over again in the newspaper. His mind flooded with questions. He searched for a few dim memories about Bembenek, and he repeatedly asked himself while he waited, What if she didn't do it? What if she didn't do it and the killer is still out there? What if an innocent woman is in jail?

CHAPTER 32

December Nights

Lawrencia Ann Bembenek couldn't have entered Robins' life at a better time. He was forty-two, had just left a job that he loved, a new business venture was failing, and after sixteen years of marriage he was suddenly single again. Robins was devastated when all the ends of his life took off in different directions at the same time.

First it was the job. For fourteen and a half years Robins had worked in Wauwatosa, just west of Milwaukee, as a city police officer. His work was the center of his life. Close friends had never known a guy who loved his job the way Robins did. "This is what I was born for," he would often tell his buddies.

For Robins, a guy raised on the streets of Chicago, the police job offered him more than the security of a paycheck. He was the only child of a hardworking, middle-class Jewish family. His father, Albert Robins, had spent several years as a special police officer for the city of Chicago, and his stories of those days sparked something inside his young son.

"My dad will always be my hero," Robins told his good friend Jim Strauss early in his police career. "There isn't anything I wouldn't have done for him, and he taught me to believe in justice and to do what I had to do to see that justice was done."

After a stint in the Army, Robins moved back to Chicago and investigated burglar alarm calls for an alarm company. Robins then started working for the Chicago Northwestern Railroad Company. He hustled bums, vagrants, and thieves off railroad company property that ran through the heart of skid row. After a promotion, Robins was transferred to Milwaukee. He thought his new assignment was too tame, and he took a job as a department store detective. Robins finally landed full-time work as a police officer in the close-knit, insulated city of Wauwatosa.

Heroes don't always come out in first place. Although Robins worked hard to be a decent cop, the cards in the Wauwatosa Police Department were not stacked in his favor. On May 21, 1981, just seven days before Christine Schultz was murdered, Robins wrote a letter of resignation from the department and then met with his wife, Sharon, and a close friend at a small restaurant near the police station.

For fourteen and a half years Robins had listened to fellow officers call him a "dirty kike" and a "dumb Jew." He had listened as commanding officers degraded women and other minorities. He had seen police reports disappear and had watched unethical confrontations on and off the streets. Finally, when he could not reconcile what he had heard and seen with what he was trying to do, Robins quit the only job he had ever really loved.

"I can't do it anymore," he told his wife, crying softly as he lifted his badge out of his wallet. "I can't work under these conditions any longer. I quit." Robins pulled out his off-duty revolver, handed it to the owner of the restaurant as a gift, and said, "I won't need this now." His days as a highly decorated police officer were over.

Robins eventually filed a discrimination suit against the police department. He won the case but he would never stop grieving for the one true love of his life—police work.

The loss of his job threw his personal life into turmoil and his sixteen-year marriage fell apart. A new venture in the restaurant business failed. Robins filed for bankruptcy and then for divorce. By 1984 he was a financial and emotional wreck. He and his wife came to a mutual agreement about the end of their relationship, but it was Robins' job to tell their four-year-old son the bad news. It was a moment Robins will never forget.

"Mommie and Daddy aren't going to live together anymore," Robins told his son. They were standing outside a department store in the cold morning air. David Robins huddled close to his father. He was cold and scared. He had never seen his father cry before.

"Daddy, it's okay," he said. "I know you love me."

Robins promised his only child he would always be there for him, no matter what. He said he would always live close to him.

"I'll be there whenever you need me," Robins said, scooping up the boy and holding him close to his chest. "I'll never really leave you."

Robins moved into a tiny, sparsely furnished apartment on the east side of Milwaukee. For months he grieved for all the losses in his life. He

missed the feeling that had permeated his entire
being when he was patrolling the streets and
tracking down criminals. At a loss for what to do,
Robins knew he couldn't get too far away from
police work. He did some investigative work for a
Milwaukee attorney, but it wasn't quite enough.
Robins rightfully decided he had nothing to lose
and began advertising for his own high-risk private investigating services. He loved living on the
edge and soliciting dangerous cases. He placed the
following ad:

TROUBLE WITH THE POLICE?

If you have been arrested or are under investigation for drugs or serious state or federal
crimes, you need my help. I conduct defense
and counter investigations. I have 25 years experience, have qualified and testified as an expert
witness, go anywhere, anytime and specialize in
high-risk assignments.

Ira B. Robins
Investigative Services
414–527–1101
(24 hours)

Robins' phone book and newspaper ads worked.
He also advertised that he specialized in covert
operations, including secret photography and in-
filtrating gangs. Motorcycle gang members, crime
families, drug dealers, and troubled business ex-
ecutives began using his services. Robins felt half
right in his new business. He liked helping the
guys no one else wanted to help. Just because a

guy had a record didn't mean he was automatically guilty of someone else's crime. If you were innocent, you were innocent. No matter who you were, where you'd been, or what color you were. Robins enjoyed defending the underdogs, the guys everyone walked over to get someplace else. But what he loved even more was winning.

By his forty-third birthday on December 12, 1984, Robins had a few things going for him. He had decided he was going to check into the Bembenek case. It was already out of his control. His head hadn't stopped buzzing since he'd gotten the tip about the wig. Ira Robins' sixth sense—the police genes inherited from his father—were sending him signals, and he was listening.

While Robins toasted his birthday with a bloody mary at his favorite bar, Lawrencia Ann Bembenek, now twenty-five, sat on the edge of her metal bed at the Taycheedah Correctional Institution, sixty-five miles away in Fond du Lac, Wisconsin.

That night wasn't much different from the hundreds she had already spent in the same place, in the same clothes, in the same hell. Bembenek had been in prison two and a half years.

The cold, damp Wisconsin winter air seeped into her tiny cell. The night, as always, was endless and offered dark dreams and memories that were already becoming distant and foreign. The unanswered prayers that had piled up for months and months tightened inside her. She would try one more that night. Something desperate. Something uncontrollable. A silent cry from her heart—from her soul—for someone, somewhere, to help her.

CHAPTER 33

The Second Victim

Once Ira Robins started asking questions about the Christine Schultz murder, he knew he was onto something. The streets were full of gossip about the case. All his contacts had heard something. He was also determined that Laurie Bembenek would not have to continue suffering the same kind of discrimination he had suffered at the Wauwatosa Police Department. He was Jewish. She was a woman. That was not a reason to put someone in prison.

Robins sat at his desk the last week of January, planted in the middle of his apartment living room, and dialed the phone. He was calling Thomas G. Halloran, Laurie Bembenek's attorney, and he had no idea what he was about to discover. There was always a way to get someone a fair trial if you worked hard enough. Halloran was nonchalant when Robins identified himself and told him he had some information about the Bembenek case. He told Robins to come on in to the office.

The minute Robins saw Halloran his guts started to churn. It was an odd emotion, a feeling of instant hate. The tall, thin attorney had slick brown hair and a nose that constantly ran.

When the two men talked, Robins thought Halloran was somewhat disinterested. There was a hand-stitched sign hanging behind Halloran's desk, NEVER PLEAD GUILTY. Robins found it easier to look at the sign than at Halloran. He asked, "What about the wig?" and waited for a response from Halloran. He was certain the attorney would be happy to have some kind of break in the case. But Robins was wrong.

Robins was also surprised to find out that Halloran needed an investigator to help with the case. He didn't say much when Robins told him about the wig, but he did say he could use some help. A paralegal named Bill Roddick was doing some work on the case. Halloran told Robins he would arrange for them to meet Laurie's parents. He also gave him the names of two potential witnesses to talk to. By the time Robins left Halloran's office he was hooked. All the feelings he had about the case were now magnified. There were way too many unanswered questions.

Robins met Laurie's parents in Halloran's office the following week. It was February and the temperature was dipping close to zero. Joe and Virginia Bembenek huddled together in the small office. He instantly liked the Bembeneks, but they were uneasy about him. They had seen investigators and attorneys come and go. They had no idea whom they could trust.

Robins, who prided himself on being open, honest, and straightforward, wasn't put off by their lukewarm attitude. He could easily imagine what it was like to have a daughter convicted of a crime she might not have committed. He had seen pictures of Laurie and he told Virginia that she and her daughter could pass for twins. Laurie was tall and slender like her father but she had her mother's beautiful eyes, soft face, and high cheek-bones.

"You will know whatever I know about the case," Robins told them. "I won't bullshit you and I'll work my butt off and do whatever it takes."

The Bembeneks gave Robins a check for $400 and promised another $600 for his work on the case. Robins stood, shook their hands, ignored Halloran, and walked out into the frigid Wisconsin air. He had lots of work to do.

Robins continued to work on other cases while he started digging into the Bembenek case. He had an assistant who eventually took all the other cases while Robins spent more and more time investigating leads in the Christine Schultz murder case. He talked on the phone with Laurie once or twice, but he came away from those conversations with no overwhelming feelings about her. It would be August of 1985, almost a year after he started working on the case, before Robins and Laurie would meet face-to-face. Until then there was more than enough to do.

Robins wanted to read all the documents pertaining to the case, but Halloran wouldn't let him take anything out of the office. Robins thought that was strange. If he was going to do the kind of job he always did, he needed everything he could get his hands on. Robins also noticed that everything he told Roddick, Halloran's paralegal, was quickly relayed back to Halloran.

Halloran did let Robins use a corner of his office, and Robins also had access to the copy machine. When he knew Halloran would be out of the office, Robins began making copies of court documents, police reports, witness statements—the entire Bembenek file.

While Robins started to read the files, Halloran was preparing a motion for a new trial that was woven around a somewhat complicated hit-man theory that had been developed and manufactured by a man named Jacob Wissler. Wissler read a story about Laurie in *The Milwaukee Journal* of September 18, 1983, and immediately became obsessed with her. He began writing her love letters, promised her a diamond ring, and offered to help pay some of her mounting legal fees. He claimed to be independently wealthy and said he would do anything to get her out of prison. "Anything" apparently meant lying, cheating, stealing, and fabricating an elaborate story about a hit man.

When Wissler touched base with reality, he would occasionally admit that he was in actuality a slick con man who had once operated a male escort service in Madison, Wisconsin. But starting in the fall of 1983 his new job was to win Laurie's love and her freedom.

The bizarre set of events that followed would eventually make Laurie wonder if she hadn't already gone crazy. When Wissler visited her in prison, she had already lost several motions and appeals for a new trial. Robins hadn't shown up yet to save her and she was desperate for anyone who could prove that she was not a killer.

Wissler had worked his way into Virginia and Joe Bembenek's lives. They were as desperate as their daughter and they said, "Yes, please do what you can." Then he worked out a plan with Roddick, Halloran's assistant, to trap Detective Michael Durfee, Elfred Schultz's partner the night of the murder. In January of 1984 Roddick and Wissler contacted Durfee and offered him $25,000 if he would come forward with the truth about what had happened the night Christine Schultz was murdered. When Durfee received a telegram from the two men, he notified his superiors and then talked with Wissler on the phone. He agreed to meet the men at a Ramada Inn on Michigan Street in Milwaukee. He didn't tell them he would be wired and under surveillance.

A Milwaukee County deputy district attorney, Michael Malmstadt, who reviewed the contract Wissler and Roddick prepared for Durfee to sign, decided not to press charges against them. He said it was possible that the two men were acting in good faith in seeking new evidence that would help Bembenek.

Wissler then decided that he had to come up with something else to get his true love out of prison. He decided to pay a convicted killer, Joseph M. Hecht III, $20,000 if Hecht would admit that he was the man who had killed Christine Schultz. When Wissler contacted Hecht in 1984, Hecht was serving a life sentence plus fifty-three years for the contract slaying on October 14, 1983, of Carolyn Hudson, of Madison. Hudson was a Madison police officer's wife.

Hecht admitted that he walked into the woman's Madison home and pumped five bullets into her chest while her fourteen-year-old daughter watched. Following his conviction, Hecht told Madison police it was not his first contract killing. When Wissler read about the case, he thought he had also found the real killer of Christine Schultz.

While Halloran and Roddick worked on the Hecht theory, Laurie and her parents were beginning to realize that Jacob Wissler was not all he claimed to be. He became very jealous of Laurie and accused her of having sex with a prison guard. Then he listed her parents' family home for sale in a Milwaukee newspaper. His behavior became more and more erratic. He posed as a police officer and began threatening people.

When Hecht was allowed to take the witness stand during Laurie's hearing to determine whether she could get a new trial, a strange thing happened. He invoked his constitutional right not to incriminate himself.

Wissler, who threatened to blow up Taycheedah, the prison where Laurie was incarcerated, suddenly was nowhere to be found, and the authorities were looking for him. A fugitive warrant was filed against him claiming that he had made harassing phone calls and impersonated a police officer.

While Wissler hopscotched around Europe, Laurie still sat in prison and tried to understand how every weirdo in the world could find his way to her. Suddenly, Wissler began sending rambling affidavits to Halloran.

"I have put the woman I love, hate or whatever, I have put her through hell," he wrote. "My anger and the horrible things I said about her, my many attempts to destroy her appeal, were based on a broken heart and my rage at not having the most desirable woman I have ever met."

Wissler admitted that he had used his money to finance a vendetta against Laurie after she had spurned him. He said he had sabotaged her murder appeal on purpose.

"Lovely, elegant, proud Laurie had become a skinny, pale ghostlike figure," he wrote. "It seems she has not had a decent meal in a long time. Her pale skin needs some sun . . . I fabricated evidence and other things to hurt Laurie, mainly to make it look like I had bribed Joe Hecht to help her, thus discrediting him, rather than having bribed him to shut up. If Laurie stayed in prison I know that she would sleep alone."

It was not much of a surprise when Laurie's motion for a new trial was not granted. Wissler was eventually spotted by U.S. Customs agents as he was reentering the United States from Canada, and he was charged with numerous crimes.

Laurie also found out that Eisenberg was not going to get back his license to practice law. The state supreme court found out that he had represented clients in California while his license had been suspended. He waited until the second period of suspension was up and then the court found out that he had represented another client during that suspension. Eisenberg ended up in Florida working as an executive with a Florida air transport firm. He never did any more work on her case and told reporters that his lost license was "such a waste of talent."

While Halloran was scurrying around with Wissler, Hecht, and Roddick, Robins was poring over trial transcripts and police reports. There were over six hundred pages of police reports that had to be read through. In quick succession he

discovered four important and incredible facts—
facts that had been available to Eisenberg or anyone else but for some reason had been overlooked
or ignored.

First, when the Wisconsin State Crime Laboratory inspected Elfred Schultz's duty gun, the gun
he was wearing the night Christine Schultz was
murdered, they discovered blood on it. Christine
Schultz's blood was type A blood and the blood on
the barrel of her ex-husband's gun was type A.
There were no reports from the Milwaukee Police
Department stating that tests had been done to
determine where the blood on Schultz's gun had
come from.

Robins knew that Eisenberg and even Laurie
had known about the blood—but without explanation it had never been used in her defense.

Robins also discovered that on the morning of
the murder, Milwaukee Police Detective Drew
Halvorsen recovered suspected bloodstains from
both sides of the hallway at the head of the stairs
leading up to the bedrooms in Christine's home.
Halvorsen had the blood tested. It was presump-
tive positive, that is the blood was from a human
being. The blood could not have been from Christine Schultz, because once she was attacked she
never left the bedroom. But no further testing was
done on those stains either, even though the police department knew about the blood on Schultz's
gun. The source of the blood had never been determined.

Third, there was Durfee's claim that he had
thrown away his police officer's notebook from the
day of the murder. As an ex-cop, Robins knew it

was against regulations to discard those small brown notebooks.

Section 69 of the Milwaukee Police Department Rules and Regulations was clear about how to handle the notebooks: "Members of the police force shall at all times keep with them a regulation memorandum book in which they shall enter the names of the persons taken into custody by them and such particulars in each case as may be important in a trial thereof, and in which they may be called upon to testify; and also all alarms and other transactions, information and matters of importance relative to the discharge of their official duties."

Robins knew there was a very good chance that Durfee's notebook hadn't just disappeared. For one thing, Durfee had helped in the Christine Schultz murder investigation and had written numerous detailed reports about it. It would have been impossible to write the reports without notes—notes Durfee claimed he didn't have.

Flabbergasted by the shoddy police and investigative work, Robins then discovered something even more disturbing. He was going through the prosecution's "damning" evidence piece by piece when some interesting information jumped right out into his lap.

Elfred Schultz's off-duty .38-caliber revolver, the gun he kept in his apartment, was eventually determined to be the weapon that had killed Christine. Robins thought it was highly unusual that the very gun that Durfee and Schultz had checked and cleared the night of the murder suddenly turned out to be the murder weapon. It was unheard of. No attorney or investigator in his right mind would believe the gun could be used as valid proof of a murder.

Schultz had also carried the .38 Smith & Wesson into the police inspector's conference room the night of the murder. Surely the gun was passed around and there were reports about that meeting.

Durfee had checked out the gun and had said numerous times it had not been fired. Then twenty-two days later that same .38-caliber pistol had been called the murder weapon.

Robins kept reading. Surely Durfee, a trained cop and a detective, had written down the serial number of the damn thing.

Maybe it's in that brown notebook he conveniently lost, Robins told himself.

Robins could not find one report that mentioned the serial number. It was as if someone had just decided that the .38 was the murder weapon.

He immediately thought the gun had been switched. Anyone could have gotten into that apartment, including Fred Schultz, and changed weapons. His own years of police work told him that something was terribly wrong with the case. Police officers are trained not to break the chain of evidence. No one had ever placed that gun in Laurie's hand. Her own attorneys, one after the other, had never properly challenged the validity of the chain of evidence.

Robins' joy was mixed with anger. He was going to get the bastards who framed her. It was time to meet Lawrencia Ann Bembenek.

CHAPTER 34

Beauty and the Beast

The countryside between Fond du Lac and Milwaukee is littered with farms and tiny towns. The edge of the city of Milwaukee is like a long, thin line. One minute there are traffic signals, blaring horns, and steamy sidewalks. Then suddenly a visitor smells cow manure and waves to men who are wearing brimmed hats and driving tractors.

When Robins crossed the city line, he immediately felt uncomfortable. He owned the concrete sidewalks and back alleys. He rarely wandered beyond the city limits.

August in Wisconsin is always hot and humid. August 1985 was no different. No matter how hard Robins pounded on his dashboard, his beat-up car's air conditioning wouldn't start. He gave up and stuck his arm out the window. He had fifty minutes to think about what he was going to say to Lawrencia Bembenek. After almost six months of phone conversations, Robins needed to meet the woman he was working for.

His initial thoughts created a vivid picture of Laurie, her hands ensnared in metal cuffs, sitting in a prison van, moving along the same highway, quietly watching the world pass behind her. He knew she had been on the same road several times during the past few years. Once on her way to

Taycheedah and then back and forth, back and forth, for one depressing appeal after another.

Robins kept his other thoughts and feelings in check. He knew that when he met Laurie, he would be able to tell within minutes if she knew anything about the murder. He already suspected that she was an innocent victim, but he couldn't be sure until he watched her eyes.

His instincts about people, especially bad people, had proved to be 100 percent right. He could pick out a thief in a crowded department store, and he had picked out more than one murderer over the years, too, when he worked as a police officer and as a railroad detective. He had a list of questions for Laurie and he also had a few things to tell her.

Robins had been to his share of prisons and he was always glad when he was on the outer side of the locked doors and barred windows. The sound the doors made when they closed always distressed him. He could not imagine what it would be like to be innocent and in jail.

Taycheedah prison looked wonderful from a distance. The grass was green and the prison was surrounded by thick shrubs and trees. If you could hover above the prison, you would see a sweeping view of Lake Winnebago, a huge, shimmering blue-green lake just a few blocks from the edge of the prison property. There are no armed guards standing in towers, and at first visitors are often fooled by its serene exterior.

Despite its outside appearance, Taycheedah is a prison. A place where women are kept locked in tiny cells behind doors and barbed wire. The women are told when and what to eat, when to sleep, what to wear, when to go to the bathroom. There is no privacy and buzzers and bells ring around the clock. Rules govern every movement every second and every hour of every day.

Robins walked through a double glass door and across a small lobby. "I'm here to see a prisoner, Bembenek," he said into a small opening slit in a glass window. Robins signed his name and listed his address, and then he flashed his driver's license to the guard behind the thick window.

"Relationship?" the guard asked.

"I'm a private investigator who works for her."

"All right, just sit tight."

The guard picked up the phone and called to the unit where Laurie was housed. Robins moved away from the window and looked down the long tiled hall to his left. He knew he would be meeting with Laurie in a private room. The one privilege permitted inmates was to meet their attorneys and assistants in private. While he waited for Laurie to be transferred to the administration building, Robins wondered what this Lawrencia Bembenek would be like.

Ever since he had begun work on the case he had heard about how beautiful she was. Guys that he ran into after work would inevitably make some kind of sexual comment about Lawrencia Bembenek and how she would pay Robins off for all his efforts.

Robins wasn't shy when it came to dirty jokes, but he had little tolerance for sexist comments, especially after all the problems he had on the Wauwatosa police force. His motives were very simple. Someone was being treated unfairly, and Robins couldn't live with that.

When a guard came for Robins, he followed him just a short way down the hall and then made a right turn into another hall and through a locked door. The guard told him to wait in a small room, about six by ten feet. The walls were bare. In the middle of the room stood a small desk and two chairs.

"Hi, Ira," Laurie said, extending her hand as she walked through the door.

"Hello," Robins said. He immediately liked her.

Laurie wore blue jeans, a sweatshirt, and tennis shoes. She pushed up the arms of the shirt and slumped into a chair. Her hair was cut very short in front and long in back. Her face showed only a trace of makeup. Robins would have to agree that Lawrencia Ann Bembenek was beautiful.

"You know, we met once before," she told him.

"When?"

"More than a year ago and you were working on Kathy Braun's case. She's a friend of mine in here."

"Oh," Robins said, slapping himself in the head, "now, I remember."

"Yeah, I was working in the kitchen brushing up on my skills so I can get a good job when I get out of here."

"Well, there's a real shortage of ex-cons who know how to scrub toilets and peel carrots, you know."

"I remember you had on the geekiest pair of white tennis shoes that I had ever seen in my life," Laurie said.

"I try to dress for success."

Robins and Laurie hit it off immediately. He

thought she was quick-witted, funny, kind, and one of the most intelligent women he had ever met.

Laurie was amazed by Robins' knowledge of her case. She had told and retold her story so many times, she could recite every detail of her arrest and trial in her sleep. Other attorneys who came to visit her did not know that Elfred Schultz had a duty gun and an off-duty gun. No one, not even her trial attorney, David Eisenberg, knew what Robins knew about her and Schultz and the case. Laurie looked into his eyes about as deeply as he was looking into hers.

Are you for real? she said to herself.

Robins was eager to ask her some questions. He wanted to know every little detail about every moment of her life. He took out a small notebook that fit in the palm of his huge hand and jotted down notes. Robins had done this before. He knew what to ask and how to lead someone so if he knew something about a crime, he would eventually divulge the information.

"Their eyes tell you a lot," Robins would explain to men and women he trained in investigative techniques. "If they know something, if they are guilty, they will shift their eyes away from you as much as possible. They will also drop hints and clues and lead you in some kind of direction just to get you the hell out of there and away from them."

Laurie's eyes never shifted and she didn't send Robins in any direction. Four years following the murder of Christine Schultz the woman who supposedly had killed her knew less about the murder than Robins did.

"Did you kill Christine Schultz?" Robins asked her.

"No, I did not kill Christine Schultz."

"Okay," Robins said. "I believe you, Laurie."

During the next several hours Laurie told Robins everything she could remember about the past five years of her life. Before Robins left her late in the day he would lean across in his chair and tell her something he had never said to anyone else.

"I promise you on my father's grave that I will make justice happen and get you a fair trial."

He had no idea justice would be so elusive and that he was just beginning a journey that would consume every waking moment of his life for months and years to come.

But Robins was a man of his word, and as Laurie started to talk, he could almost see a huge weight shift from Lawrencia Bembenek onto him. It was a burden he was determined to carry until he saw her walk through the prison gates a free woman.

CHAPTER 35

The Circle Widens

By the time Robins was asked to leave the prison, he was certain that Lawrencia Bembenek had not killed Christine Schultz. Not only did no concrete evidence exist to suggest that she had anything to do with the murder, but Robins was convinced that she wasn't capable of committing such a terrible crime, especially against another woman.

Back in Milwaukee, Robins' enthusiasm about the case was met with little interest by the Bembeneks and Halloran. Robins kept presenting the items he discovered to Halloran and Halloran wouldn't do anything about them. Because Halloran was not interested in what Robins was doing, the Bembeneks decided he must be on the wrong track, too.

The blood on Elfred's duty gun, the missing notebook, the bloodstains on the wall, and the twenty-two-day lapse before the off-duty revolver was turned in didn't seem to faze the attorney. Robins couldn't believe it.

Robins decided to take matters into his own hands. Using a borrowed typewriter, the investigator and a close friend would spend hours each day writing affidavits about the information he had found. Halloran would look over the affidavits but would not let Robins use his office staff to help with corrections. Robins worked many eighteen-hour days, and his friends thought he had disappeared.

"If Halloran isn't interested in this thing, maybe the district attorney will be," Robins told a close friend.

Robins submitted four affidavits to District Attorney McCann. His main focus was on the prosecutor's claims about the alleged murder weapon. Robins was certain that the off-duty .38 pistol could not have been the murder weapon.

There were too many unanswered questions, and he could poke huge holes in their theory. In one detailed affidavit Robins pointed out that it was Elfred Schultz who had asked to have the off-duty gun tested at the state crime lab. Robins said doing so immediately made Lawrencia look guilty and shifted any blame away from Elfred. It looked as if Fred doubted the innocence of his own wife and wanted the gun tested to prove she had committed the murder.

Robins said that the police department relied totally on Schultz's representation that the gun in his home was the only gun that he owned other than his service revolver. He said the gun was also taken to the police administration building, examined by police officers up to the rank of inspector, and then taken back to Schultz's apartment.

He said that neither the Schultz apartment nor Laurie's parents' home was ever searched by the Milwaukee Police Department. Robins also included some trial testimony from Elfred Schultz.

Question: Pursuant to your duties as a detective, did you have weapons?
Answer: Yes, I did.

Question: Did you have any handguns?

Answer: Yes, I did.

Question: What type of handgun did you have when you left your wife, Christine Schultz, and moved in with Mr. Honeck?

Answer: At the time I left Christine and moved in with Stu Honeck, I had five weapons.

Robins wanted the district attorney to see that Schultz could have had other weapons in the home the night of the murder that Laurie did not know about. Fred never did say where his other guns were kept and Robins had an idea that the guns could have been switched. Robins also wanted the D.A. to know that when Fred Schultz turned in the murder weapon, he had passed a polygraph and the police had told him that he was not a suspect in the murder of Christine Schultz. If Fred knew he was not a suspect, Robins surmised that he would have quickly acted to shift the blame away from himself so any investigation aimed at him would be stopped.

As Robins developed his theories about the real killer of Christine Schultz, he was also developing some theories about his relationship with Halloran. One afternoon Robins carried a pile of files and books into Halloran's office and put them on the edge of the lawyer's desk. Hidden inside the files was a tape recorder. Robins wanted to find out once and for all what Halloran was planning to do.

"As soon as this appeal is over with, I'm done with this damn case," Halloran said.

"What if you don't win?"

"Who cares? I know I probably won't win. I'll just get the money and forget about it."

The conversation droned on. It was obvious that Halloran didn't care about getting Lawrencia Bembenek out of prison.

"Well, I'm going to take these documents over to the Bembeneks," Robins said, setting the bait. He knew that Halloran would call the Bembeneks and tell them to be wary of Robins. He was trying to make himself look good so the Bembeneks would think he was earning his money. That had been Halloran's set pattern since Robins started working with the attorney. This time he would be ready to tell the Bembeneks the truth.

When Robins arrived at the home of Laurie's mother and father, they treated him coolly. Robins wanted to tell them the truth about Halloran and he wanted the Bembeneks to know there was no way they were going to win the latest appeal.

"Did Halloran call before I got here?"

"Yes, why?" Virginia Bembenek asked.

"Did he tell you he was working hard for you and that he would do whatever he could to get Laurie out?"

"Yes."

"All right. I want you to listen to this. I just taped our conversation."

Robins played back the tape and the Bembeneks dropped their heads. Visibly shaken, Joe and Virginia lifted their eyes and looked at Robins.

Joe asked Robins, "Will you help us get Laurie out of prison?"

"That's all I ever wanted to do."

That afternoon Robins and the Bembeneks forged another bond. They turned over all their hopes and fears to Robins. Financially ruined and always on the brink of emotional disaster, Joe and Virginia Bembenek had joined their daughter in her gruesome nightmare. Their twice-weekly visits to see Laurie in prison were impossible journeys. They would stand and watch week after week as Laurie raced into the visitors room to greet them. Their beautiful, talented baby daughter always struggled to maintain her composure, but she never fooled her parents. Lawrencia Bembenek was hanging on to the edges of her own sanity. How much longer can she last—can we last? her mother asked herself.

Robins sat quietly as the Bembeneks released years of anger, frustration and depression. He saw a retired middle-class couple. Tall, thin, soft-spoken Joseph Bembenek was a gentle man. His wife had the strong face of a woman who had lived through good and bad times. She was kind and generous. He embraced them and he made the same promise to them he had already made to their daughter.

Soon after Robins' visit to the Bembeneks, Halloran stopped taking their phone calls. Robins told Joe to tell him he had a new case for him. That's exactly what Joe did and Halloran took his phone call immediately. Joe wondered if there was an attorney anywhere in the entire world who was really interested in helping get their daughter out of prison.

Robins agreed to work on the case without payment until Laurie's parents could come up with some money. The couple had already spent

$50,000 on legal fees, borrowed money from relatives, and mortgaged their home.

Robins approached several attorneys and asked if they would be interested in working on the case. One who was particularly interested was a well-known Milwaukee lawyer and the kind of man who Robins thought could finally do something positive for Laurie. Their meeting with Laurie went well and as Robins and the attorney walked through the prison parking lot and back to the car, Robins asked him if he would take the case.

"If I win this case and get her out of prison, do you think I can get a blow job?" the attorney asked Robins.

"Not from me you can't," Robins responded.

Robins was beginning to see the hopeless circle that Lawrencia Bembenek had entered.

Back in Milwaukee, Robins clicked on his answering machine. He stopped the machine and wound it back to the third call.

"Stay away from the Bembenek case or you are a dead man."

Robins had received his first death threat and that made him happy. Now he was positive he was onto something. He must be getting close, and someone must be getting scared.

He was certain some of the subsequent threats came from crackpots who had read his name in the paper and he was equally certain that some of the phone calls came from police officers who knew he was getting too close to the truth. Most of the calls were recorded on his answering machine. Some he answered personally. Some of the voices sounded familiar and some did not. Robins knew the threats were part of his job, and he was used to them.

The threats were always in the back of his mind and they would continue until there were close to twelve hundred. The majority were delivered over the phone. Some days the same person would call over and over and tell Robins he was a dead man. There were also letters, and some people stopped Robins on the street and verbally threatened him. Robins even wondered if the real killer of Christine Schultz had called to threaten him. But there was no way in hell he was going to quit.

CHAPTER 36

Files and Follies

Laurie's appeal for a new trial dragged on into 1986. She was beginning her fifth year in prison, and at twenty-five she knew that these should have been some of her best years, not her worst. Although Ira Robins knew that Attorney Halloran's efforts to win the motion were halfhearted, Robins could not begin another appeal or find a new attorney until the latest appeal had been completed, and the waiting frustrated him.

In April, Circuit Court Judge Janine P. Geske ruled that a lie detector test Laurie had taken the previous month could not be used as evidence to gain a new trial. Geske said the Wisconsin supreme court prohibited the use of lie detectors and she didn't even want the subject brought up during the appeal hearing.

Laurie had passed that lie detector test with a high score. The man who had administered the test said Laurie Bembenek did not kill Christine Schultz.

Assistant District Attorney Robert Donohoo, who was now handling the case for the D.A.'s office, had negative comments about every piece of evidence Halloran presented to gain Laurie a new trial. Robins was particularly frustrated by Donohoo. Every time Robins would approach him with an affidavit, Donohoo would simply look at him and say, "So what, so what?" Robins tried to explain to Donohoo that there was new evidence in the case. He used Judy Zess's testimony as an example.

"Look, this woman admitted she was coerced into making statements that were not true," Robins told Donohoo. "If the jury would have known that, there is no way Lawrencia would have been convicted."

Robins started soliciting help from the public to free Laurie Bembenek. Using a list of names he had been gathering, Robins developed a network of concerned citizens who were willing to write letters and make phone calls to state, local, and federal officials on Laurie's behalf. The people working with Robins had written letters to the editor, called in on local radio talk shows, and contacted Robins asking what they could do to help. Robins kept track of all their names on a computer and started a phone-call chain whenever he needed some help.

Laurie Bembenek's supporters included grandmothers and grandfathers, professional men and women, police officers, attorneys, and representatives from just about every conceivable social, racial, and economic background. Surprisingly, almost none of the people were involved because Laurie Bembenek was "a beautiful ex-cop, Playboy Club waitress." The men and women recruited by Robins were simply concerned citizens who wanted to make sure the justice system did what it was supposed to do. In Laurie Bembenek's case these people felt that justice had failed.

Laurie was encouraged by the surge of support

from the public but she knew that would not guarantee her a new trial. Five years following the murder of Christine Schultz she was still a prisoner at Taycheedah.

Her ex-husband, Fred Schultz, had remarried and his construction business flourished in Florida. When Laurie's case made the television news, Fred, looking very tan, was pictured driving a big boat off the coast of Florida.

Laurie also knew about the problems with Halloran. Robins told her not to count on the motion for a new trial being accepted. He also promised her that he would stay with her and work for her until she gained her freedom.

In late April 1986, Laurie decided to write to Judge Geske. Laurie told the judge that before her murder trial she had rejected a plea bargain that would have given her a reduced sentence. Laurie said she rejected the offer because she was innocent and she could not bring herself to admit that she had committed a crime, when in fact she had not.

"Please, please have the courage to right this wrong," Laurie wrote Judge Geske. "As friends and eventually my own husband betrayed me and emotionally tore me limb from limb, as people in power took away my freedom with such defiant ease, I believe in the criminal justice system."

Laurie told Geske several times in the letter that she was not seeking sympathy or empathy. She was just hoping to find someone who had the courage to look at the real facts of the case.

"I refused to plead guilty to this horrible crime that I did not commit," Laurie wrote. "The result was being given a sentence four times longer than what I could have received for exercising my right to plea bargain."

She told Geske that her wrongful conviction had broken her parents' hearts. She said she herself felt lonely and heartbroken each time she watched her mom and dad drive away from Taycheedah.

"My feelings are intense and I hurt and cry and hope just like any other woman in my four-year battle to prove my innocence. No one knows how desperate I have become at times."

Two weeks later Judge Geske rejected Laurie's motion for a new trial. She did not accept the hit-man theory presented by Halloran. Halloran wanted Judge Geske to believe that Joseph Hecht had been paid to kill Christine. Although Hecht signed a confession admitting he had been paid to kill Christine Schultz, when he took the stand he refused to testify. She also said that statements from Christine Schultz's divorce attorney claiming Fred Schultz had threatened to kill Christine were available during the trial; Eisenberg hadn't bothered to use them.

That same month Laurie filed for bankruptcy. Eisenberg's law firm claimed she still owed them $30,035. Fred Schultz had turned over his half interest in Christine's home to Eisenberg shortly after the murder, but court officials later said doing so was illegal. Eisenberg's former law firm said when Fred did not pay her attorney's fees, it was Laurie's responsibility to pay for Eisenberg's services. Laurie had a total of $68.83 in her prison account. Eisenberg had charged her up to $150 an hour.

* * *

By the end of her motion for a new trial, Laurie had become familiar with legal proceedings. She had also gained a reputation as a staunch supporter and defender of prisoners' rights. She joined several fellow prisoners in filing lawsuits against overcrowding at Taycheedah. Laurie also worked to obtain phone privileges for female inmates and to try to bring the living standards of female prisoners up to the same standard as that of male prisoners.

Other prisoners also knew they could come to Laurie if they had legal problems or questions. Many women had no idea what, if anything, their attorneys were doing for them on the outside. Laurie would go over their legal papers with them and let them know what they could expect.

By the time Laurie moved into her fifth year as a prisoner, she was seeing prisoners who had been released come back into the prison for second and third offenses. For many of the women, prison was like a revolving door. Because the majority of the women incarcerated at Taycheedah were there for short periods of time, it was difficult for Laurie to develop close relationships with them. Just as she grew comfortable with a new cellmate, the woman would be paroled. Then Laurie got a new roommate, another lifer, someone who would most likely be at Taycheedah as long as Laurie was.

By the summer of 1986 Laurie had developed a close relationship with Kathy Braun. Braun, an intelligent woman and mother of four, was serving a life sentence for a drug-related murder, and at one time Ira Robins had done some work for her Milwaukee attorney. Laurie and Kathy were roommates and they helped each other stay sane. Laurie said her friendship with Kathy was her salvation.

"Kathy became the sun and moon in my life," Laurie said. "We were like sisters. We shared each other's burdens, losses, sorrows, and we knew that the other person would always be there if something bad was happening."

Once, Laurie and Kathy got caught using contraband hair dye to keep their dark hair blond. Even though Laurie was trying to keep her hair blond, the same color it was when she came into prison, she was charged with using contraband and using a disguise.

"I immediately said it was my fault so I would get the punishment," Laurie said. "But we were both laughing so hard, we thought they were going to line us up and shoot us."

Kathy and Laurie brainstormed on legal matters, traded books, and tried to keep each other from going insane.

"I realized if I was going to make it through this thing as a survivor, I would have to maintain a sense of humor," Laurie said. "Kathy helped me laugh at myself, at the system, at having a urine check at 3 A.M., at eating cold food, and, when I couldn't laugh, she was there to let me know it was okay to cry, too."

The longer Laurie stayed in prison, the more she realized she had been a fool to marry Fred Schultz, to believe him, and to believe Eisenberg. Robins had thought all along that her legal representation had been some of the worst he had

ever seen. He was especially interested in the role
Fred had played in her defense.

Robins told her, "If you look at everything, at
the gun, at the motive, at what appears to be a
police cover-up, then Fred Schultz should have
been the number-one suspect and not you."

Robins contended that if Fred had been a suspect, then it was totally improper for him to work
with Eisenberg or to secretly pay him. He said
Eisenberg had a duty to pursue other suspects and
he did not do that. He said that any money Eisenberg accepted from Fred would have been a conflict of interest.

"Fred Schultz was allowed to be at the scene of
the murder and to help in the investigation," Robins said. "He was even allowed to identify the
body at the morgue, which is unbelievable if you
know anything at all about police work. Suspects
at crime scenes are usually removed quickly so
they cannot alter evidence."

Robins was also certain that the police were still
concealing something. He thought it was possible
that Fred Schultz knew what that "something"
might be. Robins spent hours going over Fred's
testimony, and he listened to a taped interview
that had been made on July 17, 1981, by Bill Watson, the private investigator who worked for Eisenberg.

In that interview Schultz admitted that he had
experimented with drugs, including cocaine, and
that he enjoyed some interesting sexual practices.

Watson: Have you heard Honeck talk in terms
of any kind of kinky sex or anything like
that?

Schultz: Yeah, yeah, yeah, as a matter of fact since this is for Don Eisenberg, Honeck used to have a girlfriend that came over and I'd screw her while he got a blow job from her.

According to Schultz, he also had been out with Honeck drinking one night and both men "picked up a couple of hookers" and performed the same ritual.

During the interview Schultz said that the Milwaukee Police Department had spent $32,000 "following me internally." He told Watson that perhaps the police department was trying to get rid of both him and Lawrencia.

Schultz also knew that Judy Zess had a tap on her phone during the murder investigation of Christine Schultz. He said that a friend, George Marks or George Markovich, the owner of George's Pub and Grub, told him to be careful when he called Judy because of the wiretap. Fred never told Laurie about the tap.

During that interview, Fred Schultz admitted to Bill Watson that he and Durfee had gone to several bars on May 28, just an hour before the murder. He said even though he was on duty as a detective for the police department, he was trying to collect some money that the bar owners owed him for carpentry work.

Schultz said that after they left the bar, they drove to the El Matador Restaurant on the east side, out of his jurisdiction, because he knew the waitresses would treat him well. His memory was not so clear after 2 A.M. Schultz fumbled through his notes and said he got a call to go to a burglary around two.

Robins kept paging back and forth between the police reports Durfee had written about the events on May 27 and 28 and the reports Fred Schultz had written. He noticed that three weeks following the murder of Christine, both men wrote new, more detailed reports about their actions that night. For Robins that could only mean one thing—there had been some kind of internal investigation. Durfee had mentioned at the trial that he had been instructed to write new reports. Robins knew that would only happen if the police department had tried to cover up something.

Is Durfee covering for Schultz? Robins asked himself. Where in the hell were they between one and two the night of the murder?

Those weren't the only questions Robins sought to answer. He also wanted to find out what had happened in the inspector's conference room just hours after the death of Christine Jean Schultz. According to Laurie, Fred had carried his off-duty revolver into the Police Administration Building when they had gone to identify Christine's body. It was in his briefcase even though he still wore his duty revolver. Then, while Laurie waited in the coffee break area, Fred and Durfee went upstairs. Durfee had said that officials were waiting to see them. Laurie knew the meeting was being held on the same floor as the police chief's office. Fred took his briefcase with him into the meeting.

Robins looked everywhere for a report about that meeting in the inspector's conference room. There was none. No one mentioned it during the course of the trial, but Robins knew there had been a meeting and he knew that Schultz's off-duty revolver had been part of that meeting. When Robins wrote to the police department seeking information about the meeting with Durfee, Schultz, and the high-ranking officials, he received a curious response:

Further as to your request for information that occurred on the morning of 5-28-81 at the Inspector's conference room, Milwaukee Police Headquarters, as to why Detective Elfred Schultz, Jr., appeared before a high-level investigative committee and as to what occurred at that meeting, be advised that we have no record of such a meeting as you described taking place.

The mystery surrounding Fred's off-duty revolver continued to grow. Robins wondered why Eisenberg or somebody had not investigated the origin of a third shell casing that had been turned over to Monty Lutz. Lutz was the crime lab technician who had determined that Fred's off-duty gun was the murder weapon.

After Fred's off-duty gun had been fired by Lutz on June 18, 1981, Lutz sent Schultz and Detective Gauger back to the green ammunition box he had stored at Christine's house to bring him some 200-grain bullets. The bullet alleged to have been taken from Christine's body was a 200-grain bullet manufactured by the Speeris Company. That bullet arrived at the crime lab the day after the murder.

Fred said the bullets had been issued years before as standard ammunition to be used while on duty. He said he still had some of the ammunition left. Schultz gave Lutz six unfired bullets and one bullet casing that had already been fired. Three of the bullets were test-fired through the off-duty gun and the other three were fired through the duty gun. Lutz reported that there were enough consistent markings on the barrel of the off-duty gun that matched the bullet that was allegedly taken from Christine's body to lead him to the conclusion that the off-duty gun had fired the bullet that killed Christine Schultz.

Comparison of the bullets test-fired from the duty gun and the slug purportedly taken from the body did not match. The already fired shell casing was microscopically compared with the firing pins on both the duty and off-duty guns to see if they matched. The shell casing did not match either of those guns. It had been fired through a third gun. Robins immediately thought that the third gun could have been the weapon Durfee inspected on May 28, 1981. After all, Fred Schultz—or anyone for that matter—had had twenty-two days to switch guns once the murder had been committed.

There has to be some reason why Eisenberg ignored all this information, Robins told himself. If a jury had heard these things, they never would have convicted Laurie of first-degree murder. The prosecuting attorney would have been laughed out of the courtroom.

Robins thought it was time to step up his efforts to get Laurie a new attorney. He was sure Laurie could obtain a new trial because she certainly had not received adequate legal counsel.

CHAPTER 37

Lawyers and Liars

Just after Christmas in 1986 Robins received a phone call from one of his clients, Martin E. Kohler, a young defense attorney from Milwaukee who was building a reputation as a soft-spoken but diligent lawyer. Kohler wanted Robins to go into the inner city for him and pick up some money. One of his clients owed him $18,000 and Kohler knew Robins had no fears about driving into the heart of Milwaukee to get it. When Robins dropped the money at Kohler's home, he decided to ask if Kohler would be interested in representing Laurie Bembenek.

The case intrigued Kohler and he agreed to take it on. He told Robins that Laurie had a good chance of getting out if a motion for a new trial were filed. He worked out an agreement with Laurie that if he won the case he would get $50,000. If he lost, he would be out his time and energy. He told Laurie he was confident that he could win her release from Taycheedah.

Robins' first concern was to get all the files and records on the case from Halloran. He was certain there were still memos and letters concerning the case that he had never seen. Kohler called Halloran and said he would send someone over to pick up the files from the Bembenek case. He said he was thinking about taking the case and he needed to see all the documents. Robins had been hoping to see the complete set of files compiled by Eisenberg and Halloran since he had started working on the case.

Kohler asked Robins to pick up the files for him and Robins had a friend of his do the job so Halloran wouldn't know Robins was going to see them. Robins' friend dropped the files at Robins' office.

One of the first things that fell out of the stack of files was a pink message note written by Eisenberg's secretary. A waitress from Sally's Steak House in Milwaukee had called to let Eisenberg know that someone from internal affairs in the Milwaukee Police Department had been in the restaurant asking about Fred Schultz. They were investigating him as a possible suspect in the murder of his ex-wife. Eisenberg apparently never followed up on the phone message, but it was more proof that Elfred O. Schultz, Jr., had indeed been a murder suspect.

Included in the files were dozens of letters written by Laurie to Eisenberg. Robins read them all at once and was struck by their pathetic, helpless tone. Laurie was thoroughly convinced that Eisenberg was going to get her off. She did not have the faintest idea of what Eisenberg was doing for her.

Robins quickly noticed that Fred Schultz had played an important role in Laurie's defense. Fred Schultz attended almost all of her conferences with Eisenberg even though he had at one time been considered a suspect in the murder.

Then he picked up a pile of yellow legal pads. The bright notes were Laurie's writings to Eisenberg during the trial. "Why are we doing this . . .

why aren't we doing that?" she had asked Eisenberg over and over again. Laurie's notes were an endless stream of questions that apparently went unanswered.

Tucked away in the files Robins also discovered a letter that a *National Enquirer* reporter had written to Eisenberg thanking him for help with a story about Laurie. Robins couldn't believe that Eisenberg would sell a story about one of his clients. Laurie had never given him permission to do it. Robins looked up the story.

Killer Wife Demands Alimony While Serving Life for Murder blared the headline. The article called her a "coldhearted killer."

Robins threw down the paper in disgust. If selling an article about your client to a paper like *The National Enquirer* wasn't a conflict of interest, then nothing was.

While Robins started working with Kohler to gather evidence for their motion, he also struggled financially. He occasionally took other jobs to help pay the rent, but the energy and amount of time needed to pursue leads in the Bembenek case overshadowed everything else. He was evicted from one apartment and then another. When he started having problems meeting his child-support and alimony payments, he went to talk with his ex-wife, Sharon Robins.

"I know you could have me thrown in jail," he told her. "But you know me, I just can't let go of this. If I don't do it, who in the hell will?"

Sharon believed in what her ex-husband was doing and she agreed to release him from his financial obligations until he was able to regain his private income. She had a full-time job and was living with her father. She and Robins had a good relationship concerning their son. Robins promised his ex-wife that someday he would pay her back everything he owed her. Someday, when Lawrencia Bembenek was a free woman, he would make it up to Sharon and to David.

Robins continually talked with Sharon and his seven-year-old boy about the case, too. He wanted his son to know that he was going to win. Robins also wanted his boy to know that if you really believed in something, nothing should stop you from going after your dreams.

"I can't take you to some of the places your friends are going and I can't buy you expensive presents," Robins told David. "But I want you to know there are other things that are much more important."

In the spring of 1987, Robins' devotion to his son was put to the ultimate test. The anonymous threats that had been consistently made against his own life suddenly shifted to the boy.

"We know where David is," the caller said. "We know where he is and we are going to go get him and you'll never see him again."

Robins taunted the callers. He wanted to flush them out. He was prepared to do whatever it took to protect his family. "You are just like some of those assholes on the Milwaukee Police Department," he said. "Why don't you come out where I can see you and pick on me instead of a little boy?"

The calls continued. They would come at every and any hour of the day. The voices changed, always a man, and the callers also called Robins names and threatened him.

"Who am I going to call for help—the police?" Robins asked Marty Kohler. "Just thinking about making the call is a joke."

Robins did what he always did when he had a problem, he took matters into his own hands. For six weeks in a row he stood guard by his son's house. Armed with two handguns that he carried in plastic bags, "so they won't be considered concealed weapons," he walked up the street and settled into the bushes close to his son's bedroom window. He was going to shoot anybody who even came close to his son. If "anybody" happened to be a Milwaukee cop, Robins was prepared to shoot him in the head because he knew the cops wore bulletproof vests.

Whoever had threatened Robins and his family never appeared, and Robins finally gave up his nightly vigil. The calls continued, however, and even though Robins had the phone company install a phone tap, he was never able to find out who called.

In May 1987 the state court of appeals upheld Judge Geske's May 1986 ruling, stating that no new evidence existed to warrant giving Laurie a new trial. Laurie became angry and depressed. She found it hard to believe that she was still in prison, wasting the best years of her life, for a crime she did not commit. She talked to Robins and asked him what was going to happen next. "Will I ever get out of here, Ira? Why is everyone against me? I just don't understand why no one will take the time to see what we have."

Robins was just as disturbed. "Justice has not been done here, Laurie," he said. "There is a cover-up here and it's starting to stink. If District Attorney E. Michael McCann thinks I'm like a little mosquito that you swat and I will just go away, he's in for another big surprise."

He promised Laurie that he wasn't going to give up. He reminded her of his original promise. He was going to be there when she walked out of the prison a free woman. Laurie called Robins "my own real-life pit bull" and she talked with him often on the phone. They exchanged letters about the progress of her case.

While Robins plugged away, Laurie continued to work toward her bachelor's degree and continued to fight for prisoners' rights. She had learned how to write her own legal briefs, and she continued to vent her frustrations through her writing. An untitled poem, written in 1987, was a summary of her deepest feelings and fears.

It now takes more than one hand
to count all the birthdays I've spent here.
Waiting in a dark office one cold morning
I glanced up at the tree branches outside,
noticing that they already looked like
veins stretching skyward,
and realized
I can no longer live like this.

You would think
that after years of being subjected
to so much dehumanizing
degradation and intrusion, after being

strip-searched while menstruating
(to the obvious delight of two lesbian guards)
after being forced to use the toilet
in front of many strangers,
after being seized in the middle of the night
to shovel snow or to urinate into a cup—on command,

after year upon year of sensory deprivation,
   of mental sodomy,
of being harassed,
   blamed
   controlled
   embarrassed
   segregated
   confined
   humiliated
   put-down
   accused
   criticized
   discouraged
   threatened and discouraged

you would think
the small punishments could be ignored—
when we are loudly warned
   not to let a visitor kiss us again,
when we are ordered to do meaningless work
and then lose two days' pay for being late,
when we are helplessly moved from place to place,
when we are denied a package of cookies from home.
but this meaningless oppression only grows worse—
   becomes more unbearable.

I'm tired of wondering
how many fascist assholes read my letters

(and wonder if they will reach their destination)
of being monitored by cameras
   deprived of sex
ruled by a lack of alternatives and the
   sound of bells, keys, walkie-talkies.

I can no longer watch the children
outside the fence, crying "But mommy!
   I don't want to say good-bye!"
I have no children, but I feel like that child.
I look quickly away
   from the red-eyed woman.
I don't want to see anymore.
I can't stand the paranoia, the worry and despair.

Sometimes of late
it feels as though I could explode:
   but then They would win.
I would only trade my poignant reality
for psychotropic drugs and paper gowns.
So I gather up another armful of resistance
and so go on,

for now.

In early summer of 1987 Robins was working
with Marty Kohler in the Staff Office Building in
downtown Milwaukee. While walking through the
halls, they met an attorney who was always doing
something for the rights of the accused. He walked
Kohler and Robins to the side of the hall and set
down his briefcase.

"I know what you guys are doing," the attorney
said. "There are lots of us who are on your side
and who feel that Lawrencia was taken to the
cleaners."

The attorney then took out a piece of paper, jotted down the names of two men, and handed it to Robins. "You might want to check into these two men," he said and then turned and walked away.

Robins quickly unfolded the paper and his jaw dropped. He was looking at the names of Frederick Horenberger and Daniel L. Gilbert.

"Marty," Robins said, "these are the guys who were convicted in the Judy Zess robbery, and there was a Danny L. Gilbert stopped on the freeway just above the murder scene the night of the murder."

Kohler and Robins immediately knew there must be some connection between these two men and the Christine Schultz murder. Robins now realized that Horenberger knew Judy Zess and that he had been convicted of robbing her just months following the murder. He remembered the affidavit that Horenberger had sent to Eisenberg outlining a plan to pin Christine's murder on Laurie.

There must be more, Robins thought. There's got to be some kind of connection.

Robins quickly went to the clerk of court's office at the Safety Building to look up Horenberger's and Gilbert's files. First, he discovered that the attorney who had represented Horenberger was Robert Weidenbaum. Weidenbaum had been the attorney who helped Laurie with her divorce as well as with a portion of her motion for a new trial. He had been recommended to Laurie by Donald Eisenberg.

Then Robins saw that one of the men who had been arrested in connection with the Judy Zess robbery was indeed Daniel L. Gilbert. Could it have been the same Danny L. Gilbert who had been stopped on the freeway above Christine Schultz's house the night of the murder? The coincidence seemed unlikely but not impossible. Robins immediately began trying to locate a truck driver named Daniel L. Gilbert.

Robins did find that a Daniel L. Gilbert worked for an Illinois trucking firm and that his address was a post office box. The trucking firm would not release any information about the man. Even though Robins called him repeatedly, Gilbert would not return his phone calls.

While he tried to reach the Illinois Gilbert, Robins found that two Milwaukee police detectives had located him and interviewed him. The two detectives said the Illinois Daniel L. Gilbert was not the same Daniel L. Gilbert who was involved with the Judy Zess robbery. But Robins could never find a police report about the Illinois Gilbert. There was nothing about him in Christine Schultz's homicide file. Robins kept trying to find out if the two men were related, perhaps cousins with the same name, but he was never able to get the cooperation of the police department.

Robins also thought that the connections among Eisenberg, Weidenbaum, and Laurie Bembenek were strange. Weidenbaum and Eisenberg had been close friends and professional associates. Robins discovered that Weidenbaum had been Eisenberg's law clerk at one time. Eisenberg knew that Frederick Horenberger was supposed to be a key witness in Laurie's trial. Robins also knew that Weidenbaum had represented Horenberger in the Judy Zess robbery, which Robins suspected was somehow tied in to the Christine Schultz murder case.

During Horenberger's trial, Robins also found out that Weidenbaum contacted Daniel L. Gilbert twice even though Gilbert's attorney had denied him permission to do so. Weidenbaum was reprimanded for unprofessional conduct by the Board of Attorneys for Professional Responsibility.

Robins asked Laurie if she had given her permission for Weidenbaum to review her files. She told him she had not.

In all his years of investigative and police work Robins had never seen a more clearly defined conflict of interest.

"Here is Eisenberg, supposedly representing a murder suspect, and he is taking money from the suspect's husband, who is also a suspect," Robins told Kohler. "The client is never allowed to meet with the attorney alone and the attorney doesn't even pursue the more likely suspect—the husband."

Kohler and Robins decided to pursue the conflict of interest as a major theme in their motion for a new trial. Kohler told Robins to try to find check stubs that showed Fred had actually helped pay for Laurie's defense prior to trial. He also told Robins to look for any other problems that related to Eisenberg and Weidenbaum. Robins had Kohler issue a subpoena to the First Wisconsin Bank for records of Fred's checking account and was able to locate a canceled check for $1,500 written to Eisenberg on February 15, 1982. The money was for the defense of Lawrencia Bembenek.

While Robins pieced together all the information he could, he continued to be Laurie's spokesman to anyone who would listen. Any news relating to Lawrencia Bembenek ended up in the newspapers or highlighted on the evening news. However, it proved difficult to get a serious reporter interested in the real story of the Christine Schultz murder.

In mid-1987 Robins decided to approach Channel 12 in Milwaukee with a list of everything that he had uncovered since he had started working on the Bembenek case. He had constructed a list of the main characters in the Christine Schultz murder case and had accompanying information about how everyone knew everyone else. In his investigative work Robins had built up a connection between Fred Schultz and Fred Horenberger. The two men had been business partners. Robins found out that George Marks, the owner of George's Pub and Grub, had introduced the two men and they had been in his bar and had worked on several jobs together.

"Everyone knows everyone else," Robins told the reporters and officials gathered for his Channel 12 meeting. "Marks knew Horenberger and Schultz and the other men involved with the Zess robbery."

Robins looked around the room as he was talking. Marty Kohler was with him and so was Bob Donohoo, Mr. "So What . . . So What?" from the district attorney's office. Dave Begel, the Channel 12 news director, was there as well as Mark Siegrist, one of their reporters. Michael Malmstadt, also with the D.A.'s office, sat quietly with his eyes focused on Robins.

Robins showed how Elfred Schultz knew absolutely everyone who had come close to the murder of Christine: Marks, Horenberger, Weidenbaum, Eisenberg, Christine, and Honeck.

Every time Robins said anything, Donohoo said his *so whats* and Robins could tell he was getting absolutely nowhere. It was like talking to a brick wall. Everyone had his mind set and no one would listen to anything new.

Finally, Robins sat down and ate a corned beef sandwich that had been provided by Channel 12. He chewed on his meat and looked at Donohoo. The guy in the white hat always wins, you rotten bastard, Robins told himself as he stared at Donohoo. Before this is over, people all over the world will know what kind of man you are and the truth will be known.

CHAPTER 38

Freeze Frames

In August 1988, Laurie Bembenek spent her twenty-eighth birthday at Taycheedah. By then Laurie had already spent over twenty-three hundred days in prison since her conviction.

Friends from Milwaukee sent her letters about her high school class reunion. There was news of new babies, college graduations, job promotions. A classmate had been to Europe. Another had just purchased a new home and made a final payment on a car.

Laurie was doing manual labor in a prison. She was cleaning toilets, making license plates, scrubbing floors, and trying to stay away from the seductive voices of insanity. Her writing and her few close prison friends continued to be her major sources of comfort. Her longing for things that were familiar never faded, and one morning, feeling lonely, and remembering friends and moments of the past, she sat on her bed in her cell and wrote "Freeze Frames."

FREEZE FRAMES

In a room as dark as a garnet
my thoughts turn to face themselves;
a return to earlier times
filtered through the prism of maturity,

questions:
what on earth have I learned?
I still cry over a dog that died,
years pass
and I see my family less and less.

When I was a child
I always dreamt I could fly
Sometimes I would only fly
a few feet above the sidewalk,
my arms spread like an airplane.
That's how I felt
as I looked out my window this evening,
at the yellow light after the tornado
making the wet, black highway shine.
Lightning lapped at a fat rainbow
that slid to earth.

My mom. Always calm and fresh
as the rain-drenched peonies
by the backyard swing,
her skin cool and clean.
I can picture the wind swaying tree branches
above her, at the park
in her sleeveless '50s blouse.
Safe arms to come home to.

I call old friends, hear the sounds
of their homes in the background
and get that odd, sad longing
to relive the past.
But I've grown so tired, lost and afraid
and the only thing I look forward to
are the painless dream journeys
that sleep bestows to those confined.

Somehow Laurie managed to maintain her sense of humor. Every now and then she would drop her pants and moon one of her friends. During holidays she would often dress up in ridiculous outfits with Kathy Braun and entertain the others. Sometimes Laurie and Kathy would put on heavy makeup and parade through the halls like Avon ladies. They would stuff their sweatshirts full of clothing so they looked pregnant. The women did whatever it took to make themselves and the other inmates laugh.

Laurie couldn't call what she did her life. That had all stopped a long, long time ago. "I'm existing," she said to a friend who wanted to know what it was like inside a women's prison. "The best years of my life have been spent here. It is like living in hell. There is nothing like it, nothing at all. I can write about it but unless you are here, unless you have everything taken away from you, there is no way to really know what this is like."

Supporters continued to write to her and to do whatever they could in her behalf. Many of the men and women who wrote to Laurie had never met her but had read about her case in the newspapers. Her relatives and coworkers also wrote. Those who continued to keep in touch with Laurie did so because they were convinced she had not murdered Christine Schultz. Some wrote letters to the governor. Others lobbied the district attorney's office or the United States attorney's office. It seemed that anyone who had ever heard about Lawrencia Bembenek had a hard time forgetting her and what had happened to her.

* * *

At the end of 1987 Robins and Kohler had announced plans to file a motion for a new trial. Kohler said much of the information they were going to use in the motion was not new material. Everything had been available to Laurie's previous attorneys. They just hadn't used the information properly and that was why she deserved a new trial.

By poring over Laurie's files and reinterviewing witnesses Robins had also come up with some interesting information.

He found out that Christine Schultz had been followed for at least three months before her death. She told several people that she thought it was the internal affairs division of the police department but she hadn't been sure. She said there were strange cars parked outside her house at all hours of the day and night. Christine said there were cars following her, too. Maybe it was internal affairs and maybe it wasn't.

Robins also learned that Virginia and Joe Bembenek had received a strange phone call from Stu Honeck on December 4, 1982. Honeck called to talk about Christine's murder. "I heard Police Officer Stewart Honeck state $300,000 worth of drugs disappeared from the Christine J. Schultz home the night that she was murdered," Joe told Robins. "He also said that Elfred Schultz probably took the drugs."

Laurie also told Robins that Honeck had called her parents months after the murder and was asking about all the plants that Christine had in her house. He wanted to know who had them. Robins knew that many drug dealers hid drugs in their plants because it was difficult for the drug-smelling dogs to find them.

"This would have been a motive for the murder and for a robbery," Robins said. "I can't believe Eisenberg never pursued this information."

Robins needed to obtain Honeck's statement on tape. So he called him at work and told him Mr. and Mrs. Bembenek already had the information about the drugs on tape from the time Honeck had called them. Robins was able to get Honeck to talk about the drugs and he told Honeck he would give him the tape so he could stay out of trouble. No earlier tape existed, but Robins was secretly recording his conversation with Honeck.

The drug connection also tied in with the Zess robbery. Horenberger knew that Gaertner was involved with drugs, and Robins thought that was probably what he had been looking for when he had robbed Judy Zess.

By comparing the Zess robbery and the Christine Schultz murder, Robins was able to see many similarities between the two crimes.

1. There was a man with a wig at both crime scenes.
2. Both victims were gagged.
3. The victims were held at gunpoint with a weapon held against the body.
4. A .38-caliber revolver was used in each instance.
5. Both victims' hands were bound.
6. In the Zess robbery, the codefendant was a Daniel L. Gilbert. Within thirty minutes of the Schultz murder a Danny L. Gilbert was questioned by police because his truck was parked on the freeway, just above the Schultz home.

7. Both homes were entered with no signs of forced entry; apparently keys were used.
8. Both homes were ransacked and stereo equipment was tampered with.
9. Drugs were involved in both cases.
10. Violence was used in both cases.
11. Elfred O. Schultz, Jr., had lived with both victims.
12. Detective Frank Cole of the City of Milwaukee Police Department was the complaining witness in both criminal complaints.

Robins' interviews with Christine Schultz's friends also yielded other important information that had been available to Eisenberg before the trial. Several of her friends said that Christine was afraid of Fred and that he had been violent with her on a number of occasions. There was also the interview with Eugene Kershek, Christine's divorce attorney, who said that Fred had threatened to kill his ex-wife. At least one of Fred's girlfriends also told Robins that Fred had been violent with her.

The motion for a new trial that Kohler filed for Laurie in December of 1987 seemed perfect. Kohler outlined the conflict of interest between Eisenberg and Fred Schultz. Eisenberg knew that it was Fred's gun and that Fred had a key to Christine's house. He knew that Fred and Laurie had marital problems and he had them marry again anyway. Eisenberg accepted money from Fred even though he knew Fred was a suspect in the murder.

The motion included mention of Eisenberg's

connection to Weidenbaum and Horenberger, Horenberger's connection to Fred, and Fred's connection to Eisenberg. It also outlined the similarities between the Zess and Schultz crimes and explained that several people had seen a person matching Horenberger's description not far from Christine's house. Horenberger actually lived just seven blocks from Christine's house. The problems with the off-duty revolver and the wig were also mentioned. Everything in the motion made it clear that Elfred Schultz, not Lawrencia Bembenek, should have been the suspect.

Just after the motion was filled with Circuit Judge Robert W. Landry, Assistant District Attorney Donohoo was quick to say there was absolutely nothing new in it. Donohoo said he would do his best to see that the motion was denied.

While lawyers prepared their cases, Laurie was busy filing a class action suit along with Kathy Braun and another inmate, Rhonda Ambuehl. Laurie and her friends were working with Attorney Diane Schwerm Sykes to protest overcrowding and inadequate programming for the inmates at Taycheedah. Their suit claimed that prisoners' constitutional rights were being violated. There were 247 prisoners at Taycheedah when the women filed the suit and the prison had been built to hold 126 women.

Laurie at least had another cause to work on. Although she was optimistic about her chances for a new trial, she was more optimistic about winning the class action suit.

Even though the motion for a new trial was already in the courts, Robins didn't stop working on the case. He answered every call that came into his office about the Christine Schultz murder case. Robins met one Milwaukee-area woman at a restaurant because she told him she had some information about the murder that could help him. The first thing the woman said when Robins showed up was "Lawrencia didn't do it."

Robins couldn't wait to hear her story, but she made him order lunch first. While they waited, she told him the big news. "Christine Schultz told me who murdered her," said the woman.

"When did you talk to Christine?" Robins asked.

"Just last week," the woman replied.

Robins almost succumbed to an irresistible urge to stick his fork into the woman's forehead. He ate as fast as he could and left.

Continually worried about the sorry state of his finances, Robins also had to dodge bill collectors. Robins' spirits were bolstered when the Wisconsin Department of Revenue and the Internal Revenue Service gave him indefinite extensions on his overdue taxes.

In 1988 he also came up with a unique way to get some attention for his efforts to get Laurie out of prison. He made up two huge signs, one for each side of his car. The signs read, E. MICHAEL MCCANN—THE CITIZENS OF MILWAUKEE COUNTY DEMAND HONESTY AND INTEGRITY OR A NEW DISTRICT ATTORNEY. Robins signed the bottom of the signs.

The signs generated lots of attention. People were constantly pulling Robins over to talk about the case and to ask what they could do. When he drove up and down the main streets of downtown Milwaukee, cars would often fall in line behind him and beep their horns. Robins knew that he had the support of the general public. Most people felt that Laurie Bembenek had been wrongly convicted. But he wondered how fair and impartial the courts would be.

CHAPTER 39

The Long, Winding Road

Ira Robins and Marty Kohler believed Laurie would win a new trial. Their optimism made Laurie believe everything they told her. "We've put together a motion that is straightforward and everything is right there," Ira said. "This time we are going to win."

Everyone's hopes were quickly dashed when Judge Landry, considered by many to be the most experienced judge in the state, relinquished the case so it could go back to Judge Michael Skwierawski, the judge who had sat at the original trial.

"I can't say enough bad things about him," Robins said during several interviews. "At the original trial he spent most of the time arguing with Eisenberg, and he allowed things to be presented that no other judge anywhere would allow. If he couldn't see something wrong then, he can't see it now."

Kohler was still confident that the motion had a chance, but having Skwierawski as the judge was not a good omen.

Robins also knew that Eisenberg had a terrible reputation in Wisconsin and was still not practicing law. He thought the conflicts of interest were very obvious.

The hearing finally started on May 9, 1988. Judge Landry had set aside three days for the hearing, and Kohler told Judge Skwierawski that he was going to prove that Laurie Bembenek had not received a fair trial. Donohoo stood up and said, "State's position is that there was no conflict factually."

Laurie was the first witness, and she said she had put her total trust in Eisenberg. She said there were only three times that she had met with Eisenberg alone and the other times Fred had done all the talking.

"Well, there were certain things that I really couldn't talk about because I had no personal knowledge of certain subjects that Don wanted to discuss with Fred," she said. "It was Fred's ex-wife. It was Fred's gun. These were Fred's two children. Fred was a detective, I wasn't."

Laurie admitted that she probably should have been more assertive but that she didn't know any better.

"I really didn't think there was anything wrong. I was emotionally at the lowest point in my life, and I just looked at Don and Fred as the only two people on my side. And I really—I just didn't question the situation. I was looking to them for all the help they could give me, and I didn't know any other way."

During the first day of testimony Kohler was set to call a series of expert witnesses but Judge Skwierawski allowed Donohoo to call some witness from out of town. That threw off Kohler's plan but he did not object. He was also surprised that Judge Skwierawski allowed Donohoo to call the witnesses. It was not standard procedure. Usually the defense was allowed to present its witnesses first because the defense was the party requesting some new court action.

Kohler and Robins thought that Skwierawski had set aside several days for the hearing. They were ready to go. But Robins didn't know what had happened earlier, just before the hearing began, when the judge called Kohler into his chambers. Robins sat and waited. He had no idea what was going on.

After just a few hours of testimony Judge Skwierawski announced that the hearing would be postponed for a month until June. Robins was furious. Something was wrong with the way the hearing was progressing. Robins felt as if the entire hearing had already been decided. Kohler's assistant, Ann Reilly, said she had no idea what was happening, either, but it seemed as if the hearing was a mere formality.

When the hearing resumed in June, Kohler was able to call his witnesses—all legal experts and all certain that Donald Eisenberg had done the law profession a disservice in his representation of Lawrencia Bembenek.

Thomas G. Cannon, a former law professor at Marquette University in Milwaukee, an ex-member of the City of Milwaukee Board of Ethics, executive director of the Legal Aid Society, and a partner in his own firm, said there was more than enough evidence to suggest that Fred Schultz was the principal suspect in the murder of his former wife, Christine Schultz. Cannon, well respected among his peers, said Eisenberg should have considered a number of factors when representing Laurie.

First of all, the murder weapon belonged to Fred

Schultz. He had threatened to murder his ex-wife and he had at least three possible motives. There was a financial motive, his anger over Christine's residence in his house, and his jealousy and anger over her relationship with Stu Honeck.

Cannon also said that Schultz had keys to Christine's house; there was blood on his holster that matched Christine's blood; Schultz lied about his whereabouts the day of the murder; he had access to the crime as an investigating officer; his occupation as a police detective gave him a knowledge of crime and crime detection; the police considered him a suspect; and he asserted his Fifth Amendment right when he was called to testify.

Cannon testified, "It is my opinion to a reasonable degree of certainty in the fields of criminal law and legal ethics that Lawrencia Bembenek was deprived of the effective assistance of counsel guaranteed her by the constitutions of the United States and the State of Wisconsin."

Two other legal experts, attorneys Michael K. McChrystal and Stephen E. Kravit, agreed with Cannon. "Lawrencia Bembenek put her complete trust in the hands of her attorney," Kravit said. "She mistakenly believed her interests would be protected. Regrettably the only interests served were her husband's, as Attorney Eisenberg served the master who paid the fee."

The statements of all three experts were strong and the men were all good witnesses.

McChrystal, who had helped write the code of ethics used by attorneys in Wisconsin, said that Laurie Bembenek should have been advised by Eisenberg that a conflict of interest existed because of Horenberger, because of her husband, and because confidential information about her was shared with Horenberger's attorney, Weidenbaum.

McChrystal said, "Attorney Eisenberg's representation of Ms. Bembenek was riddled with serious conflicts of interest that adversely affected the representation. These conflicts were so serious and so central to the representation that the integrity of the representation was thoroughly undermined."

Just when Kohler was getting warmed up, Judge Skwierawski announced that he was going to have to adjourn again.

Robins thought the entire courtroom, including the judge, had fallen asleep. He knew that once a defense team's witnesses were not called to the witness stand in order, it was a tough battle to make everything fit together. Robins also had a feeling the adjournments were being scheduled to give Donohoo time to go through the testimony and to take apart all the evidence. It was clear to him that something was going on behind closed doors.

Each time Laurie was transported to the Milwaukee County Courthouse, she had to go through a series of humiliating rituals. She was strip-searched several times and had to spend endless hours in a police van, chained to other inmates. In August, when she was brought back for the third time to continue the hearing, she was chained to a mentally disturbed black man who threatened her all the way to Milwaukee.

In Milwaukee she was taken to a tiny holding pen behind the judge's chambers. It was no bigger than a small closet and there was one window in the door. She was nervous and excited. Kohler came back to tell her that everything was just about ready. He said the judge had another case but it would be not more than twenty minutes before they started her hearing.

Laurie waited. She had nothing to read, no one to talk to, nothing to do. An hour went by, and finally Ann Reilly came back to see her. She said things were taking longer than expected but that everything would start soon. Laurie continued to wait. She heard Judge Skwierawski's secretary come into her office and call her mother.

"Mom, hi, it's me," said the woman. "Listen, Bembenek is here and I'm going to be on television tonight, so watch. I gotta go. Bye."

Laurie couldn't believe the woman had the gall to make the phone call knowing that she was sitting right next to her office and could hear every word.

Laurie waited another hour and one more after that. Finally a sheriff's deputy came back and told her she had to go back to the jail cell in the county building. She waited several more hours in a filthy county cell. She tried calling her parents and Marty Kohler's office but there was no answer at either place. Finally, Kohler contacted her and said she would have to go back to Taycheedah because there had been another delay.

Laurie was devastated and furious. She knew immediately that there was no way they were going to win the motion for a new trial.

"I want to wind him up, kick him in the butt, and give him a shove," Laurie told Robins. "He isn't doing anything. He isn't objecting to anything."

Robins couldn't have agreed more, but there was nothing he could do about it. Marty Kohler was the attorney and Robins, as an investigator, had no right to stop the proceedings or protest what was happening. He was just as angry at Kohler. Kohler wouldn't tell him what had gone on in the judge's chambers, but since that meeting Kohler had become quiet and subdued.

When the judge told both parties to submit briefs and gave them deadlines, Kohler met his deadline but Donohoo didn't. Robins and Laurie were furious, but Kohler didn't object. It happened again and again. They went back into court and there was another delay. Donohoo missed another deadline and Kohler didn't object to that, either.

By the end of September, Laurie just wanted the entire matter settled. She didn't want to be shuttled back to Milwaukee and she knew there was no way Judge Skwierawski would rule in their favor. She was right. In October of 1988 Judge Skwierawski made numerous rulings against her contention that Eisenberg had not properly defended her. The judge said he believed Eisenberg, an attorney who had been disbarred in Wisconsin, and not the list of experts that Marty Kohler had assembled to prove otherwise.

The following month Skwierawski formally denied her motion for a new trial. He said there was absolutely no evidence that Lawrencia Bembenek had been denied a fair trial because of a conflict of interest on the part of her attorney. Kohler immediately announced plans to appeal the decision. Back at Taycheedah, Laurie could only wait for

Kohler to prepare her appeal. But she did have several legal victories of her own to celebrate.

First, her federal lawsuit alleging overcrowding and violent conditions at Taycheedah was settled out of court. As part of the settlement, state officials agreed to reduce the population at the women's prison and the inmates who filed the lawsuit agreed not to pursue any other legal action.

The settlement also extended medical coverage for female inmates to twenty-four hours a day and guaranteed annual review of health policies and procedures. Disparities between men's and women's programs were to be corrected, at least 6 percent of the inmate population would be guaranteed jobs in prison, and drug- and alcohol-abuse treatment programs would be expanded.

Then a state hearing examiner ruled that one of Laurie's supervisors in the prison's silk-screening shop had acted unprofessionally by harassing her on numerous occasions. The officer, Dave DePrey, had pushed a doughnut in Laurie's face, spit in her coffee, put yellow-colored soda into her coffee cup and told her it was urine. He also called her names. The officer was ordered to apologize to Laurie.

She was allowed to quit working at the silk-screening shop and started answering phone calls about the state lottery. (The inmates answered questions about the lottery from a special 800 number that had been installed at the prison.) Laurie also kept studying for her bachelor's degree.

Robins continued to work with Kohler on the appeal, but his relationship with the attorney had more than cooled. Robins felt that Kohler had let

Laurie Bembenek down by handling the motion for a new trial in a less than aggressive manner. Robins felt that the motion was a strong one and with the expert witnesses they had a better than average chance to succeed.

Although Kohler continued as Laurie's official attorney, Robins started meeting daily with another Milwaukee attorney, Robert Sosnay. Sosnay, a criminal defense attorney in private practice, believed in Laurie's innocence. "It's one thing to be in prison and to be guilty," Sosnay said to a local reporter. "But to be there and to be innocent. That's something that I can hardly believe."

Sosnay, a short, stout chain-smoker, quickly became Robins' legal sounding board. Every time Robins wrote a letter, tracked down a new lead, or was about to make another public statement chastising the Milwaukee County district attorney's office, Sosnay would make sure everything was legal. Robins was convinced that with Bob Sosnay's help, they would eventually win Laurie's freedom. The defeat of that motion for a new trial had not slowed him down and he looked to 1989 with hope. "This should be a good year," he told Sosnay over one of their many cups of coffee. "They can't all keep lying forever."

CHAPTER 40

Film, Friends, and Fright

The Lawrencia Bembenek story gained a new surge of national notoriety during the first few months of 1989 when filmmaker James Benning released a movie about Laurie called *Used Innocence*. The movie was not designed for general release but was shown at small theaters and at some universities. Although a large number of people never saw the film, critical reviews appeared in newspapers and magazines throughout the country.

A native of Wisconsin, Benning was an avant-garde film maker praised for the movies *Landscape Suicide* and *One-Way Boogie-Woogie*. He taught at the California Institute of Arts. In 1986 he saw a newspaper photo of Laurie and was captivated by her beauty. Benning, who was living with a woman when he befriended Laurie, claims he was never in love with her, but simply interested in her case. He started writing to her.

Laurie responded, and soon Benning and Laurie became friends. He went to visit her. After becoming convinced of her innocence, he decided to make a movie about her.

Most reviewers panned the movie. Janet Maslin of the *New York Times* said Benning's belief in Laurie's innocence was "touching" but lacked a clear thesis. She wrote, "Benning has faith in his

subject, good intentions, and not much more."
Other critics said that Benning's friendship with
Laurie dominated the movie and he should have
concentrated on her story instead.

Partly filmed in and around Milwaukee, the
movie had no big-name stars and used excerpts
from the letters Benning and Laurie wrote to each
other.

The publicity renewed Robins' hope that something could finally be done to free Laurie. Although an appeal on her denied motion was still
in the works, Robins wasn't hopeful it would be
granted. Laurie was not allowed to see the movie
and it only played for two nights at the University
of Wisconsin at Milwaukee.

Benning had started out to make a movie about
Laurie's case and the injustices that seemed to
surround it. But suddenly he changed his mind.

"My beginning objective was to remain objective (stay outside), and look for a solution. Be a
journalist and/or detective. Find out if she was set
up," Benning said. But then, he added, his own
life fell apart. His long-time lover moved out, and
he was heartbroken.

"For a month I didn't write or visit," he wrote
in the promotion material for his film. "Then I
started again and it was entirely different. She became my friend. She helped me through. She and
prison life interested me as much as her case. I
no longer remained outside. I could no longer
make a story just about her case. It had to reveal
more of her. And some of me."

Laurie had hoped that the movie would be an
in-depth look into her case instead of a story about
Benning's relationship with her. She was still

waiting for someone to investigate the Christine Schultz murder.

During the first two months of 1989 an alternative Milwaukee newspaper, the *Shepherd Express*, ran a series of articles outlining the case. Robins had asked the paper's editors to write the stories. He was having a hard time getting anyone else interested. The series proved a good forum for him and helped renew interest in Laurie's case.

One afternoon when Robins was sitting at the *Shepherd Express* office, he overheard the secretary talking to a woman on the phone about photos of nude Milwaukee police officers dancing in public. He knew that Laurie had turned in similar photos of parties sponsored by Tracks tavern. Robins jumped up and grabbed the phone out of the woman's hand.

On the other end was a former girlfriend of the man who owned Tracks. She said she had access to lots more photos. Robins was convinced that photos of Tracks parties could hold some kind of answer to the murder of Christine Schultz.

He had already seen the photographs that Laurie had turned over to the Milwaukee Police Department in 1981, including pictures of Fred Schultz posing nude in a Milwaukee park. Robins knew that dozens of Milwaukee cops had attended those parties and if he could get photos of them dancing naked or participating in other illegal activities, he might find a motive for someone from the police department wanting to frame Laurie Bembenek. The Tracks tavern could also be in trouble if it had sponsored parties during which illegal activities took place.

In the following weeks Robins learned that a man named Peter Wolberson owned Tracks and had been convicted three times for the sale and distribution of drugs. He learned that Wolberson had employed Fred Schultz as a carpenter and that Wolberson owned at least one eight-family apartment building with Milwaukee Police Detective William Vogel. Detective Lieutenant Vogel was a commander in the homicide squad that had helped investigate the Christine Schultz murder. Robins thought the connections between Fred and Tracks, and between Detective Vogel and Tracks, were much more than coincidental.

Robins told Sosnay, "If high-ranking police officials were involved in illegal activities such as drugs, gambling, after-hours drinking, and nude parties sponsored by Tracks, and these same high-ranking officials realized that Laurie Bembenek knew about the parties and had turned over photos of illegal activities, they would sure have good reason to frame her for the murder of Christine Schultz so she would be kept quiet."

Channel WVTV in Milwaukee also began working on a news series about the Bembenek case. Robins worked closely with the reporters and was impressed when the first part of the series was aired. But something strange happened the following day when the next segment was to be shown. Robins, who had been privy to the series, didn't recognize the next set of stories. They had been dramatically toned down and many references to a police cover-up had been removed.

When Robins contacted Duane Gay, the news reporter who was putting the story together, he discovered that E. Michael McCann, the district attorney, had called Gay and demanded some changes. He had threatened Gay with legal action and Gay and his producer were threatened by the station manager. References to certain Milwaukee police officers and to Tracks tavern were left out.

Even with the changes, the series won the Associated Press Best Investigative Story of the Year in 1989. But Robins was more convinced than ever that the real story about the murder of Christine Schultz had not been told.

On April 17, 1989, Marty Kohler filed a twenty-five-page appeal with the Wisconsin Court of Appeals requesting a new trial for Laurie. His appeal was based on the motion for a new trial denied by Judge Skwierawski. Kohler still claimed that Laurie Bembenek's constitutional rights to fair representation and a fair trial had been hampered by her attorney, Donald Eisenberg.

Ironically, Milwaukee County Circuit Judge Robert Landry publicly stated that he had some serious questions about how the Bembenek case had been handled. Landry was the judge who earlier had been assigned to hear Laurie's motion for a new trial. But he had been removed from the case at the request of the district attorney's office and it had been reassigned to Judge Skwierawski.

Judge Landry told several reporters that the more he learned about the case, the more upset he became: "I just have the feeling that with this case we were never able to get the whole truth and nothing but the truth." The judge said it was too bad that Laurie Bembenek had been so naïve when she was charged with first-degree murder.

He said if she had known better, she could have raised some conflict-of-interest complaints with Judge Skwierawski during the trial or before it started.

In private, other judges throughout Wisconsin also told Robins that they thought his client had not received a fair trial. "Keep after them," the judges would say, slapping Robins on the back when they passed him in the courthouse halls. "Lots of us are counting on you to bring the truth out in public."

Just after the motion was filed, some of Laurie's supporters held a series of get-togethers throughout Milwaukee to show their belief in her innocence. The Friends of Lawrencia Bembenek had also been formed by Robins to funnel donations for her legal defense and to do whatever they could to help her. Comprised of Robins, Virginia Bembenek, and four or five friends of Laurie, the nonprofit group met occasionally to discuss potential fund-raisers and letter-writing campaigns. Robins had organized the group because small donations for Laurie's legal defense had been trickling in to the Bembeneks for years and the group could help decide how to use the funds. A treasurer handled all the money. Robins also thought the group would offer people interested in Laurie's case a chance to get involved.

The friends' group raised about $2,000—hardly enough to cover expenses and pay legal fees that had grown to $105,000. Laurie's parents, living on a small fixed income, had virtually no money left. They had mortgaged their small home and Joe Bembenek worked odd jobs doing carpentry, repair, and remodeling to help them buy food and clothing. They still owed Robins for the work he was doing and about $25,000 in attorney's fees.

Robins' financial situation was not much better. He had finally moved to a friend's basement and was pretty much living out of his car. Sosnay let him work in his office and when the Bembeneks had it, they would give him twenty or thirty dollars for gas and food.

While her supporters were busy doing whatever they could, Laurie was busy in the Taycheedah library. With the help of Attorney Ann Reilly and Robins she was writing a complaint against Judge Michael Skwierawski. Laurie filed a request with the Wisconsin Judicial Commission for an investigation into how Judge Skwierawski had handled her motion for a new trial. She had researched what she thought to be numerous judicial rule violations and oversights committed by Judge Skwierawski.

Laurie wrote, "He gave the District Attorney complete immunity from court rules, deadlines, court orders, and court procedures while requiring the defense attorney to abide by the same. He cost the defense a great deal of both personal anguish and torment and money in witness fees and other expenses due to arbitrary delays, postponements, and adjournments caused intentionally by the judge."

Laurie said that what should have been a simple two-day postconviction motion turned into sixteen scheduled appearances. She also detailed the emotional strain of being transported back and forth to the Milwaukee courthouse.

"These trips to and from court were extremely stressful, degrading, frightening, and humiliating," she wrote. "Strip searches are required before and after. Women are transported in a Milwaukee County van with men prisoners—some of them dangerous, mentally ill, or physically sick. All of us are handcuffed to waist chains. It is horrendously dehumanizing."

Then she shared with the judicial commission something very few people had known: "I had named two inmates in my motion as suspects, Daniel L. Gilbert and Fred Horenberger, and had to ride in the same van with them and about five other men. Both were obviously angry with me and I was scared all the way to and from court. Gilbert is incarcerated at Waupun and Horenberger is at Columbia."

After outlining all the delays and missed deadlines by Assistant District Attorney Donohoo, Laurie attached a statement from Kohler's secretary who had been sitting outside the courtroom when Judge Skwierawski announced that he was denying the motion for a new trial. The woman watched and listened as Judge Skwierawski turned to a courtroom bailiff and said, "Now I can get on with something important."

While Laurie filed her complaint, Robins filed another one with the Milwaukee City Fire and Police Commission. Robins knew that the commission had a history of denying citizen complaints against the police and fire departments. Out of 116 complaints that had been filed in the past few years, all but two minor disciplinary actions had been denied. Robins wanted to go on record with his complaint anyway.

Robins alleged that from the summer of 1980 the City of Milwaukee assistant chief of police Orval Zellmer had personal knowledge that certain police officers and detectives had engaged in illicit and illegal activities in violation of state and city rules and regulations. He said that Laurie Bembenek had even turned in visual evidence, the pictures from the Tracks parties showing police officers dancing naked in a public park, but nothing had been done about it. Robins included a detailed list of what Zellmer had known and not acted on. He said Zellmer had known that at least fifteen police officers, several attorneys, and one judge had been involved with the lewd and lascivious parties at public parks.

According to Robins, Zellmer had also known that Fred's partner, Michael Durfee, had broken many police department rules by throwing away his notebook, not recording his true activities on the night of the murder, and failing to report Fred Schultz for his non-job-related activities the night Christine was murdered.

Stu Honeck had also broken department rules and never been disciplined, Robins said. Honeck had had sexual intercourse with a woman who was not his wife, had denied having a drinking problem, had lied to and then threatened a newspaper reporter, had had information regarding drugs involved in the murder, and had had information that one potential witness had been threatened.

Robins also filed complaints against several

other police officers, including Michael Durfee, but those complaints were also dismissed.

On August 15, 1989, Ira Robins threw a party in a Milwaukee hotel for several hundred friends, supporters, and relatives to celebrate Laurie Bembenek's thirty-first birthday. There were balloons and party favors but the mood was serious. While partygoers waited in line to sign a huge birthday banner for Laurie, Robins worked the crowd, shaking hands and answering questions. The guests were an interesting mix. There were several police officers and at least one Milwaukee detective. Two attorneys sat together at one of the back tables. The father of a state senator made it known that he thought Laurie's murder conviction was wrong. There were reporters, a few grandmothers and grandfathers, and lots of people who had never been able to forget Lawrencia Bembenek. They believed an innocent women was in prison.

Robins had announced that he would offer evidence of a police coverup during the party. Taped on the walls in the corner of the hotel ballroom were dozens of photos of naked police officers. The photos had been taken at the now famous Tracks parties. Hotel employees joined the partygoers to get a glimpse of some of Milwaukee's finest. When Robins addressed the group, he told them that the pictures offered evidence that the police department had tried to keep Laurie quiet because she knew about illegal activities by many police officers.

"She turned in these pictures," Robins said. "She had obvious evidence that police officers were committing crimes and they wanted her quiet, and they kept her quiet by putting her in jail!"

During the course of the evening Robins shared his affidavits with the crowd. He talked about the inspector's conference room, the delay in deciding which gun was the murder weapon, Durfee's "lost" notebook, the drug connection.

Robins also told the crowd they should be appalled at the way the D.A.'s office had handled the case. "This could happen to you or to anyone," he said, pointing at various people in the crowd. "There is a woman in prison right now for a crime she did not commit and it's up to us to get her out."

Miles away, Laurie was trying to get through her seventh prison birthday.

CHAPTER 41

The Great Escape

Just after her thirty-first birthday Laurie was talking with some friends from Milwaukee in the visitors room at Taycheedah when she noticed a good-looking man walk into the same room. He had on white tennis shorts, a white tennis shirt, and tennis shoes. Starved for even a glimpse of a man, Laurie noticed that he was sitting with an inmate, Mary Beth Kline.

When visiting hours were over, Laurie walked out with Mary Beth. Laurie knew that the woman was in prison because she had a drug problem and had forged prescriptions. She had only met her once or twice in the prison library.

"Hey, who was the guy in the white tennis shorts?" Laurie asked Mary Beth.

"That's my brother, Nick Gugliatto."

"Is he gay or married?"

"Neither," Mary Beth laughed. "He just got divorced. He noticed you, too, and asked who you were."

The two women talked about how terrible it was to be two sex-starved prisoners.

"Why don't you write him?" Mary Beth asked.

"No way," said Laurie. "You can tell him to write me and if he writes, I'll write him back."

Dominic Gugliatto, thirty-four, a divorced father of three from Milwaukee and a factory worker, didn't know anything about Lawrencia Bembenek. When his friends knew that he had started writing to Laurie, they couldn't believe he was actually corresponding with the infamous Bambi. "You must be the only man on the face of the earth who doesn't know who she is," his friends kidded him.

Laurie and Nick wrote back and forth several times and he finally suggested that he come to visit. Laurie agreed and Nick Gugliatto quickly became a regular visitor. Laurie was cautious with Nick. She had been through her share of losers and didn't want to pin her hopes on a relationship that would most likely end before it started. Laurie knew it would be very difficult for any man to maintain a relationship with a woman who was in prison.

"It's not like there are men lined up to see a woman in prison," she said. "I noticed him because I play tennis and he looked like a tennis player."

Nick wasn't a tennis player, but he was kind and outgoing, and Laurie realized how easy it would be to fall in love with him. He called, sent her gifts, and visited several times a week. His visits and conversations added a new dimension to her life.

"I guess I have just as much of a right to be happy with a man as anyone," she confided to a close friend. "My life has been on hold for so long, waiting for this appeal and that appeal, and Nick is someone I can love and care about right now."

Laurie kept her relationship with Nick a secret from many of her friends and from her family for several months. When she finally told her mother that she was serious about Nick Gugliatto, the news was not well received.

"Laurie, how do you know he isn't like everyone else?" her mother asked, remembering Fred

Schultz and Jacob Wissler. "I don't want to see you get hurt anymore. Please be careful."

Laurie already knew that she was falling in love with the dark-haired Italian and his skinny legs. She wanted to enjoy every moment she was able to talk with him on the phone or see him when he visited. She was allowed to kiss Nick when he first arrived for visiting hours and then again when he left. Conjugal visits are not allowed at Taycheedah, and for Laurie two kisses were better than nothing.

Laurie's judicial complaint against Judge Skwierawski was rejected, and Robins was still waiting to hear about his complaint with the Police and Fire Commission.

But in October of 1989 the state court of appeals asked the state supreme court for some help with the appeal Laurie had filed claiming Eisenberg had not given her effective representation. The court of appeals asked for a clear statement of the standard of effective assistance of legal counsel. They wanted some help in deciding if Eisenberg had met his duty in his representation of Lawrencia Bembenek.

Kohler said it was a good sign that they were struggling with his appeal. He said the court of appeals was actually asking the state supreme court to rule on her appeal. He said that was also good because it would mean a new set of people would look at the evidence.

But the following month, on November 8, the supreme court gave the case back to the appeals court. They said it was not their duty to make a decision and it was more appropriate for the appeals court to decide. Kohler said there was still hope that the appeals court could rule in their favor. Robins said if this latest appeal failed, he was working on a few new leads anyway.

Robins wrote to Michael J. Barron, the chief judge in Milwaukee, and asked for a John Doe Investigation of the City of Milwaukee Police Department covering the years 1980 to the present. In a John Doe a special prosecutor calls witnesses before a judge and, working with a special investigator, attempts to unveil corruption or conspiracy. The investigator and judge then have the power to file criminal charges if they find wrongdoing. Robins asked that Judge Robert Landry be assigned to investigate his claims of wrongdoing because Judge Landry was set to retire and would not be worried about reelection.

Robins knew that a John Doe investigation would allow the judge in charge to have access to any and all records in the police department. The investigators working with the judge would pretty much have free rein to do whatever they wanted to get at the truth, something that Robins had been working toward for over six years.

In his John Doe request, Robins outlined everything from the Tracks parties to the reluctance of the police department to release information that could be used to help free Lawrencia Bembenek. He also asked that the district attorney's office not be involved in the investigation.

"The District Attorney's office is no help because either they allowed themselves to be duped or are now active participants in the current cover-up," Robins wrote. "That office refuses to acknowledge the existence of a wiretap on one of their main witnesses against Bembenek, Judy Zess (interestingly, this witness has recanted her testimony and says she was subjected to strong influences from the police department prior to trial), has hidden the existence of the Inspector's conference room, and refuses to sit down and even look at the information I have gathered."

Robins also made visits to Milwaukee Mayor John Norsquist's office and Milwaukee Police Chief Phillip Arreola to ask for investigations into the police department. (Arreola had replaced Chief Breier, who had retired in 1989.) The mayor and police chief never responded to Robins' complaints.

In January of 1990 Robins also discovered that two sets of unidentified fingerprints had been found at the scene of the murder. Robins used the State Open Records Law to obtain copies of several police reports that discussed the fingerprints. The records stated that the fingerprints were found on Christine Schultz's bed and on the rear door of her home. The fingerprints did not match the prints of Fred Schultz, Christine Schultz, or Sean or Shannon Schultz, and they were not made by Lawrencia Bembenek.

Not only was Robins excited about the fingerprint report, he was also certain there was more information that the police department had kept hidden. Defense attorneys are entitled to receive any relevant evidence obtained by police investigators. This exculpatory evidence has to be presented before a trial so the defense can use it if they want to. Bob Sosnay, the attorney advising Robins, immediately told him that the failure of the police department to release the fingerprint information could be used to seek a new trial.

But when District Attorney E. Michael McCann

heard about the fingerprints, he just shrugged. He declared houses were full of fingerprints and he was more convinced than ever that Lawrencia Bembenek had murdered Christine Jean Schultz. In February McCann said he was not going to reopen the case just because of the fingerprints. Assistant District Attorney Donohoo said he was pretty sure the information about the fingerprints had been turned over to Eisenberg. When he ran the prints through the police computer, Donohoo said he was unable to determine whom they belonged to.

"They were not in any way connected to the crime," Donohoo said. "They were just some fingerprints found in a home."

Robins was beginning to think he was going to have to find someone who had videotaped the murder before he could get the district attorney's office to listen to him. He knew that other murder convictions had been overturned with less new evidence.

By following up leads Robins was also able to develop two more interesting pieces of information about Fred Schultz. First, a former neighbor of Fred and Christine Schultz told Robins that Fred had tried to force Christine into participating in wife-swapping. The neighbor said she heard Fred and Christine arguing and when Fred left she went downstairs to talk to Christine. Christine was crying and told the woman that Fred wanted to try out some new sex partners. He told Christine that if she loved him she would participate in wife-swapping.

The woman said she asked Christine why Fred wasn't concerned about her getting pregnant by some other man and Christine told the woman that she was already pregnant.

Then another Milwaukee police office, Laura Schwefel, a tall blonde who didn't think she had ever owned a green jogging suit, told Robins that she, not Laurie Bembenek, was the woman two other Milwaukee police officers and their wives had seen with Fred Schultz. The officers and their wives had testified during the trial that they had seen Laurie Bembenek, wearing a green jogging suit, at a Milwaukee-area movie theater. Schwefel said that she hadn't come forward with the information because she was afraid for her life and that she would lose her job.

Robins was also notified by the Police and Fire Commission that his complaint against the police department didn't have standing because he wasn't the aggrieved party. The complaint would have to come from Laurie, and she could file it when and if she ever got out of prison.

Judge Michael Barron, who had received Robins' request for a John Doe investigation, told him immediately that he would have to rewrite the request in affidavit form. Robins threw up his hands. He felt as if he were bashing his head against a wall.

While Laurie suffered through her latest disappointments, she did have something and someone else to occupy her thoughts and time. She was going to marry Nick Gugliatto. Robins would be their best man. If they could get the necessary permission from the warden, Nick and Laurie planned on marrying in the prison chapel in August. Laurie's family had finally accepted the idea. They could see that Nick had made a difference in their daughter's life.

For months Laurie's mother had been dogged with a nagging feeling that something was going to happen to Laurie. The feeling kept her awake at night, and she eagerly awaited phone calls from her daughter. Virginia Bembenek knew that 1989 had been a rough year for Laurie. Just when she would get excited about the possibility of a hearing or motion going in her favor, her hopes would be dashed. She knew that Laurie had been attending a suicide prevention group at the prison. The thought of spending more years in prison was too much for her daughter to take.

Although Laurie would be eligible for parole in 1993, after serving eleven years and three months, it was common knowledge among inmates that the first parole date was just that, a date. The busy bureaucrats in the state capitol in Madison had changed sentence classifications that made it almost impossible for someone with a sentence like Laurie's to get out of prison until she had been there at least fifteen years.

"At least with Nick, I know that someone cares about me and he has given me something to hope for and to wait for while I wait for everything else," Laurie told a friend in Milwaukee.

The warden agreed to let them marry in the prison chapel on August 5, 1990, and she busied herself with wedding plans. She ordered a dress and shoes and wondered what it would be like to be making the same plans somewhere besides a state prison.

In May Laurie made headlines again when the University of Wisconsin–Parkside campus announced that she would be a member of the grad-

uating class of 1990. She had completed all but
one class requirement for a bachelor's degree in
humanities and had maintained an almost perfect
grade-point average for four years. But Taycheedah officials wouldn't let her attend the graduation ceremonies. They said because she still had
to finish up one class, she couldn't technically be
considered a graduate.

Laurie was devastated by the news. She had
been planning on attending her graduation ceremony for five years and had worked hard to maintain her grades.

Then the following month, on June 20, the court
of appeals announced in an eighteen-page decision
that they were rejecting Laurie's bid for a new trial.
The court did not want its decision published. The
court said that Fred Schultz's contribution to her
defense was small and that it was not uncommon
for a husband to pay his wife's legal fees.

The decision left Laurie totally depressed. It
seemed as if the whole world was against her.

How many husbands paying for their wife's defense are murder suspects for the same crime?
she asked herself. Laurie knew there were no easy
answers for her questions, but she also knew that
Robins would keep trying to find them anyhow.
Somehow that didn't seem to be enough.

She had been in prison for eight years. Each
year had seemed like a hundred. Everything she
had ever called her own had been taken from her.
All she had left was her sanity and Nick.

At 9:25 P.M. on July 15, 1990, prison guards at Taycheedah were doing a routine check to make sure
all the inmates were in their cells. Everyone was
accounted for except Lawrencia Ann Bembenek.

CHAPTER 42

Finding Fate Again

By midnight Taycheedah officials had searched the entire compound and there was no sign of Laurie Bembenek. Warden Nona Switala used dogs to cover the grounds, and the guards had looked through every building. The guards did find a section of barbed-wire fence that had been pulled down with a woman's belt. They also found that the screen in the basement laundry room of Laurie's housing unit had been pushed out. The last time anyone remembered seeing Laurie she had been doing her laundry.

By early morning on July 16 the news of Lawrencia Bembenek's escape from prison was the biggest story throughout the Midwest. Police officials didn't have much to say about how Laurie got out of the prison. They said they found some footprints leading into a wooded area near the prison. But no one knew where she was. They also hinted that Laurie might be on the run with her fiancé, Dominic Gugliatto. He had not shown up for work that morning and was also missing.

Police stations throughout Wisconsin received phone calls about the missing couple, but no one had actually spotted Laurie and Nick. Most of the callers wanted the cops to know that if Lawrencia Bembenek showed up at their house, they were not going to turn her in.

The Milwaukee County district attorney's office was quick to let the world know that a convicted killer was on the loose. They were also eager to check out Robins as a person who may have helped her escape. Police detectives called Robins to find out where he had been the night Laurie escaped.

Fred Schultz told reporters that he was fearful that Laurie Bembenek was on her way to Florida to kill him. When a Florida woman was murdered, Fred also said he was certain that Laurie had something to do with it. He had no proof that Laurie was even in Florida but Fred told reporters she should be considered the number-one suspect.

Supporters of Laurie Bembenek prayed that she was safe. Rumors immediately circulated that some Milwaukee police officers had killed her so that she would not be able to testify against them. Someone called in to say that he knew Laurie and Nick were in Mexico. Someone else spotted her in northern Wisconsin near some land that Nick Gugliatto owned.

But not one really knew where she was. Laurie Bembenek had disappeared. Nick's gray GMC truck was found three days after the escape in a department store parking lot just outside the Milwaukee city limits. When it was dusted for fingerprints, the police didn't find any that matched Laurie's.

Gugliatto's friends and relatives speculated that the two ran off together because they were in love and because they were frustrated by the legal system. Five days following her escape, authorities were certain that Gugliatto had helped her. But they still had no idea where Nick and Laurie had fled. A nationwide alert for Laurie was issued and the Fond du Lac sheriff said he was confident that she would be found.

News of Laurie's escape gradually drifted across the United States and magazines and newspapers resurrected her story. "Geraldo," "Inside Edition," "Hard Copy," "A Current Affair," and every major newspaper in the country ran stories about her. Reporters called her close friends in Wisconsin looking for any piece of information that could be used in a story. Nick's family held a news conference outside their Milwaukee home to say that they supported their son and they believed in Laurie Bembenek's innocence. They said they hoped the escape would help Laurie get a new trial.

Days passed and still there was no trace of Gugliatto and Bembenek. Friends and relatives of Laurie were put under surveillance. Phones were tapped. Once, when a moving van pulled in across the street from Joe and Virginia Bembenek, undercover Milwaukee police officers rushed in. They were certain Laurie was in the truck and had come to visit her parents.

Milwaukee restaurants and bars immediately capitalized on Laurie's escape. Someone printed up bright pink RUN, BAMBI, RUN bumper stickers. Other cars sported white stickers that said GO LAWRENCIA GO. There were Bembenek Burgers and "going-to-Mexico" burgers. One bar held a Laurie Bembenek look-alike contest. Another sold T-shirts that depicted a picture of a belt hanging over a barbed wire fence and a leg disappearing into the woods.

* * *

Robins and Laurie's former attorney, Marty Kohler, did not know that Laurie Bembenek had planned to escape. They both told authorities they had no idea where she was.

"I hope she is safe," Robins said on television. "I know that being on the run can be a worse prison than being in jail."

Although Robins could understand Laurie's frustration with the legal system, he also knew that his work would come to a standstill until she was captured. Without Laurie in custody, new appeals and motions could not be filed.

While he waited, Robins capitalized on the renewed interest in Laurie's case. He gathered several thousand signatures on a new petition to try to get her a new trial and organized a rally to show support for her. About five hundred people gathered on the lawn in front of District Attorney E. Michael McCann's office to listen to Robins. Some supporters attending the rally wore Lawrencia Bembenek look-alike masks and shouted, "We want a new trial."

One local television station conducted a random poll asking viewers about Laurie's innocence or guilt. The phone lines were flooded with calls. The overwhelming majority of callers thought that Laurie Bembenek was innocent.

Joe and Virginia flew with Robins to New York City and appeared on "Geraldo." It was a good forum for Laurie's story, Robins thought, and generated lots of support. Fred Schultz appeared via satellite on the show and with him was a surprise guest, Donald Eisenberg.

Somehow Fred and Eisenberg had gotten together. Eisenberg said that he now believed Laurie was guilty. Geraldo introduced Fred as "the very man some suspect is responsible for the murder." When he asked Virginia if she saw anyone who might be the real murderer, she immediately pointed to Fred Schultz. "He had the most to gain," she said.

Back in Milwaukee Robins took advantage of the publicity and asked for the district attorney's resignation. McCann reacted by telling Robins he was welcome to bring in any new evidence any time he wanted. He said the courthouse was open from eight to five.

By the beginning of September Laurie had been free for almost sixty days. Supporters counted each day she was gone as a good omen. They knew the longer she was missing, the harder it would be for authorities to locate her.

Robins continued to check out leads on the case. One proved particularly fruitful. He contacted Sharon M. Niswonger, the woman who had lived in the apartment next to Laurie and Fred on 20th Street. The wig that was recovered and subsequently tied into the Christine Schultz murder had been pulled from Niswonger's drain.

Niswonger told Robins that something strange happened just a few weeks following the murder. She said Judy Zess called to ask her if she wanted to go to the gym and work out with her. Niswonger thought the call was strange because she rarely saw her neighbor. That same day Judy arrived at her apartment. She was wearing a dress and had a gym bag with her. Niswonger let Judy into the apartment and then Judy asked if she could go into the small bathroom and change her clothes. Judy took the gym bag into the bathroom with her. Then she left.

The next person who used the toilet discovered that it was clogged and wouldn't work. Niswonger said when the toilet was inspected by a plumber, the reddish wig was pulled out of it. While no one had actually seen Judy Zess put a wig in the toilet, Robins thought there was a good chance that is exactly what had happened. Sharon Niswonger agreed to give him a written statement of her story.

George Marks, the owner of George's Pub and Grub, also admitted to Robins that Detectives Durfee and Schultz had been drinking with him on the night Christine was murdered. He said the men drank at two different bars and once, around 2 A.M., Schultz disappeared for a short time.

"I thought he was just using the bathroom," Marks said.

Marks also admitted that Fred had been with friends and a working companion, Fred Horenberger. Horenberger was the same man Robins suspected had something to do with the Christine Schultz murder and the same man who had robbed Judy Zess. Marks said he had introduced the two men, and they had been seen together numerous times in his bar.

Robins thought that Marks's statement was a major breakthrough in the case because it linked Fred Schultz and Horenberger. It also obliterated Fred Schultz's alibi the night of the murder. During Laurie's trial, Fred claimed he had been working all night and had never left Durfee. Marks said that was not true.

"I have thought all along that Durfee and

Schultz have been lying about their whereabouts on the night of the murder," Robins told Sosnay, his attorney friend. "They were supposedly taking care of a robbery that night, but when they wrote their initial reports, they didn't even have the name of the robbery victim."

By researching the police reports Robins could see that initially Durfee and Fred said they had been on patrol, stopped to eat, and then investigated the burglary. But when Robins read through the court testimony, he realized that Eisenberg knew that Fred and Durfee had been at George's the night of the murder. Eisenberg had asked him about it in court and Fred had admitted they had been there but said he had not gone there to drink.

Kramer and the entire district attorney's office also knew that Fred Schultz had lied on the witness stand. No one but Fred and Durfee knew exactly where they were and what had happened on the night Christine was murdered.

When Robins requested the police reports from the burglary that Fred and Durfee had allegedly handled the night of the murder, half of the report was missing. Using covert means Robins finally got the rest of the report and saw that two uniformed officers had done the work on the burglary that night. Usually detectives handle all the investigative work at a burglary crime scene. Durfee and Fred had been the detectives on duty that night and they had not even known that there were suspects in the burglary.

Robins was positive he had finally broken Fred Schultz's alibi for the night of the murder. But even with the new information received from Marks, Robins was unable to get the D.A.'s office to consider looking into the case. As far as they were concerned, there was no new evidence.

As the weeks passed, interest in the Bembenek case continued. By the beginning of October Robins was still getting phone calls from people throughout the world who wanted to know about Laurie. Magazine and newspaper reporters from London, Japan, Australia, and France talked to him. During the second week of October a segment on Laurie was aired on the television program "America's Most Wanted." Just days after the show aired, the FBI received a tip from a man who had recently visited Canada. He told an FBI agent that a woman who had waited on him at a restaurant looked just like Lawrencia Bembenek.

That tip was one of dozens received by FBI agents following the show. It sounded possible, though. Canada wasn't that far from Wisconsin, and a detective from the Royal Canadian Mounted Police was sent to a small café in Thunder Bay, Ontario, a striking city surrounded by mountains and lakes on the shore of Lake Superior.

The detective questioned a waitress at the café who said her name was Jennifer Lee Gazzana. When he left he checked the identification she had given him and found out that it was not valid. The waitress was Lawrencia Bembenek. She had been living in Thunder Bay with Nick since the escape. Nick had been using the name Anthony Gazzana and was working as a short-order cook. Besides her waitressing job, Laurie also worked as an aerobics instructor.

Nick and Laurie were packing to leave when they were captured. They surrendered quietly and were taken to the Thunder Bay District Jail, on the shore of Lake Superior. Laurie assumed they would be immediately deported but that didn't happen. One day passed and then another.

Outside the prison, reporters and photographers began gathering from throughout the United States, Europe, Canada, and Japan. Laurie's new Canadian friends also came to show support for the woman they knew as Jennifer. They couldn't believe that Jennifer was a cold-hearted killer.

Louis Kebezes, Laurie's boss at the Columbia Grill & Tavern, said he would trust her with anything. "She was a terrific waitress, very popular," he said. "She was also very nice and everyone liked her."

Laurie and Nick had rented a small basement apartment from a woman named Jenny Beck just days after Laurie escaped. Beck also came to Laurie's defense and said that Laurie and Nick helped out everyone in the neighborhood. She said Laurie would cut the grass and do all kinds of jobs without anyone asking her.

Inside the jail Laurie was told to get dressed because she was going to her deportation hearing. No one came. Three hours passed. Finally, a guard came in and said that nothing was going to happen that day. Laurie hadn't bothered to call an attorney because she was certain she would just be whisked back to the United States. When the hearing was delayed, Laurie realized there had to be a problem.

"I told the guard I wanted to call an attorney," Laurie told a writer. "The first name on the list was a woman from Thunder Bay who had a great reputation. The guard left to call her and I waited some more."

The guard finally came back, hours later, and said she was having problems getting in touch with the attorney. Laurie told her to call the next name on the list. That attorney was Dave Dubinsky. A recent law school graduate, Dubinsky had no problems making his way through the crowd of reporters camped outside Thunder Bay jail. He was dressed in a pair of jeans and a stylish top. No one suspected he was an attorney who was coming to see Lawrencia Bembenek.

Dubinsky listened to Laurie's story. He took notes as Laurie told him everything she could about her case. He told her he would represent her and that he would talk to his superior, Attorney Ron Lester, about her case. Laurie waited some more and the following day Dubinsky came back to see her.

"This is an incredible case," he told her. "I think you may have a claim here for refugee status."

For the first time in ten years Laurie Bembenek felt that fate was finally being kind to her. She had figured she would be going back to the United States, but she had an attorney who said that maybe, just maybe, it was possible for her to stay in Canada and to live as a free citizen.

CHAPTER 43

Answered Prayers

Laurie and Nick's attorneys were able to obtain an immediate delay in their deportation hearings. That would give both attorneys time to do some homework, and they hoped it would lower their prisoners' profile. Dubinsky had convinced Ron Lester to help him with the case. Laurie told Lester that she didn't have any money. Lester, a soft-spoken, bespectacled man who had an impeccable record, said he didn't care. If she ever got any money, she could send him some, but until then he would do whatever he could for her. He believed she was an innocent woman. In the United States the attorneys would be keeping track of every second they spent with her so they could add it to the bill. Dubinsky and Lester were kind, concerned, and they actually cared about Laurie's claim of innocence.

While Laurie waited for her hearing, she had plenty of time to adjust to her new prison and to remember what the past three months of her life had been like. Close friends were surprised to learn that she had been relieved when she was captured.

"Actually, being on the run was like going from one prison to another," she said. "I had to be just as careful about what I said and who I talked to. The one good thing was that with these new people I had no history and they couldn't judge me by what someone else had said. They knew me for who I was."

Once they got to Canada and moved into the apartment, she was too frightened to go anywhere alone. "It was like something was holding me back. I guess I had become so institutionalized that I wanted someone to tell me it was okay to go out and do something. For ten years someone has been telling me when I can go to the bathroom, eat, sleep, or breathe."

Her months of freedom were like a dream. In restaurants, she ordered fresh vegetables, something she had not eaten in ten years, and she almost fainted when she walked into a grocery store.

"I could actually get whatever I wanted and I was overwhelmed by all the decisions," she recalled to a friend. "Just being able to ride in a car was like taking a trip to the moon. It was unbelievable."

After years of sensory deprivation, Laurie was moved to tears when she took her first bus ride. "The colors, the people, the freedom. It was all just too much. It was like moving in a dream. There was a certain sense of unreality to everything that I did and saw during those months."

Laurie's favorite pastime was sitting on the back step of the house and watching the night sky. "The Northern Lights were phenomenal," she remembers. "I could sit there as long as I wanted to, and breathing the air was like breathing in new life."

When Nick wasn't working or fishing, they spent lots of time walking. Laurie wanted to pet every animal she saw. If she spotted someone walking a dog on the opposite side of the street, she would immediately run as fast as she could to touch the animal. She wanted to bend down and smell every flower. She wanted to live every day like it was her last day on the face of the earth.

One night Nick took her fishing on a lake close to Thunder Bay. The lake was surrounded by pine trees, and the moon hung over the edge of the trees like a big orange ball.

"That scene is embedded in my mind now," Laurie said. "Years ago I would never have become so emotional by simply watching the moon, but it was something I had not seen in many, many years and it was all very intense."

After sleeping alone for almost ten years, Laurie was also glad to have someone to hold her. Just to be able to have someone touch her openly was something she had not been able to experience in years, either. Because she was a prison escapee, Laurie could not really open up with anyone besides Nick. She was afraid to write down her feelings and she was lonely.

"I would write something and then immediately tear it up and burn it," Laurie said. "I missed my family and wondered constantly if everyone was all right. It was very, very exhausting living like that, day after day."

Once she was captured Laurie could at least remember the sunsets, the bright colors of early morning, and the smell of fresh food simmering on the stove. Her memories were no longer ten years old.

The Thunder Bay jail was one of the worst Laurie had ever been in. Designed as a holding facility for short-term inmates, the jail was not equipped to handle women. It was no more than a cage inside a room. There were three cells and three bunkbeds and a picnic table soldered to the bars. The men were allowed to work but not the women. There was one small television, and the female inmates had to beg for recreation. The men were allowed to leave the prison to play bingo and participate in sporting games outside. But the women had no planned activities. It took days of negotiation for the female inmates to win approval for just a few minutes of fresh air.

Prisoners were not allowed to make phone calls but cigarettes could be purchased at the canteen. Because smoking was not permitted throughout the jail, the guards would congregate in the women's section to smoke. Mail was censored and the guards made Laurie erase anything they disagreed with.

While many of the guards were sympathetic to Laurie, she had particular trouble with two young male guards, Brian McNeil and Dan Haig. Once, when Ron Lester was coming in to see her, Haig turned to him and said, "When the fuck are we getting rid of her? She's a pain in the ass and she gets about forty fucking letters a day that we have to process."

Laurie quickly became ill. The women's jail often filled up with psychiatric patients who walked the streets and carried an assortment of diseases. By the time she was allowed to see a doctor, she was so sick she had to be pumped full of antibiotics. Jail officials did allow a contact visit between Laurie and her parents. At an emotional meeting, they embraced, cried, and then cried some more. Her mother was relieved that her daughter was safe and that she could hold her in her arms once again.

In November Laurie's good news continued. Canadian Immigration Minister Barbara McDougall rescinded a certificate that she had signed the previous month declaring Laurie a danger to the Canadian public. That certificate had also barred her from applying for refugee status.

To help with her latest legal battle, Ron Lester contacted Frank Marrocco, of Toronto. Marrocco had helped write the Canadian immigration laws, and he was often referred to as the F. Lee Bailey of Canada. After talking with Lester, Marrocco agreed to help with the case. Once he went through Laurie's legal files, he was hooked. Marrocco told Laurie if her case had come before the Canadian courts, it would have been dismissed. His professional integrity would not allow him to abandon Lawrencia Bembenek, a woman he thought had been wrongly accused of a terrible crime.

Marrocco and Lester immediately began work on a case that they hoped would show Laurie had a credible basis for applying for refugee status. They were going to prove that she had been persecuted in the United States.

Marrocco told a reporter, "It's obvious the U.S. justice system failed her, but I'll be damned if I'll stand by and watch the Canadian immigration system fail her. I don't think Canada should be a party to this."

Robins and Marrocco immediately began working together. When Marrocco said he needed everything Robins could give him, Robins pulled out his file drawers, threw them in his car trunk, borrowed some money, and drove up to Canada.

Laurie's attorneys had several bridges to cross before she could actually apply for the refugee status. First, they had to show that she was entitled to apply. They had to prove that if Laurie Bembenek returned to the United States, she would be further persecuted. Then they could proceed to a hearing before an immigration adjudicator and an immigration board member. If those officials agreed that there was a credible basis for her fears, then she could be passed on to another panel that could allow Laurie to stay in Canada.

While her attorneys worked to prepare her case, Nick was deported back to Fond du Lac and charged with helping Laurie escape from jail. He was released on $10,000 bail while he waited for his September hearing. But after several weeks, he returned to jail because it was impossible to come up with the bail interest payments each month.

Laurie was transferred to a detention center near Toronto so she could be closer to the hearings site and because Marrocco wanted to see her on a regular basis. The detention center was a more modern facility and although the prison population was transient, Laurie had more privileges. She could make phone calls, participate in some activities, and have visitors for twenty minutes twice a week.

In February of 1991 Marrocco filed a ninety-one-page brief with Canadian immigration officials outlining why Laurie should not be returned to the United States. The brief outlined the entire case and focused on the circumstantial evidence that had been used to convict Lawrencia Bembenek. Marrocco picked apart each piece of evidence—the wig, the gun, the green jogging suit, the hair, and the testimony of the witnesses. He wanted the officials to know that they should not even consider her murder conviction when deciding if Laurie should be granted refugee status. Marrocco also pointed out Laurie's actions to show that male police officers were treated differently from female officers in Milwaukee, Wisconsin. He wanted the men and women deciding her fate to know that there had been more than one reason to get rid of Laurie Bembenek.

While Marrocco was championing Laurie's cause in Canada, someone else had taken it up in Milwaukee. For months, a Milwaukee attorney, Mary Woeherer, had been thinking about the Bembenek case. A deeply religious woman, Woeherer had always believed in Laurie's innocence and she had included Laurie in her daily prayers.

Woeherer, whose legal expertise included pathology, had always thought that the bullet removed from Christine Schultz's body had been switched and replaced with a bullet from Fred Schultz's off-duty weapon. She knew the key to the case would have something to do with pathology. Co-teacher of a class on medical ethics at the Medical College of Wisconsin, Woeherer felt that she was being guided by a higher force when her co-teacher in 1991 turned out to be Dr. Chesley Erwin. Erwin had been the chief medical examiner in Milwaukee when Christine Schultz was murdered, and he agreed with Woeherer's theory about the bullet.

Mary Woeherer, a petite blonde, quickly became a driving force in Laurie's bid for freedom. She worked closely with Robins and found that her theory about the switched bullets was correct. She also told Robins and the Bembeneks that her work was pro bono; she wouldn't accept a dime.

First, Robins and Woeherer contacted Dr. Elaine Samuels, the assistant medical examiner who had handled Christine Schultz's body. Samuels had never wavered in her belief that the body had been tampered with and that Laurie Bembenek had not killed Christine. Woeherer quickly discovered that when Samuels had removed the bullet from Christine's body she had written the initials CJS, for Christine Jean Schultz, on the bottom of the bullet. But the bullet that was presented at the trial had six initials on it.

"You could tell that the other three initials were not even the same handwriting," Woeherer said during an interview. "One set had been written with one kind of pen, and the other set had been written with another kind of pen."

Woeherer then pursued another idea. She wanted to see close-up photos of the bullet wound in Christine Schultz and she wanted to compare that hole with the muzzle of Fred Schultz's off-duty gun. She asked several experts if the wound could be larger than the muzzle of the gun. "Absolutely not," the experts told her. "The wound in Christine's body could not be larger than the muzzle of the gun used to make the hole."

"When we went to look at the guns and com-

pared them with the wound, we were all amazed,"
said Woeherer. "There is no way that the off-duty
gun could have been the weapon that killed Christine Schultz."

To bolster her theory, Woeherer got her two experts to write detailed affidavits concerning the
size of the bullet hole and the muzzle. Dr. John
Hillsdon Smith, director of forensic pathology in
the Ministry of the Solicitor General in Ontario, a
renowned pathology expert, said the diameter of
the off-duty gun was 13.29 millimeters and the diameter of the wound was 17.21 millimeters.

Another well-known pathology expert from the
United States, Dr. Werner Spitz, examined the
same weapons and photos of the bullet hole. He
was emphatic in his findings, too. "The alleged
murder weapon identified at the trial of Lawrencia Bembenek is not the weapon that murdered
Christine J. Schultz," he told reporters.

Mary Woeherer still wasn't finished. She knew
that Dr. Samuels had always claimed that there
had not been a blond hair, supposedly from the
recovered wig, on the body of Christine Schultz
when she examined it.

Woeherer said to a writer, "The witnesses were
sequestered at the trial and Dr. Samuels, who is
one of the most brilliant women I have ever met,
did not know during the trial that the blond hair
had been introduced as evidence against Laurie.
She was never allowed to say that she thought the
chain of evidence had been broken and that the
hair had been planted in the gag used on Christine."

Robins and Woeherer finally obtained all the
crime lab reports concerning the murder, some-

thing Robins had been attempting for almost seven years. For some inexplicable reason the police department and the district attorney's office both agreed to release the crime lab reports. By going through the records Woeherer was able to see that a number of things had interfered with the chain of evidence.

It would have been simple for someone to remove a hair from one of Laurie's police uniforms and put it on the bandana. She was more certain than ever that Laurie had been framed.

"This gets to be a very frightening thing," Woeherer said. "You wonder how many people are involved in this and how high up the corruption goes. We are talking about a person's entire life here. Laurie Bembenek needs to be out of prison. She has been there way too long for something she did not do."

By closely working over the pathology reports, Woeherer also determined that the tests done to see if Christine had been sexually assaulted were inconclusive. The lab did find traces of a fluid that could have been semen. Robins knew that Christine had been cross-referenced in the crime lab records as a possible sexual assault victim and Woeherer's findings boosted that theory.

In April, Canadian immigration adjudicator Carmen DeCarlo claimed that Lawrencia Bembenek was entitled to a credible basis hearing. That meant Marrocco could proceed with a hearing and present any information he had to show why Laurie should be allowed to stay in Canada. The hearing was postponed until June so Marrocco could line up his witnesses.

When the hearing resumed in June, James Morrison, the attorney who had once worked for Laurie and who had assisted in her discrimination suit against the Milwaukee City Police Department, took the stand. Morrison, now in private practice in Washington, D.C., told the Canadian officials that Laurie Bembenek had been a key witness in his investigation against the City of Milwaukee. Once Laurie was charged with murder, his investigation was stopped. "The heart of the investigation had been cut out," Morrison said.

Morrison's testimony supported Robins' claim that Laurie had been discriminated against and that she posed a threat to a number of corrupt officers.

When Robins took the stand, he spent hours detailing the work he had done for Laurie during the past seven years. Dr. Samuels' affidavit was also presented, and Robins asserted that the police department was still hiding evidence. A polygraph examiner for the Canadian Defense Department, John McClinton, also testified that Laurie had passed an extensive polygraph exam with flying colors.

Marrocco's witnesses were the most respected in Canada. They were experts who had testified at hundreds of other hearings. When the hearing recessed until August, Laurie was more positive about her chance for refugee status. She had finally been able to tell her side of the story. Marrocco had also promised to push for her to be released on bail.

Back in Milwaukee Robins worked with Woeherer to get the police department to release a key piece of evidence. Robins had been trying for years to get the police department to release a photo album that had been tied to the murder. The photo album had allegedly been recovered at the murder scene and Robins knew the police department had lifted several fingerprints from it.

In a stormy court session on June 28, 1991, Milwaukee County Circuit Judge William J. Shaughnessy, visibly angry, ordered the police department to turn over the photo album and any accompanying information "immediately."

Robins and Woeherer were led into a back room and spent hours going through the records. What they discovered was shocking, even to them.

The photo album, which had been turned over but kept secret just weeks following Christine's murder, contained the fingerprints of Fred Schultz and of Carl Ruscitti, a high-ranking police officer and the chief investigator into the murder. That could tie either man to the murder of Christine Schultz, and to Robins and Woeherer it was a final proof of a police cover-up.

In the album were many nude photographs. There was also a picture of a police woman in uniform and a Milwaukee attorney. But even though the police department had been ordered to turn over all the evidence, Robins was able to determine that some photos had been removed. There was still missing evidence. Some fingerprints that had been recorded in evidence had also disappeared and there was no explanation from the police for that.

The police had claimed that due to personnel matters they would not turn over the album. No police officers were identified in the album. Rob-

ins thought either the pictures of the police officers had been removed or the city attorney had
filed a false defense for not releasing the album.

Included in the released information was a
lengthy report about an internal investigation of
Fred Schultz. The report revealed that Fred had
been involved in numerous illegal activities and
the department had been considering charging
him with numerous rule infractions when they
met with him on December 10, 1981—the day he
had quit the police force.

The police investigators discovered that Fred
had filed false information about his marital
status, had illegally married Laurie, and had lied
at a Department of Industry, Labor and Human
Relations compensation hearing in September of
1981. At that hearing Fred had said he did not
carry a weapon to and from work—but Fred
Schultz did carry a weapon because he was a
Milwaukee police officer.

For Robins, the material contained in the once-
secret files proved his point. The police department had been concealing evidence.

"If this information would have been made
available to her before her trial, it would have
helped clear her," Robins told reporters. "This
proves that Fred Schultz was a liar and those police officers let him testify anyway and helped him
get immunity, knowing that he had already lied
under oath."

Robins knew that somehow he had to get the
rest of the photos and fingerprints.

"What else are they hiding?" he asked Woeherer during one of their late-night work sessions.
"What else don't we know about?"

CHAPTER 44

While Laurie Waits

The weekend of July 19, 1991, Ira B. Robins worked almost around the clock on a detailed affidavit requesting a John Doe investigation. Across town Dr. Chesley Erwin worked on another affidavit supporting Robins' work.

On July 22 Robins took his documents to Mary Woeherer. She already had Dr. Erwin's statements. They spent several hours reviewing and revising them. Woeherer composed a letter to Judge William Shaughnessy formally requesting an investigation into the handling of the Lawrencia Bembenek murder case. She told the judge that enclosed in the affidavits was information that showed evidence had been falsified, that there had been a conspiracy, and that there had been police misconduct.

Robins hand-carried the John Doe request to the judge's office.

On July 26 Mary Woeherer was notified that the court had assigned Milwaukee County Circuit Judge William J. Haese to decide if a John Doe investigation into the murder conviction of Lawrencia Bembenek would be initiated. Woeherer began supplying Judge Haese with documents. Woeherer also asked for a special prosecutor and investigator if a John Doe was granted because she believed the district attorney would either be a witness or a target of the investigation.

An editorial in *The Milwaukee Journal* supporting a John Doe stated, "Ideally, an investigation would determine once and for all the guilt or innocence of the police or Bembenek. However, a John Doe probe, with all of its uncertainties, seems the only possibility right now to clear the air."

When Milwaukee reporters tried to contact Fred Schultz for a comment about the John Doe investigation, someone who answered the phone at his Florida home said that he was living and working in Kuwait. But several weeks later, Canadian reporters talked with him on the phone, and he said he was still laughing about the Kuwait statement and that he had never been in Kuwait.

Laurie's refugee hearing continued during the second week of August 1991. When Laurie took the witness stand, she was wearing the same dress she had worn during her 1982 murder trial. Prison officials would not allow her to wear makeup or curl her hair for the proceedings. She looked tired and pale.

When Frank Marrocco asked Laurie if she had killed Christine Schultz, Laurie looked into his eyes and said, "Absolutely not, no."

During her testimony she told the Canadian tribunal hearing her case that she had been verbally abused by police officials. She said she had been humiliated by the treatment she received at the police academy and from police officers during her training period. Laurie also said she was certain she had been singled out for harassment because of her feminist beliefs and because police officers thought she knew more than she really did about their illegal activities.

Her hearing was adjourned at the end of the week and rescheduled for the second week of September. But a massive workers strike in Canada postponed the hearing to October 17, 1991. Ironically Laurie and Nick had been captured on October 17, 1990. Laurie had now been a prisoner in Canada for one year.

When Laurie was returned to the detention center, one of the female inmates immediately began harassing her and threatened to kill her. "When this woman found out that I was an ex-cop, she confronted me and told me she was going to stab me with a knife," Laurie said to a Wisconsin friend.

Even though Laurie often formed friendships with guards and inmates, she said there were always a number of prisoners who hated her because she was an ex-cop and a number of guards who hated her because she was a prisoner.

"I try and explain that the reason I am even in prison is because I am an ex-cop and was framed, but with some of these people it doesn't matter what you say," Laurie said. "They can hate you just because you have on a pair of tennis shoes."

Back in Wisconsin, Nick Gugliatto, accused of helping Laurie escape from prison, waited in the Fond du Lac County jail for his September 4 trial to begin. Just before he was taken to jail, Nick had an old tattoo on his right upper arm replaced with the word *Lawrencia*. Nick quickly fired his attorney just weeks before the trial because the lawyer wanted him to say that Laurie had planned the escape. Nick refused to do that, and Robins' friend, Bob Sosnay, agreed to represent him at his trial.

The entire trial took less than one day. Several witnesses said they had seen Nick Gugliatto with Laurie Bembenek during or after the escape. Nick did not take the witness stand, and Sosnay said to the judge, the only witness he could have called, Laurie Bembenek, was in Canada and might never come back. Laurie and Nick have never publicly discussed any details of the escape.

It took the jurors a little over one hour to find Nick guilty, and he was taken back to the Fond du Lac jail to await sentencing during the first week of October 1991.

Following the sentencing Nick's father appeared distraught and bitter. He told every reporter who could hear that Laurie Bembenek climbed over the fence at Taycheedah herself. He said it wasn't right that his son was found guilty for helping Laurie escape.

Laurie was not surprised to hear about Nick's conviction. Although she was able to correspond with him, phone calls were not possible because all calls from prison have to be collect calls. "Maintaining any kind of relationship in prison is very difficult," Laurie told a close friend. "My relationship with Nick is uncertain right now mainly because of the distance between us."

Laurie's stay at the Metro Toronto West Detention Center took an unexpected turn on September 12, 1991. Laurie was working in a hobby class on her latest painting when she was summoned for her weekly detention hearing by a guard. The hearings are mandated by Canadian law and are designed to give men and women behind bars a chance to say why they should be released on bail. Week after week Laurie had attended the hearings with her attorney only to have her request for bail denied. She thought the September 12 hearing would be the same old thing.

"I live for my painting because it is the only thing I can do in here," Laurie told a friend. "When the guard came to get me, I didn't even want to go so fast. I begged him to let me stay because I had just opened up all the paints."

But the guard insisted, and Laurie was led to a small meeting room, where she was surprised to see a new immigration adjudicator presiding. Carmen DeCarlo had been handling her case but DeCarlo, a member of the Public Service Alliance of Canada, was on strike along with hundreds of other Canadian workers. The new adjudicator told Laurie he thought she should be released immediately on bail.

"Everything happened so fast, I just sat there for a minute," Laurie told a Wisconsin writer and friend. "I sat there with tears running down my face trying to believe what this man was saying. He assured me it was for real."

In a private conversation the adjudicator also echoed the sentiments of the majority of Canadians when he told Laurie that he thought she had been wrongly convicted of murder. He said that she should be a free woman. Other Canadian officials, however, tried to get a federal court order to keep Laurie in prison. But her Canadian attorneys were working just as hard to set her free. The following day, September 13, 1991, Laurie

Bembenek was finally released from the detention center.

"Because of everything else that has happened to me, I knew that something could stop me at any moment," Laurie said. "I wanted to think that I could stay out of the detention center and be really free for the first time in ten years."

Released on $10,000 bail and ordered to report to immigration authorities once a day, Laurie was whisked from the detention center by a carload of her attorneys. Frank Marrocco had arranged for Laurie to stay at a halfway house in downtown Toronto run by the Elizabeth Fry Society, a non-profit group dedicated to working with women involved with the criminal justice system. In Milwaukee, Laurie's parents quickly boarded a plane for Toronto.

Laurie spent her first hours of freedom with her attorneys, who knew they would have to work miracles to keep her out of prison. News reached them at the halfway house that Fond du Lac authorities were pursuing an extradition request to have Laurie sent back to Fond du Lac immediately. "I was exhausted because the night before I was too excited to sleep," Laurie said to her friend. "I had one small piece of pizza and then met with my parents for a few hours before I fell asleep."

By six the next morning Laurie was dressed and ready for a round of meetings with attorneys. By early afternoon she was back in prison. A federal prosecutor acting on behalf of Wisconsin had successfully sought a new warrant for Laurie's arrest, and the Royal Canadian Mounted Police quickly and quietly took her back to the detention center.

"I managed to eat a Twinkie and that's about it," Laurie said, back in her cell. "For me this is like mental torture. One minute I am free and the next I am not. All I have left now is the hope that the truth will come out and I will be set free—forever."

An extradition hearing was scheduled for November and immigration officials told Laurie her refugee hearing would continue on October 17 as scheduled.

On October 4, 1991, Nick was sentenced to one year in the Fond du Lac county jail and was ordered to pay extradition costs of $2,500. When Nick stood before the judge, he said, "As God is my witness, if Lawrencia Bembenek came in here now and asked me to help her escape, I would say no."

Nick claimed he still loved Laurie, but he said he had no idea that so many people, including his own family, would be hurt by Lawrencia's escape from prison and his sudden disappearance.

Back in Canada, despite their strained relationship, Laurie was glad to hear that Nick had received a light sentence. He could have been fined up to $10,000 and sentenced to five years in prison.

"If it wasn't for Nick, I might not have made it to Canada, and I might not have this chance," she told a close friend. "All I can do now is what I have done since the day I was arrested for a crime I did not commit. I can wait and I can hope."

On October 11 Milwaukee County Circuit Judge William J. Haese announced that he had made a decision concerning a request to hold a John Doe investigation into the handling of the Christine Schultz murder case. A John Doe is an investigation conducted by a judge to determine whether a crime has been committed. Haese said he would make a formal announcement concerning his decision the following Monday in his courtroom.

Robins, Woeherer, and two friends and supporters of Laurie sat in the back of Haese's courtroom at 8:45 A.M. on October 14 to wait for the judge's decision. The room was crammed with television reporters and their cameramen. Laurie's parents decided not to attend the hearing because they were afraid of how they would react in front of the cameras if the decision went against the investigation. "Another setback might just be too hard to handle," her mother told a writer.

When Haese started to talk, it seemed as if everyone in the courtroom stopped breathing. The judge had told no one what his decision would be. He had decided to grant the request for the John Doe. Robins and Woeherer grasped hands and fought back tears when they heard Haese's decision. Across the courtroom, Deputy District Attorney Bob Donohoo sat quietly with his head bowed.

Haese said that Robins and Chesley Erwin, the former Milwaukee County medical examiner, were the men who had requested the investigation. "Questions have been raised and allegations have been made concerning the handling of evidence and the prosecution and conviction of Lawrencia Bembenek," Haese told those attending the hearing. "A John Doe proceeding will enable the complainants and others with knowledge to come forward with any evidence they may have so as to determine whether there is in fact proof to the degree required to issue a criminal complaint."

Haese then appointed a Milwaukee area attorney, E. Campin Kersten, fifty-nine, to head the investigation. He said a normal John Doe would be handled by the district attorney's office, but because that office would be under investigation, a special prosecutor would be needed.

Kersten, a soft-spoken, gray-haired man, said Haese would ultimately decide whether any criminal charges would be filed once his investigation was completed.

"This is not an investigation into the guilt or innocence of Lawrencia Bembenek," Kersten said. "We are going to determine if there was criminal activity during the murder investigation that led up to her conviction."

According to Kersten, if criminal wrongdoing was uncovered, Laurie Bembenek's murder conviction would most likely be affected.

Haese also ordered the investigation to be conducted in secret. He said that some witnesses might be reluctant to come forward if they knew their remarks would be made public. He said that under the guidelines of a John Doe, Kersten had the power and authority to subpoena witnesses and secure any information that he needed.

Kersten said that he wanted to move quickly but added that it would still take several months to go through materials, court records, and reports. He said it would be well into 1992 before he completed his work.

Robins was elated by the news. All he ever wanted was someone not associated with the case to investigate it. He told reporters that he was "very confident" that the investigation would prove there had been criminal activity involved with the murder investigation.

When Laurie heard that the John Doe had been granted, she tempered her feelings with the Milwaukee track record for the past ten years. "It's hard to think of anything positive as a possibility after all these years," she told a friend during a phone conversation. "I want to think that it is good and that justice will finally be served, but it is hard to think that way after all these years."

Less than two weeks later, another Milwaukee Police Department internal affairs report, written on November 19, 1981, was discovered by Robins and Woeherer in a pile of police documents.

In that November 1981 report, police investigators told Kenneth Hagopian, former inspector of detectives, that they had proof that Elfred Schultz had committed several crimes. Those crimes included disobeying a court order not to marry within six months of his divorce, committing perjury during a Department of Industry, Labor and Human Relations meeting, and being involved in the Tracks parties.

According to the report, two detectives, Lieutenants Craig Hastings and James Kelly, asked District Attorney E. Michael McCann to charge Schultz with perjury or a similar charge. McCann's response, according to the police report, was "Do you want Bembenek or do you want Schultz?" McCann then told the detectives to make another appointment if they wished to talk further about the allegations.

After the release of the police records, Robins

said publicly that the information concerning Schultz should have been given to Laurie's attorneys before her case went to trial. He said that the information could have had a drastic effect on the outcome of the trial.

At the same time Laurie's Wisconsin team uncovered the internal investigation reports from the Milwaukee Police Department, her Canadian lawyers charged that Donohoo "actively undermined" Laurie's claim for refugee status. Laurie's attorneys said in their court documents that Donohoo aided immigration officials when he should have been a silent observer.

Those charges were part of a writ of habeus corpus filed on Laurie's behalf. This writ is meant to protect a person against illegal imprisonment, and Laurie's attorneys knew that by filing the writ, the Canadian authorities working to send her back to Wisconsin prison would have to prove that she actually committed a crime. They realized this was a task that would be impossible to complete.

The weeks of October and November were filled with one delayed immigration and extradition hearing after another. Laurie told friends and family that she felt as if she were part of a "circus." She spent hours in holding cells waiting for court adjournments so her attorneys could better prepare her case.

On November 30 the Milwaukee investigation into the Schultz murder took a dramatic and bizarre turn when Frederick Horenberger, forty, shot and killed himself following an armed robbery. Horenberger, considered by Robins to be the prime suspect in the murder, robbed a bakery not far from the Bembeneks' home on Milwaukee's south side early Saturday morning. Horenberger and an accomplice were chased by police from the bakery. The two suspects then abandoned the truck they were driving and ran into a residential area. Horenberger forced his way into a home in the 4000 block of Second Street and held an elderly couple at gunpoint for several hours before descending into the basement of the home and shooting himself in the head.

Horenberger was released from prison in December of 1990 after serving a ten-year sentence for robbing and beating Judy Zess just weeks after the Christine Schultz murder. Although Horenberger denied being involved in the Schultz murder, Robins said it was only a matter of time before he gathered up the necessary information to link Horenberger to the crime.

"Horenberger knew that he was going to be a target of the John Doe investigation and he also knew that he could end up back in prison for a long, long time," Robins said when he heard about Horenberger's death. "There are many, many people who will now be willing to talk about the murder because they know Horenberger won't be around to do anything to them."

Robins said he had numerous informants who had information linking Horenberger to the murder of Christine Schultz. He said he had been working for years to get those people to go on record, some of whom purportedly claim that Horenberger confessed to murdering Christine Schultz.

"The police considered Horenberger a suspect in the Schultz murder from the beginning, but any police records indicating that were never turned over to us," Robins said. "I know they looked into him as a suspect, but the reports have somehow disappeared."

When Laurie learned of Horenberger's death, her reaction was similar to that of Robins. She said that although he could not be part of the John Doe, others who had information about his involvement would now be more likely to come forward.

For Laurie Bembenek life had become nothing more than a waiting game. While the legal jockeying continued in Canada and in Wisconsin, Laurie remained confined in the Metro West Detention Center and spent her nights and days waiting for the moment when she could walk from prison a free woman.

After ten years of incarceration, waiting was something she knew how to do all too well.

AFTERWORD

June 4, 1992

In December 1991, Toronto, Canada, was cold, dreary, and ominous. Laurie's view of the outside world, the world beyond the steel cell bars and locked doors, continued to be framed by a tiny window that overlooked a prison parking lot. Cars, prison workers, and visitors passed in and out of view. Laurie wondered where everyone was going, where they lived, what they did after work. "What's it like to have a normal life?" she wondered. "What's it like to be safe, to be free, to be happy?"

When her attorneys, parents, or friends from Wisconsin visited her at the detention center, Laurie always watched with face and arms pressed up against the cold window as her guests walked across the snow-covered parking lot. Her friends would watch Laurie with tears streaming down their faces. Laurie watched them too, until distance obliterated her vision. She wanted to remember every detail, every second of each visit. It was all she had.

"There are no activities in here, and having a visitor, receiving mail from someone I care about, and tutoring the other prisoners are about all I have to look forward to," she said during one of her many long conversations with a Wisconsin friend. "The days simply go on and on and on."

As her tenth Christmas behind bars loomed, Laurie tried hard to remain optimistic. Every move she made seemed to bring her back to her starting point. Appeals, escapes, boyfriends—nothing mattered. She was still serving out someone else's life sentence for murder. Laurie talked to her friends and relatives about their holiday plans, knowing December 25, 1991, would be pretty much like any other day of the year for her. Christmas would be just another day in hell.

But Laurie Bembenek's Christmas was not as bad as she expected. A Toronto-based women's organization planned a Christmas day party for the inmates at Metro West, and Laurie found herself laughing, enjoying some Christmas cookies, and talking with friends in Wisconsin on the phone. It wasn't one of the golden, warm holidays she had spent in Milwaukee, years and years ago, but it was something.

"These women put together little baskets for us with real soap and shampoo that smell wonderful," Laurie said. "It was a very nice thing for them to do and it made the day just a bit more livable for all of us."

The best part of Laurie's Christmas was a surprise contact visit with her parents. Joe and Virginia Bembenek had traveled to Canada hoping to see Laurie on Christmas Day. It was a long shot, but Virginia and Joe would do anything to keep Laurie's spirits positive.

Visitors at Metro West usually sit in a tiny room and talk with inmates over a black phone, separated from their daughters, sisters, lovers, or friends by a scratched and stained piece of glass. But Steven and Johanne LeLacheur, a Toronto couple who became avid supporters of Laurie, petitioned prison officials for a private, hands-on visit between Laurie and her parents on Christmas Day. "It was wonderful, just wonderful to be able to actually touch her and hold her," said Mrs. Bembenek. "The three of us just stood there and cried. It was the best Christmas we have had in years and years." Laurie met with her parents in a private room for several hours, sharing hugs, laughs, and a few wishful thoughts about upcoming holidays. There was still some hope, still a chance that someday life would become what it was supposed to be.

Laurie was also boosted by news from Milwaukee that a judge had ordered the city of Milwaukee to pay Ira Robins $21,000 for refusing to turn over public records to him concerning the Christine Schultz murder. Using Wisconsin's Open Records Law, Robins had petitioned the court to release a photo album confiscated at the murder scene and several police files. The records and files included the information that Fred Schultz had lied under oath as to whether or not he habitually carried a loaded gun and had eventually been pressured to leave the Milwaukee Police Department because of misconduct.

Robins considered the financial award a huge victory for the Bembenek camp. He said the award would be the first of many Milwaukee taxpayers would have to pay for keeping an innocent woman in prison for ten years. He also said the award was further proof that there was indeed a police cover-up.

Laurie Bembenek ended 1991 in her Toronto jail cell, listening to one of her four cellmates cough, and the other three discuss life on the streets. There were no champagne, no dancing bands, no midnight buffet; just the constant hum of the over-head heater, the muffled sounds of women, crying into their pillows, and the promise of absolutely nothing better for 1992.

Despite her limited existence, the beginning of the New Year, 1992, was not a quiet one for Laurie Bembenek. Publicity surrounding her case continued to escalate, and reporters and television crews were constantly trying to get an "exclusive" interview with her. "These people keep forgetting something very important," Laurie told a friend. "I'm in prison and I am not allowed to give interviews. There is some kind of idea floating around out there that I live at a hotel and can do whatever I want. This is a prison and I am a prisoner." Stories about her continued to crop up in magazines and newspapers throughout the world, and ABC, CBS, and NBC all announced plans to air movies based on her story.

Fred Horenberger's December suicide added to the barrage of questions surrounding her case. Several major newspaper articles investigated the incident, and rumors were flying that the police department actually had something to do with the death of a man who could have been a key witness for the ongoing John Doe investigation. Shortly after Horenberger's suicide, Thomas Eckert, a friend and accomplice to Horenberger, publicly stated that Horenberger had confessed to him on numerous occasions that he had killed Christine Schultz.

Eckert said the way the Schultz house was entered, the description of the man seen leaving the

Schultz home, and everything associated with the case fit Horenberger's mode of operation. "I know," said Eckert, "because I worked with him." Eckert was subpoenaed to testify in front of the John Doe panel and had promised that he would cooperate and tell officials "everything possible" to get at the truth.

While January was a good month for Laurie Bembenek, it was the beginning of hard times for Nick Gugliatto. Nick had been transferred from the Fond du Lac jail to a work release program in Milwaukee. He was working as a bartender at two Milwaukee taverns and staying at the Community Correction Center on 10th Street. When officials ran a random drug test on Gugliatto during the first week of January, he tested positive for cocaine and was immediately transferred back to the Fond du Lac prison. He was ordered to spend the rest of his one-year sentence at the prison.

By January, the relationship between Laurie and Nick had all but disappeared. Nick stopped answering Laurie's letters and frustrated by her attempts to maintain communication, Laurie stopped writing to him. She confided to friends that their relationship had been far from perfect and that it had been impossible for her to antici-pate what it would be like to live with a man she had only seen a few times a week on prison visits. "There were many things that I did not know about him," Laurie said.

When Gugliatto was released from prison in April 1992, he announced plans to write a book and appear on national television shows to let the world know what Laurie Bembenek "was really like." Nick appeared on "A Current Affair" and compared Laurie to a piece of cheesecake. "I could only imagine what it would be like to be with a woman that hasn't had sex for eight and one half years. Come on. It's every man's dream." Nick's comments did nothing for his public standing. Angry men and women wrote letters to the editor in Milwaukee newspapers chastising Nick for his crude behavior.

Two close friends of Laurie's then refused to appear on the Geraldo show with Gugliatto. "This isn't a story about his relationship with Laurie," the women told a producer of the show. "This is a story about a woman who was wrongly convicted of a crime—a woman who has spent ten years, ten good years, trying to prove her innocence. Appearing on the same show with a man like that would only give credence to his existence. This is yet another example of someone getting involved with Laurie and then turning the story into his own." An ABC reporter who contacted one of Laurie's supporters in Wisconsin said that she was told Gugliatto would not talk to anyone "unless he had $7,500 on the table for starters." "This is nonsense," said the reporter. "What kind of man is this?"

On January 31, Judge David Watt of the Ontario Court General Division signed an extradition warrant for Lawrencia Bembenek and sent it to Kim Campbell, the Canadian Minister of Justice. It would be up to Campbell to sign the warrant and send Laurie back to Taycheedah or allow her to continue with her refugee hearing.

Lawyer Doug Hunt, an extradition specialist working with Laurie's other attorneys, appealed the extradition order in February, saying that

Laurie had a right to continue with her refugee hearing before a decision was made on returning her to the United States. With Laurie's refugee hearing scheduled to resume on March 9, Hunt said it was important to let that process continue.

But, in a decision that stunned many people, Laurie decided during the last week of February to give up her fight to remain in Canada and to return voluntarily to the United States. During a February 28 news conference held in Toronto, Hunt explained that Laurie needed to focus her energies on gaining a new trial in Wisconsin.

According to Hunt, it is up to the Wisconsin court to come to grips with the problem: It has to do the right thing and find out the truth about the murder of Christine Schultz. "With the John Doe going on, now is the time to be there and to cooperate," said Hunt.

Laurie said coming back to the United States had always been an option. She said that once she decided to cooperate with the John Doe investigation she also lessened her chances at gaining refugee status in Canada. "To get that status I had to be unwilling or unable to cooperate with officials in the United States," Laurie explained. "All I have ever wanted was an independent look into his murder, and that is what I now have with the John Doe."

Laurie said her return would allow her to help with the John Doe investigation. "If they need me, if someone has questions, if they need anything I'll be right there," said Laurie with just a hint of optimism in her voice. She also knew that in order for her to obtain a new trial she had to be living in the state of Wisconsin. "It isn't a complicated matter, and there was no deal worked out," she said. "I just want to get on with this and clear my name."

Laurie's decision to come back to the United States did not guarantee her immediate return. Campbell, the Canadian Minister of Justice, still had to sign the extradition order and allow Laurie to give up her refugee claim.

While Laurie waited for Campbell's decision she tried to prepare herself mentally for her return to the United States. She knew that she would be returned to Taycheedah, the same prison she escaped from, and that she would be forced to spend a great deal of time in solitary confinement. "I've had friends in there go off the deep end," she confided to a friend. "Promise me that you will stay in touch and write to me. If you stop hearing from me it means I need help. My silence will be me asking you to help me, and I just might need it."

Prisoners in solitary are essentially cut off from the outside world. They are not allowed to watch television, have visits, make phone calls, or listen to music. They are kept alone, in a small cell, and when they are moved from the cell they are locked in chains from the waist and ankles. That is what Laurie Bembenek had to look forward to when she was returned to Wisconsin. There would be no more phone calls to friends, no quick walks in the exercise yard, no painting classes; just another cell; another tiny window; another day and another night after that.

Laurie's mental troubles turned physical in March when she discovered a lump in her breast. Because Laurie had already undergone surgery once before for the removal of a breast tumor, she asked prison officials for immediate medical help. But the help did not come. Laurie could feel her lump growing, and still, prison authorities did not respond to her request for medical attention. Finally, desperate for some help, she told a Toronto reporter that she needed medical treatment and told him why. A newspaper article by the reporter helped speed her treatment, and a doctor drained a large cyst in her breast. The cyst was not cancerous, but Laurie was dismayed when another lump appeared just two weeks following the successful treatment for the first lump. The doctor put her on medication to try and get rid of the second lump, and Laurie was on the medication when she was returned to the United States.

On April 20, the day after Easter, U.S. marshals whisked Laurie out of her Toronto prison and onto a small plane headed for Milwaukee. Reporters who flocked to a small airport near the city were treated to a quick but sad glimpse of Lawrencia Bembenek being led from the plane to a waiting car. Laurie, wearing a dark dress, was handcuffed. She was also wearing leg irons, small handcuffs around her ankles attached by a chain. She did not want her return to become a media circus, and she asked the marshals to keep media representatives away from her. For friends and relatives who watched Laurie hobble from the plane to the car it was a dramatic and emotional scene.

At Taycheedah Laurie was quickly processed and put in medical confinement. Once she passed her medical tests, Laurie was taken to her new cell. She was back at the same prison where she had already spent eight years of her life. Other prisoners at Taycheedah saw Laurie come "home." Some shouted "Hang in there, Laurie" at her. "We missed you," others yelled. "Now that you're back they won't push us around anymore." Her prison friends, the women she had helped with legal problems, with reading skills, with self-esteem, her friends would be just outside her door. But when the door slammed shut again, even that thought was small comfort for Lawrencia Bembenek.

During her first week in solitary confinement Laurie was told she would be punished for her escape by spending 368 days there. The sentence was no surprise to Laurie or to her attorneys, but the finality of it—all those days piled one on top of the other—that would be a different matter. Solitary is solitary: Laurie Bembenek would spend over a year by herself.

During her first week back at Taycheedah Laurie was allowed to see her parents. The Bembeneks were shocked when Laurie appeared in chains, handcuffed to her waist. Her ankles were also chained and the Bembeneks and daughter Colette had to help Laurie drink soda from a can. "It's not easy to go there—to see your daughter like that," said Mrs. Bembenek. "It's horrible and I pray to God that someday, someday soon, this horrible thing will be over."

Laurie's parents were allowed to visit for two hours each week, and she was given the chance to make one ten-minute phone call once a week. She always called her mom and dad. But that was the extent of her privileges. No music. No visits from friends. No work privileges. Just the quiet; just the cold; just the endless monotony of the four walls, the floor, the ceiling, the endless waiting.

During the months of April, May, and June, Laurie's new Chicago-based attorney, Sheldon Zenner, worked with a team of five other attorneys to prepare a motion for a new trial. Zenner, a quiet, well-spoken man is considered by many to be one of the brightest attorneys now practicing. As a United States associate of Frank Marrocco, Zenner had been working on the case for over a year by the time Laurie was returned to Wisconsin.

In television appearances, Zenner talked about the case in a quiet, straightforward manner. Without pointing fingers or becoming angry, Zenner said he was surprised that an attorney of E. Michael McCann's stature had not been willing to offer Laurie Bembenek a new trial. "There is new evidence, and it is our hope that when we present this motion a judge will look at what we have with an open eye and give Laurie the chance she deserves," said Zenner.

Laurie knew Zenner was doing his best to prepare the motion, but she was impatient. Zenner told her he did not want to rush the motion. "This could be the last chance," he said. "It's got to be perfect and that is what it will be." Zenner told Laurie it could be July before he was actually ready to take his petition to court. In the meantime, investigators would follow up on new leads, work the old ones, and help prepare a motion that was airtight.

While Zenner prepared his motion, witnesses were still being interviewed as a part of the secret John Doe investigation. The secrecy surrounding the investigation continued to grow during the spring of 1992 but Laurie's supporters took that as a good sign. Ira Robins said he knew that many people would be willing to testify if they knew their identities would be kept secret. "We have no reason to believe that these men running the John Doe are doing anything but a great job," said Robins. "This is what we have been asking for and I am confident that the investigation will find some wrongdoing."

E. Campion Kersten, the man heading up the John Doe panel, said that the investigation would not be complete until "sometime in summer." He said he could not be specific. He wanted to do a thorough job—the public, Laurie Bembenek, everyone deserved that much. There was no hint from him or from any of his staff members about the outcome. Everyone would just have to wait.

While Laurie Bembenek paced the floor in her tiny cell, the world surrounding her was far from quiet. In early spring, just after she was interviewed by Diane Sawyer from "Prime Time Live," Thomas Gaertner was killed in a motorcycle crash in California. The controversial, drug-dealing boyfriend of Laurie's ex-roommate died before he had a chance to testify at the John Doe hearing.

During the first week of May there was a positive event that temporarily overshadowed Laurie's often negative existence. The University of Wisconsin–Milwaukee sponsored a showing of her art works at the UWM Art History Gallery. The university paid to ship and prepare her paintings for the show, and Laurie, who has always been serious about her art work, was excited about the show.

Some negative comments by a small group of

university students who called the show a "spectacle" did not dampen its success. Hundreds of people turned out to see the paintings, and reviews of the show were very favorable. Laurie said she was grateful for the chance to show the world a side of her that had been essentially hidden. "To be able to express myself this way is one of the few joys I have left in this world," she said. Laurie also donated one of her paintings to the Milwaukee AIDS Project for its annual art auction. Her simple, yet stunning acrylic painting, "Tenacity", depicted a single yellow dandelion growing up from the crack in the ground, away from a manhole cover.

"Was Laurie Bembenek painting herself?" everyone asked. "Is she that flower—tough, obstinate, unwilling to back down, unwilling to admit to something she did not do?"

If Laurie could answer those questions, if she was not isolated and alone she would have much to say. Today, she is still waiting for that chance.

Laurie Bembenek remains in solitary confinement at the women's prison in Wisconsin. Her final bid for freedom lies in the hands of the same system—with the same men—who sentenced her to life in prison over ten years ago.

MURDEROUS MINDS